INTEGRITY

(integrity)

Stephen L. Carter

BasicBooks
A Division of HarperCollins*Publishers*

Designed by Elliot Beard

Library of Congress Cataloging-in-Publication Data
Carter, Stephen L.
    Integrity / Stephen L. Carter.
        p.   cm.
    Includes bibliographical references and index.
    ISBN 0-465-03466-7
    1. Integrity. I. Title.
    BJ1533.I58C37   1996
    170—dc20   95-44538
                                                                    CIP

96 97 98 99 ❖/HC 9 8 7 6 5 4 3

To my mother and father,
my first teachers,
and, once more, to Enola—naturally

Contents

III
RUMINATIONS

Acknowledgments

IT must seem odd to find a book by a lawyer—still worse, a law professor—on the subject of integrity. So let me make clear that integrity is
something I only think about, not something I exemplify. I strive toward
it, as I am sure most of us do, but I do not pretend to achieve it very often.

This book is written for a general not an academic audience. Although
I hope to enrich our understanding of a virtue that most of us talk about
and all of us value, I do not pretend to make a formal contribution to the
scholarship in law or philosophy, still less in theology.

Integrity is the first of three books I plan to write about what I think of
as "pre-political" virtues—that is, elements of good character that cross the
political spectrum and, indeed, without which other political views and
values are useless. First among these virtues is integrity, which gives meaning to all the rest of what we say we believe in.

As the reader will discover, I define integrity with some care, to include discerning the right and acting on it, not simply living a consistent life according to some arbitrary set of principles. In this I am inspired by Dietrich Bonhoeffer's notion of *discipleship*. For Bonhoeffer, discipleship meant an
unblinking obedience to God. For our public morality, it means an unblinking obedience to the right.

This is a hard test. Few of us can meet it very often, and I do not consider myself one of the few. Yet the struggle itself is important. Indeed, I am persuaded that nothing but an all-out effort to demand integrity of our political leaders—and of their bosses, by which I mean *us*—will preserve democracy as we have come to know it in the century to come.

I am grateful to all those who took the time to talk with me about my ideas or the draft, especially Akhil Amar, Barbara Bradley, Lisle Carter, Bob Ellickson, Margaret Farley, Ronald Feenstra, George Jones, Paul Kahn, Tony Kronman, Jane Livingston, Jim O'Toole, Loretta Pleasant-Jones, and Reva Siegel. I have had the benefit of splendid research assistance from Yale Law School students Deborah Baumgarten, Kali Bracey, Heidi Durrow, Dina Friedman, and Lewis Peterson. I am also indebted to my editors at Basic Books, Kermit Hummel and Linda Carbone, as well as to my literary agent, Lynn Nesbit. Portions of this book are adapted from lectures I have delivered or articles I have published in scholarly journals. On those lectures and articles, I have been the fortunate recipient of helpful comments and suggestions from colleagues, listeners, and editors far too numerous to mention.

Finally, I must once more thank God for blessing me with a marvelous and supportive family: my children, Leah and Andrew, and my wife, Enola Aird, whose gifts of conversation and critique are of inestimable value and whose life and love continue to be my greatest inspiration. Without Enola, I could never have written about integrity.

New Haven, Connecticut
September 1995

One final note: All quotations from the Bible are from the New Revised Standard Version, with the exception of the quotation from Ephesians in chapter 9. That quotation, for reasons that its context will make clear, I have rendered in a more traditional form.

(i)

Explanations

The integrity of the upright guides them.
—*Proverbs 11:3*

(one)

The Rules About the Rules

MY first lesson in integrity came the hard way. It was 1960 or thereabouts and I was a first-grader at P.S. 129 in Harlem. The teacher had us all sitting in a circle, playing a game in which each child would take a turn donning a blindfold and then trying to identify objects by touch alone as she handed them to us. If you guessed right, you stayed in until the next round. If you guessed wrong, you were out. I survived almost to the end, amazing the entire class with my abilities. Then, to my dismay, the teacher realized what I had known, and relied upon, from the start: my blindfold was tied imperfectly and a sliver of bright reality leaked in from outside. By holding the unknown object in my lap instead of out in front of me, as most of the other children did, I could see at least a corner or a side and sometimes more—but always enough to figure out what it was. So my remarkable success was due only to my ability to break the rules.

Fortunately for my own moral development, I was caught. And as a result of being caught, I suffered, in front of my classmates, a humiliating reminder of right and wrong: I had cheated at the game. Cheating was wrong. It was that simple.

I do not remember many of the details of the "public" lecture that I received from my teacher. I do remember that I was made to feel terribly ashamed; and it is good that I was made to feel that way, for I had some-

thing to be ashamed of. The moral opprobrium that accompanied that
shame was sufficiently intense that it has stayed with me ever since, which
is exactly how shame is supposed to work. And as I grew older, whenever
I was even tempted to cheat—at a game, on homework—I would remember my teacher's stern face and the humiliation of sitting before my classmates, revealed to the world as a cheater.

That was then, this is now. Browsing recently in my local bookstore, I
came across a book that boldly proclaimed, on its cover, that it contained
instructions on how to *cheat*—the very word occurred in the title—at a
variety of video games. My instincts tell me that this cleverly chosen title is
helping the book to sell very well. For it captures precisely what is wrong
with America today: we care far more about winning than about playing
by the rules.

Consider just a handful of examples, drawn from headlines of the mid-
1990s: the winner of the Miss Virginia pageant is stripped of her title after
officials determine that her educational credentials are false; a television network is forced to apologize for using explosives to add a bit of verisimilitude to a tape purporting to show that a particular truck is unsafe; and the
authors of a popular book on management are accused of using bulk purchases at key stores to manipulate the *New York Times* best-seller list. Go
back a few more years and we can add in everything from a slew of Wall
Street titans imprisoned for violating a bewildering variety of laws in their
frantic effort to get ahead, to the women's Boston Marathon winner
branded a cheater for spending part of the race on the subway. But cheating is evidently no big deal: some 70 percent of college students admit to
having done it at least once.[1]

That, in a nutshell, is America's integrity dilemma: we are all full of fine
talk about how desperately our society needs it, but, when push comes to
shove, we would just as soon be on the winning side. A couple of years
ago as I sat watching a televised football game with my children, trying to
explain to them what was going on, I was struck by an event I had often
noticed but on which I had never reflected. A player who failed to catch
a ball thrown his way hit the ground, rolled over, and then jumped up, celebrating as though he had caught the pass after all. The referee was standing in a position that did not give him a good view of what had happened,
was fooled by the player's pretense, and so moved the ball down the field.
The player rushed back to the huddle so that his team could run another
play before the officials had a chance to review the tape. (Until 1992,
National Football League officials could watch a television replay and
change their call, as long as the next play had not been run.) But viewers

at home did have the benefit of the replay, and we saw what the referee missed: the ball lying on the ground instead of snug in the receiver's hands. The only comment from the broadcasters: "What a heads-up play!" Meaning: "Wow, what a great liar this kid is! Well done!"

Let's be very clear: that is exactly what they meant. The player set out to mislead the referee and succeeded; he helped his team to obtain an advantage in the game that it had not earned. It could not have been accidental. He knew he did not catch the ball. By jumping up and celebrating, he was trying to convey a false impression. He was trying to convince the officials that he had caught the ball. And the officials believed him. So, in any ordinary understanding of the word, he lied. And that, too, is what happens to integrity in American life: if we happen to do something wrong, we would just as soon have nobody point it out.

Now, suppose that the player had instead gone to the referee and said, "I'm sorry, sir, but I did not make the catch. Your call is wrong." Probably his coach and teammates and most of his team's fans would have been furious: he would not have been a good team player. The good team player lies to the referee, and does so in a manner that is at once blatant (because millions of viewers see it) and virtually impossible for the referee to detect. Having pulled off this trickery, the player is congratulated: he is told that he has made a heads-up play. Thus, the ethic of the game turns out to be an ethic that rewards cheating. (But I still love football.) Perhaps I should have been shocked. Yet, thinking through the implications of our celebration of a national sport that rewards cheating, I could not help but recognize that we as a nation too often lack integrity, which might be described, in a loose and colloquial way, as the courage of one's convictions. And although I do not want to claim any great burst of inspiration, it was at about that time that I decided to write this book.

TOWARD A DEFINITION

We, the People of the United States, who a little over two hundred years ago ordained and established the Constitution, have a serious problem: too many of us nowadays neither mean what we say nor say what we mean. Moreover, we hardly expect anybody else to mean what they say either.

A couple of years ago I began a university commencement address by telling the audience that I was going to talk about integrity. The crowd broke into applause. Applause! Just because they had heard the word *integrity*—that's how starved for it they were. They had no idea how I was using the word, or what I was going to say about it, or, indeed, whether I was for it or against it. But they knew they liked the idea of simply talking about it. This celebration of integrity is intriguing: we seem to carry on a passionate love affair with a word that we scarcely pause to define.

The Supreme Court likes to use such phrases as the "Constitution's structural integrity" when it strikes down actions that violate the separation of powers in the federal government.[2] Critics demand a similar form of integrity when they argue that our age has seen the corruption of language or of particular religious traditions or of the moral sense generally. Indeed, when parents demand a form of education that will help their children grow into people of integrity, the cry carries a neo-romantic image of their children becoming adults who will remain uncorrupted by the forces (whatever they are) that seem to rob so many grown-ups of . . . well, of integrity.

Very well, let us consider this word *integrity*. Integrity is like the weather: everybody talks about it but nobody knows what to do about it. Integrity is that stuff we always say we want more of. Such leadership gurus as Warren Bennis insist that it is of first importance. We want our elected representatives to have it, and political challengers always insist that their opponents lack it. We want it in our spouses, our children, our friends. We want it in our schools and our houses of worship. And in our corporations and the products they manufacture: early in 1995, one automobile company widely advertised a new car as "the first concept car with integrity." And we want it in the federal government, too, where officials all too frequently find themselves under investigation by special prosecutors. So perhaps we should say that integrity is like *good* weather, because everybody is in favor of it.

Scarcely a politician kicks off a campaign without promising to bring it to government; a few years later, more often than is healthy for our democracy, the politician slinks cravenly from office, having been lambasted by the press for lacking that self-same integrity; and then the press, in turn, is skewered for holding public figures to a measure of integrity that its own reporters, editors, producers, and, most particularly, owners could not possibly meet. And for refusing to turn that critical eye inward, the press is mocked for—what else?—a lack of integrity.

Everybody agrees that the nation needs more of it. Some say we need to return to the good old days when we had a lot more of it. Others say we as a nation have never really had enough of it. And hardly any of us stop to explain exactly what we mean by it—or how we know it is even a good thing—or why everybody needs to have the same amount of it. Indeed, the only trouble with integrity is that everybody who uses the word seems to mean something slightly different. So in a book about integrity, the place to start is surely with a definition.

When I refer to integrity, I have something very simple and very specific in mind. Integrity, as I will use the term, requires three steps: (1) *discerning* what is right and what is wrong; (2) *acting* on what you have discerned, even at personal cost; and (3) *saying openly* that you are acting on your understanding of right from wrong.[3] The first criterion captures the idea of integrity as requiring a degree of moral reflectiveness. The second brings in the ideal of an integral person as steadfast, which includes the sense of keeping commitments. The third reminds us that a person of integrity is unashamed of doing the right. In the next chapter, I will explain more about why I have chosen this as my definition; but I hope that even readers who quarrel with my selection of the term *integrity* to refer to the form of commitment that I describe will come away from the book understanding why the concept itself, whatever it may be called, is a vital one.

The word *integrity* comes from the same Latin root as *integer* and historically has been understood to carry much the same sense, the sense of *wholeness*: a person of integrity, like a whole number, is a whole person, a person somehow undivided. The word conveys not so much a single-mindedness as a completeness; not the frenzy of a fanatic who wants to remake all the world in a single mold but the serenity of a person who is confident in the knowledge that he or she is living rightly. The person of integrity need not be a Gandhi but also cannot be a person who blows up buildings to make a point. A person of integrity lurks somewhere inside each of us: a person we feel we can trust to do right, to play by the rules, to keep commitments. Perhaps it is because we all sense the capacity for integrity within ourselves that we are able to notice and admire it even in people with whom, on many issues, we sharply disagree.

Indeed, one reason to focus on integrity as perhaps the first among the virtues that make for good character is that it is in some sense prior to everything else: the rest of what we think matters very little if we lack essential integrity, the courage of our convictions, the willingness to act and speak in behalf of what we know to be right. In an era when the American people are crying out for open discussion of morality—of right and wrong—the ideal of integrity seems a good place to begin. No matter what our politics, no matter what causes we may support, would anybody really want to be led or followed or assisted by people who *lack* integrity? People whose words we could not trust, whose motives we didn't respect, who might at any moment toss aside everything we thought we had in common and march off in some other direction?

The answer, of course, is no: we would not want leaders of that kind, even though we too often get them. The question is not only what integrity is and why it is valuable, but how we move our institutions, and our very lives, closer to exemplifying it. In raising this question, I do not put myself forward as an exemplar of integrity, but merely as one who in daily life goes through many of the struggles that I will describe in these pages. The reader will quickly discover that I frequently use the word *we* in my analysis. The reason is that I see the journey toward a greater understanding of the role of integrity in our public and private lives as one that the reader and I are making together.

INTEGRITY AND RELIGION

The concept we are calling *integrity* has had little attention from philosophers, but has long been a central concern to the religions. Integrity, after all, is a kind of wholeness, and most religions teach that God calls us to an undivided life in accordance with divine command. In Islam, this notion is captured in the understanding that all rules, legal or moral, are guided by the *sharia*, the divine path that God directs humans to walk. In Judaism, study of the Torah and Talmud reveals the rules under which God's people are expected to live. And Christians are called by the Gospel to be "pure in heart" (Matt. 5:8), which implies an undividedness in following God's rules.

Indeed, although its antecedents may be traced to Aristotle, the basic concept of integrity was introduced to the Western tradition through the struggle of Christianity to find a guide for the well-lived life. The wholeness that the Christian tradition identified as central to life with integrity was a wholeness in obedience to God, so that the well-lived life was a life that followed God's rules. Thomas Aquinas put it this way: "[T]he virtue of obedience is more praiseworthy than other moral virtues, seeing that by obedience a person gives up his own will for God's sake, and by other moral virtues something less."[4] John Wesley, in a famous sermon, was more explicit: "[T]he nature of the covenant of grace gives you no ground, no encouragement at all, to set aside any instance or degree of obedience."[5]

But obedience to what? Traditional religions teach that integrity is found in obedience to God. Moses Maimonides put the point most simply: "Everything that you do, do for the sake of God."[6] And a Professor W. S. Tyler, preaching a sermon at Amherst College in 1857, pointed the way to generalizing the concept beyond the religious sphere: "[I]ntegrity implies implicit obedience to the dictates of conscience—in other words, a heart and life habitually controlled by a sense of duty."[7]

But this is not a book about religion as such, still less about Christian doctrine. This book, rather, tries to honor our own national understanding of the word, in a tradition that is somewhat more secular but is, in its way, equally profound. My hope is to use traditional religious understandings to illuminate a concept that now has a distinct and honored place in the American ethical narrative, but to allow the narrative to tell its own story. So, although I have quoted Aquinas and will quote him again, this book is not about how Aquinas thought of integrity; it is about how we Americans think, or have thought, or should think, of it. Our demand for it illustrates that we think about it often, and a little desperately; my hope in this book is to demonstrate the value of the concept—to show *why* we think of the word with such affection—and then to examine the interplay of the integrity concept with a range of American problems and institutions.

In choosing integrity as my subject, I have tried to select an element of good character that is independent of the particular political views that one might hold; indeed, I would suspect that all of us, whatever our politics, would value, and perhaps demand, a degree of integrity in our associates, our government, and even our friends and families. So it is best that we try to reach some agreement on just what it is that we are valuing and demanding.

A good citizen, a person of integrity, I will refer to as one who leads an *integral life.* An integral life in turn requires all three steps of the definition, to which I will occasionally refer as the rules or criteria of integrity. Once this definition is understood, there are implications, from politics to marriage, from the way bosses write letters of recommendation to the way newspaper editors choose which stories to run. In the chapters to come, I plan to discuss them all. I am, by training and persuasion, a lawyer, and so the reader should not be surprised to find many legal examples in the pages that follow; indeed, there is even a bit of constitutional analysis. But if this is not a book about Christianity, still less is it a book about law, and certainly it is not a work of philosophy. It is, rather, a book about Americans and our society, about what we are, what we say we aspire to be, and how to bring the two closer to balance.

THE THREE STEPS

Integrity, I should explain before proceeding, is not the same as honesty, although honesty obviously is a desirable element of good character as well. From our definition, it is clear that one cannot have integrity without also displaying a measure of honesty. But one can be honest without being integral, for integrity, as I define it, demands a difficult process of discerning one's deepest understanding of right and wrong, and then further requires action consistent with what one has learned. It is possible to be honest without ever taking a hard look inside one's soul, to say nothing of taking any action based on what one finds. For example, a woman who believes abortion is murder may state honestly that this is what she thinks, but she does not fulfill the integrity criteria unless she also works to change abortion law. A man who believes in our national obligation to aid the homeless cannot claim to be fulfilling the criteria unless he works to obtain the aid he believes is deserved—and perhaps provides some assistance personally.

All too many of us fall down on step 1: we do not take the time to discern right from wrong. Indeed, I suspect that few of us really know just what we believe—what we value—and, often, we do not really want to know. Discernment is hard work; it takes time and emotional energy. And it is so much easier to follow the crowd. We too often look the other way when we see wrongdoing around us, quite famously in the widely unwitnessed yet very unprivate murder of Kitty Genovese thirty years ago. We refuse to think in terms of right and wrong when we elect or reject political candidates based on what they will do for our own pocketbooks. On the campuses, too many students and not a few professors find it easier to go along with the latest trends than to risk the opprobrium of others by registering an objection. Indeed, social psychologists say that this all too human phenomenon of refusing to think independently is what leads to mob violence. But a public-spirited citizen must do a bit of soul-searching—must decide what he or she most truly and deeply believes to be right and good—before it is possible to live with integrity.

The second step is also a tough one. It is far easier to know what one believes—to know, in effect, right from wrong—than it is to do something about it. For example, one may believe that the homeless deserve charity, but never dispense it; or one may think that they are bums who should not be given a dime, yet always dig into one's pockets when confronted. We Americans have a remarkable capacity to say one thing and do another, not always out of true hypocrisy but often out of a lack of self-assurance.

We see this in our politics, where nobody wants to be the one to say that the retirees who receive Social Security payments are, for the most part, receiving not a return on an investment but direct subventions from the payments being made by today's workers toward their own retirements—which, if done by a private investment firm, would be an illegal pyramid scheme. The late legal scholar Robert Cover illustrated the point quite powerfully when he examined the puzzling question of how avowedly antislavery judges in the early nineteenth century could hand down obviously proslavery decisions.[8] Equally puzzling to many political activists is their inability to recruit support from people they know to be committed to their causes, who frequently explain that they simply do not want to get involved.

But in order to live with integrity, it is sometimes necessary to take that difficult step—to get involved—to fight openly for what one believes to be true and right and good, even when there is risk to oneself. I would not go so far as to insist that morally committed citizens living integral lives must fight their way through life, strident activists in behalf of all their beliefs; but I worry deeply about the number of us who seem happy to drift through life, activists in behalf of none of our beliefs.

This leads to the third step, which seems deceptively simple, but is often the hardest of all: the person truly living an integral life must be willing to say that he or she is acting consistently with what he or she has decided is right. When the statements of a person of integrity are the result of discernment, of hard thought, we treat them as reliable, even when they are indicators of the future—"You've got the job" or "Till death do us part." But forthrightness also matters because people of integrity are willing to tell us *why* they are doing what they are doing. So it does not promote integrity for one to cheat on taxes out of greed but to claim to be doing it as a protest; indeed, it does not promote integrity to do it as a protest unless one says openly (including to the Internal Revenue Service) that that is what one is doing. It does not promote integrity to ignore or cover up wrongdoing by a co-worker or family member. And it does not promote integrity to claim to be doing the will of God when one is actually doing what one's political agenda demands.

This third step—saying publicly that we are doing what we think is right, even when others disagree—is made particularly difficult by our national desire to conform. Most of us want to fit in, to be accepted, and admitting to (or proudly proclaiming) an unpopular belief is rarely the way to gain acceptance. But if moral dissenters are unwilling to follow the example of the civil rights movement and make a proud public show of their convictions, we as a nation will never have the opportunity to be inspired by their integrity to rethink our own ideas.

This last point bears emphasis. Integrity does not always require following the rules. Sometimes—as in the civil rights movement—integrity requires *breaking* the rules. But it also requires that one be open and public about both the fact of one's dissent and the reasons for it (see chapter 11). A person who lives an integral life may sometimes reach moral conclusions that differ from those of the majority; displaying those conclusions publicly is a crucial aspect of the wholeness in which integrity consists.

Instead of a nation of public dissenters, we have become a nation experienced in misdirection—in beguiling the audience into looking in one direction while we are busy somewhere else. The media culture unfortunately rewards this, not only because a misleading sound bite is more attractive (that is, marketable) than a principled argument, but also because the media seem far more interested in tracking down hypocrisy than in reporting episodes of integrity.

Indeed, to bring the matter full circle, the media will get a healthy share of blame in this book: blame for oversimplification and for interfering with, rather than enabling, the search for right and wrong that each of us must undertake in order to live a life of integrity. But only a share of the blame. If indeed we allow the distractions of living to prevent the discernment of right and wrong so necessary to living with integrity, we should blame neither the media nor the schools nor the government nor our employers, but only ourselves. As I will explain, we as a society can and should do far more to train our children—and ourselves!—in the difficult work of sorting right from wrong and then doing the right and despising the wrong. We can try to blame other forces that interfere; but in the end, when the children grow up, they must make right choices for themselves.

CORRUPTION

If integrity has an opposite, perhaps it is corruption—the getting away with things we know to be wrong. We say that we are a nation that demands integrity, but are we really? We call ourselves a nation of laws, but millions of us cheat on our taxes. We seem not to believe in the integrity of our commitments, with half of marriages ending in divorce. We say we want integrity in our politics, and our politicians promise it endlessly. (Try searching the Nexis database for uses of the word *integrity* by politicians and commentators, and you will be inundated.) But we reward innuendo and smear and barefaced lies with our votes.

Corruption is corrosive. We believe we can do it just a little, but I wonder whether we can. Nearly all of us break small laws—I do it all the time—laws governing everything from the speed at which we may drive to when and how we may cross the street. Few of us will stop on the highway to retrieve the paper bag that the wind whips out the window of our moving car; we may not have thrown it out intentionally, but it still came from our car and it's still littering. These I shall refer to as acts of unintegrity, not an attractive neologism, but one way of avoiding the repeated use of the word *corruption*, which might be misleading. And one who engages in repeated acts of unintegrity may be said to be living an unintegral life.

Some of these acts of unintegrity can be cured by simple calls upon the virtue of consistency. It is both amusing and sad to hear liberals who have fought against the portrayal of vicious racial stereotypes in the media now saying that portrayals of sex and family life in the media affect nobody's behavior; it is just as amusing, and just as sad, to see conservatives bash the President of the United States for criticizing hateful speech on the nation's airwaves and then turn around and bash Hollywood for speech the right happens to hate. But inconsistency is the easiest example of unintegrity to spot. There are harder examples—as we shall see, there may even be some cases in which a lack of integrity is unavoidable—and I shall deal with many of them in the chapters to come.

When I began working on this book, I shared the story about the cheating football player with a few of my colleagues over lunch in the wood-paneled faculty dining room at the Yale Law School. Like me, they are lawyers, so none could be too outraged: our task in life, after all, is sometimes to defend the indefensible. They offered a bewildering array of fascinating and sophisticated arguments on why the receiver who pretended to catch the ball was doing nothing wrong. One in particular stuck in my mind. "You don't know if he was breaking the rules," one of the best and brightest of my colleagues explained, "until you know what the rules are about following the rules."

On reflection, I think my colleague was exactly right. And that, maybe better than anything else, sums up what this book is about. What are our rules about when we follow the rules? What are our rules about when we break them? Until we can answer those two questions, we will not know how much integrity we really want in our public and private lives, to say nothing of how to get it.

•   •   •

Let me offer a brief outline of what is to follow. Part I, "Explanations," is foundational. After further refining its definition in chapter 2, I explain in chapter 3 why integrity is admirable, and distinguish honesty and other similar concepts in chapter 4.

In part II, "Applications," I apply the integrity criteria to six very different (and yet, I trust, interrelated) areas of our public and private lives: I examine our ability to say what we think is true by looking at how we evaluate students and employees; I next look at the news business, particularly the reluctance of journalists to view themselves and their world through the same critical lenses that they train on everybody else; I consider the integrity of our processes for discovering truth by examining the role of oaths, witnesses, and lawyers in civil and criminal trials; I contemplate the integrity of commitments through a discussion over two chapters of what I call the integral marriage; I return to the subject of cheating and sportsmanship; and, finally, I take up the question of civil disobedience, in which the role of integrity is crucial. In each case, I try to determine how the integrity criteria apply, and why, in some situations, they seem not to apply at all.

The third part of the book, "Ruminations," deals with my own questions and reservations as the journey nears its end. I discuss the difficulties of trying to force integrity on others, whether through "special prosecutor" laws or through making rules for political campaigns; sketch an outline of an integral politics; and conclude part III—and the book itself—with a discussion of the problem of evil.

In all of this, I see myself as on a journey toward a richer understanding of our society and of practical morality in a world where values so often seem at war with one another. I certainly do not insist that all or even most people of integrity must agree with the outcomes I reach here; I simply invite the interested reader to come along.

(two)

The Integrity of the Upright

THE historian Josephus tells a famous story of how, when the Roman general Petronius was ordered during the first century to erect a statue of the Emperor Caligula in the Temple in Jerusalem, tens of thousands of unarmed Jews protested, baring their throats and insisting that they would rather die than become idolators. After extended negotiations, Petronius pronounced himself sufficiently moved by their courage that he could not carry out his orders. He wrote to the Emperor saying that honor would not allow him to place the statue in the Temple.[1]

We would all agree, I trust, that believers who are prepared to die rather than abandon the religious commitments that provide meaning in their lives demonstrate a powerful integrity. The capacity of many believers to stand and protest when others will not is a testament to Paul Tillich's contention that religions draw believers toward the ultimate—for a genuine belief in the ultimacy of one's convictions will strengthen them against the temptation to follow the herd. Moreover, as the story of Petronius illustrates, integrity so sublime can move others to change their ways. But we also use the term to describe lesser accomplishments: keeping one's word, for example, or simply telling the truth. In this chapter, after a brief stroll through our struggles to define the word *integrity*, we will consider how some famous instances of integrity (or of its absence) help shape our understanding of and admiration for the term.

A POLITICAL STROLL THROUGH THE *OED*

Our political leaders love to talk about integrity, especially in praise or criticism of somebody else. Explaining his choice of Al Gore as running mate in 1992, Bill Clinton called Gore "a leader of great strength, integrity and stature."[2] Following Michael Dukakis's heavy defeat by George Bush in 1988, George McGovern—who knows something of heavy presidential defeats—reminded Dukakis that he still had "the respect of the American people, his health and his integrity."[3] During that same campaign, Bush called on voters to elect the candidate with "the integrity and the stability to get the job done."[4] Dukakis proposed during the campaign what he called the Integrity in Government Initiative to tighten postemployment restrictions on federal employees. (In an interesting sideshow on integrity, his aides then rushed to explain that the document as distributed to reporters actually misrepresented some of Dukakis's positions.)[5]

In 1984, the Reverend Jesse Jackson, campaigning for the Democratic ticket, praised Walter Mondale for possessing "the integrity, the intelligence and the endurance to be a true leader of the American people."[6] That same election year, in his speech renominating George Bush for Vice President, California's then-governor George Deukmejian said that Bush, "[d]uring his many years of service to our country . . . , has earned an impeccable reputation for integrity."[7] And in 1972, just a week before Richard Nixon's landslide reelection, the *New York Times*, which had endorsed his opponent, published a prescient editorial stating that "the most important virtue in politics is integrity."[8]

Having worked our way back to Richard Nixon on the subject of integrity, perhaps we have found a good place to stop and ponder. What are all these people talking about? Or, more to the point, what do they think they are talking about, and why do they think voters care? To find the answers, we must look a bit more deeply into the definition of *integrity*.

Let us first move to the location that every schoolchild would suggest as the sensible place to start. When trying to understand any word in the English language, you go to the dictionary, and when you want more than a casual definition, you go to the *Oxford English Dictionary*. The *OED* lists three definitions of the word *integrity*. Two of them are already in the nature of old friends. The first definition captures the sense of wholeness that I mentioned in chapter 1:

The condition of having no part or element taken away or wanting; undivided or unbroken state; material wholeness, completeness, entirety.

The *OED*'s citations go back to 1533 and Thomas More ("Not ye sacrifice nor oblacion, whyche to the integritie therof requyreth both the formes"), and include as well an eighteenth-century cite from Thomas Warton's essay on Alexander Pope ("The poem before us is by no means destitute of a just integrity, and a lucid order"). In these examples and others, one finds illustrated the sense of integrity as *completeness.*

The *OED*'s second definition points less to completeness than to perfection:

The condition of not being marred or violated; unimpaired or uncorrupted condition; original perfect state; soundness.

The editors of the *OED* are nothing if not erudite. Among their citations is a 1450 reference to the Virgin Birth ("When he [Christ] was born savyng his moders integritee") and a strikingly similar use a century later ("In these and other lyke factes, was faythes integrite broken, whych is the true maydenhede of ye soule"). Other citations refer to integrity of the faculties and integrity of a text, so that one finds a sense not only of perfection but actually of being in good order.

What the *OED* here fails to mention, but what the student of integrity cannot afford to forget, is that when understood in this sense—denoting perfection or an uncorrupted state—the word has been put to horrible uses. For example, the Nuremberg racial laws of the Nazi regime and many of the segregation laws of the Jim Crow era shared a common justification: protecting the "integrity" of the race. And perfectly serious people have been unafraid to offer this justification in fairly recent history. So, for example, in *Naim v. Naim* (1955), in which the Virginia Supreme Court upheld the constitutionality of the state's antimiscegenation statute, the judges made no effort to disguise either their own racism or the legislature's. The law, the court wrote, was intended "to preserve the racial integrity" of the citizens of the state.

That the word can be used this way is a reason for caution; it does not counsel abandonment of the concept. However, we can see how the notion of integrity as perfection not only is less useful than the definition

I have offered, but can actually be dangerous. So let us proceed to the *OED*'s third definition, which startles the reader if only because it is marked *Obs.*, for *obsolete*:

> In moral sense. . . . Unimpaired moral state; freedom from moral corruption; innocence; sinlessness.

The most instructive of several citations is from Thomas Traherne's *Christian Ethics*, published in 1675: "In his corruption, he might possibly retain a sence of that nature and life, which he enjoyed in his integrity." This is better, surely, for it reminds us of what the Virginia judges (and legislature) chose to ignore: the integrity of human beings is found in the purity not of the pigmentation of their skin but of their moral understanding and their efforts to do right. So one wants at once to ask: Obsolete? The idea of integrity as implying a freedom from moral corruption? Do we not use the word this way even today?

Well, maybe not. Glancing down the column, one discovers that the editors have appended a variant *b* to this third definition, perhaps to capture our modern usage:

> Soundness of moral principle; the character of uncorrupted virtue, esp. in relation to truth and fair dealing; uprightness, honesty, sincerity.

And now perhaps we have it, or rather, the remaining piece of it: integrity, applied to a person, carries more than a sense of wholeness, because a person must have something to be whole about. It carries more than a sense of perfection, because the person must have a standard against which that perfection is measured. And the thing that the person of integrity is whole about, the standard against which perfection is measured, is "uncorrupted virtue" and a sense of "uprightness, honesty, [and] sincerity."*

---

*What are "uprightness, honesty, [and] sincerity," which the *OED* says are the parts of integrity? Here, the *OED*, usually the final authority in understanding the English language, turns out to be of little help. Take the three words in reverse order. How does the *OED* define *sincerity*? As "freedom from dissimulation or duplicity; honesty, straightforwardness"—in other words, we still need to know what *honesty* is. The *OED*'s answer: "Having honourable motives or principles; marked by uprightness or probity." So we are back again to *uprightness*, which seems to be the key to it all. Except that when we select the proper volume and turn to the right page, we find . . . "The state or condition of being sincere, honest, or just; . . . moral integrity or rectitude." So we have come full circle, back to *integrity*, which is the

This sounds useful. Surely when politicians proclaim their integrity, this sense of "uncorrupted virtue" is what they have in mind; and we take it with a grain of salt because nobody is that perfect, although we seem to want everybody to claim to be. But one need not be sinless to possess integrity. As one Joseph Dana preached in a sermon at the North Meetinghouse in Salem nearly two hundred years ago: "[I]f it meant *sinless rectitude* it could apply to no man living." But instead, Dana explained, integrity conveys "an idea of *thorough principle*": not that one never fails to live a life governed by a duty to the good and the right, but rather that one always tries to.[9]

Consider the quotation from the Book of Proverbs that appears on the overleaf, which reads in full: "The integrity of the upright guides them, but the crookedness of the treacherous destroys them" (Prov. 11:3). This line, attributed to Solomon, appears in the part of the Book of Proverbs that extols the role of wisdom in life; so integrity is a part of wisdom, and it is a possession of the upright. This cannot be taken to mean, however, that integrity itself answers the moral questions; after all, the narrative of the Judeo-Christian Bible insists that the laws of God answer the moral questions. Consequently, the believer who possesses the faculty of integrity must have the desire and, perhaps, the ability to discern and do the will of God.[10]

Thus, when the Proverb says that the upright will be guided by their integrity, its reference is to the process of discerning rather than to the substance of what is discerned.* After all, it is possible to discern without integrity, to undertake moral reflection in order to get the answer on which you have already settled, rather than the genuine opening of the self to listen for the word of God that true discernment requires. The upright will, in the Proverb, do the second, not the first, and it is that *openness* to God that makes them upright.

To move from the religious background to the more general analysis we are attempting, one would say that integrity is not in and of itself a sense of right and wrong; rather, integrity is the faculty that enables us to discern right and wrong. Integrity is not by itself a guide. It is a guide to being guided. It does not so much tell us right and wrong as it helps us to see the truth of right and wrong. And at the center of that integrity lies a will-

---

word we were looking up in the first place. The dictionary has taken us as far as it can.

*The word translated here as *integrity* occurs in approximately fifty places in the Hebrew Bible. In other verses, it is translated as *perfection, simplicity,* or *uprightness,* among other words.

ingness to be open in our discernment of the right.

And if that is the meaning of *uncorrupted*, it is one that we can, in our human fallibility, surely endorse: the life that is lived with integrity is a life of striving toward the good and the true. Integrity, in that sense, may be conceived as a journey rather than a destination, an effort to live according to one's sense of duty rather than a sinlessness reserved for a handful of saints—and precious few of them. Already, one can reflect on the definition of *integrity* that I have offered: for the duty that forms the basis of the integral life is thus the duty to act in accordance with the good that one discerns in rule 1. The act itself is of course rule 2. And it is the struggle to take those two steps, and then to take the third, the step toward articulating one's reasons, that represents the integral life.

Moreover, one can begin to understand how this definition fits the way politicians use the term. When one claims to possess more integrity than another, one is claiming to be uncorrupted in this special sense; and the duty toward which the politician bends his or her efforts should be the duty to follow principle. That duty should not vary depending on circumstance. As the theologian James M. Gustafson points out, "consistency or predictability" is crucial to integrity: "if in similar circumstances he always did different things, the word integrity would not come to mind as appropriate."[11] So now it is plain why the politicians who steer close to the winds of popular opinion, changing their positions with every shift, are viewed as the ones who lack integrity. Those politicians may be described as corrupt in the sense conveyed in Joseph Dana's sermon: there is no set of principles to which they give their all.

DISCERNMENT: ANTIGONE'S INTEGRITIES

Our admiration for this capacity to sacrifice *all* for the sake of principle is a vital part of our more general admiration of integrity. Let us take a moment now to consider one of the most famous examples of this in literature: Sophocles's play *Antigone*.[12]

The facts are quickly told. The ruler of Thebes, Creon, has decreed that no citizen who dies fighting for the city-state's enemies may be buried; instead, the corpse must be left to rot. In due time, Creon's own nephew, Polynieces, turns against the city and is slain outside the walls. The king insists on imposing the punishment he previously decreed, refusing permission for burial. His niece, Antigone, acting out of love, defies her uncle and buries her brother according to tradition. A furious Creon has the unrepentant Antigone walled up in a cave; when at last he changes his mind and has the cave opened, he finds that she has committed suicide. Query: Who showed the greater integrity?

Many a high-schooler or college freshman has struggled with this question. Let us struggle along with them. First, consider the possibility that King Creon, in his unbending insistence on punishing even his own nephew, acts with more integrity than Antigone. Creon is hardly a sympathetic character, but he is clear and steadfast in doing what he believes to be right. He plays no favorites, making no exception even for his own flesh and blood. As for Antigone, she evidently made no protest when the punishment was carried out against ordinary citizens of Thebes, but only when the burial of her brother was forbidden; she asserts no principle (other than familial love) to undergird her protest.

In this Antigone is like many of the Americans who protested with such vehemence when a judge in Singapore sentenced a young American to a caning—a flogging, really—for vandalism, an offense that some in the United States consider relatively minor. The reason the protesters were like Antigone is that the ground of protest seemed to be so narrow: Treat your own citizens as you like, but you may not so treat one of ours! (No wave of revulsion has ever swept America at the way that Singapore treats its own people.) And, so stated, the objection turns out to be an argument not against brutality generally but against brutality to Americans, thus losing a good deal of its moral force.

The same may be said of Antigone: her argument, directed only at her brother, loses the universalism that might make it sound in justice, at least to the modern ear.[13] And yet it is plain to the most casual reader of the play that Sophocles means us to see Creon as the villain and Antigone as one to be admired. Consider how Sophocles builds the dramatic tension as Creon begins to have second thoughts. First his own son, Haemon, Antigone's betrothed, urges him to release her and is furious when he will not. Then Teiresias, a prophet, shows up to warn Creon: "Stubbornness and stupidity are twins." When Creon, at last convinced, rushes off to free Antigone, he is too late. She has hanged herself. Haemon, in a rage, tries to kill his father and, missing, kills himself instead. A distraught Creon returns to the palace, haunted by the Chorus, which taunts him: "You have learned justice, though it comes too late." And then he learns that his wife, Eurydice, has killed herself in despair over the death of her son. Creon cries out, "This is my guilt, all mine."

But is Creon right that the guilt is all his? If he was in his way too unbending, might we not say the same of Antigone? After all, had she submitted to the law, there would have been no tragic string of suicides. Indeed, it is fair to say that the horrible ending arose from the *combination* of her stubbornness and Creon's. The philosopher Martha Nussbaum (following Hegel) points out that "Antigone, like Creon, has engaged in a ruthless simplification of the world of value which effectively eliminates conflicting obligations."[14] So why is Antigone to be more admired?

Part of the answer comes from the conversation between Creon and the Chorus that I just quoted. Creon, on reflection, sees his error. The Chorus's position—and, I think, the reader's—must be that Creon should have thought all this out in advance. His moral error came in not being sufficiently reflective before announcing his rule. Antigone, by contrast, holds a lengthy conversation with her sister, Ismene, *before* embarking on her defiance of the king. We know that she has reflected long and hard on both right and wrong and the consequences of her action because we see her do it. So our admiration for Antigone probably stems at least in part from our realization that she, unlike Creon, *is* morally reflective, and that she undertakes this process of reflection *before* deciding what to do.

Thinking matters through before we act is always difficult and often consumes a significant part of our time. But it simply is not possible to be a person of integrity without doing it. On this point, many different moral sources agree. Socrates, of course, thought the unexamined life not worth living. Such very different contemporary philosophers as John Rawls and Bernard Williams, by exalting dialogue, necessarily exalt reflection as well. But reflection is not merely for philosophers; it is for all of us. For example, when the *Catechism of the Catholic Church* turns to the issue of conscience, it enjoins individuals to follow the dictates of conscience but also concedes that conscience can be in error—usually because the conscience "remains in ignorance." The *Catechism* continues: "Ignorance can often be imputed to personal responsibility. This is the case when a man 'takes little trouble to find out what is true and good, or when conscience is by degrees almost blinded through the habit of committing sin.' In such cases, the person is culpable for the evil he commits."[15]

Why is the person culpable? Because it is his own fault that he is morally ignorant. He either is stuck in "the habit of committing sin" or—what is, for the student of integrity, both much more important and much worse— he has not taken the trouble "to find out what is true and good"; that is to say, he has not engaged in moral reflection before choosing a course of action.[16]

DISCERNMENT AND RISK

Doing right in preference to wrong implies that one will do so even in the presence of risk. This surely accounts for our respect for this century's twin icons of nonviolent resistance, Mohandas Gandhi and Martin Luther King, Jr., both of whom were open and public and loving in their successful battles against oppressive authority. (See chapters 3 and 11.) Their example continues to inspire people who love democracy—literally around the world. As I write these words, the government of Myanmar (formerly Burma) has just yielded to intense international pressure and released from six years of house arrest Daw Aung San Suu Kyi, who won the 1991 Nobel Peace Prize for her struggle to democratize her nation and was punished for it. Also as I write, the government of China has just released Harry Wu, who spent nineteen years in Chinese prisons for his prodemocracy work but became a U.S. citizen in 1994. Since changing citizenship, Wu has often returned to China (sometimes under assumed names) to gather information about human rights abuses. Finally, the Chinese government arrested Wu, only to turn around and release him after an international outcry— fresh evidence that faith moves mountains.

Faith—the faith that we are right—also enables us to take risks for what we most deeply believe to be good and true, and that is what all of these people did. If for the sake of the right they stood in harm's way, they did so by personal choice, a choice that the rest of us can only admire. The philosopher Lynne McFall has argued that there is no integrity without risk of loss: "A person of integrity is willing to bear the consequences of her convictions, even when this is difficult, that is, when the consequences are unpleasant." And if we are never tested, we never really know how deeply we believe: "Where there is no possibility of its loss, integrity cannot exist."[17] In short, we can never really know whether we are acting from deep and steadfast principles until those principles are tested.

McFall's point is well taken, not only as a matter of moral philosophy but as a matter of human personality: we admire most those who stand up for their beliefs when they have something to lose. Much of the Biblical narrative is built around such steadfastness. Thus, Abraham accepts God's command to sacrifice his son Isaac, and Job refuses, in the face of endless tribulations, to abandon his faith (or, as he puts it, his "integrity" [Jb. 27:5]). And secular examples abound. Thus, Bobby Fischer, the tempestuous American genius who was world chess champion from the time of his victory over Boris Spassky in 1972 until his resignation in 1975, was to many observers a spoiled and irritating brat, but there was no denying his integrity. Indeed, had he possessed less integrity, he might well have been champion a good deal sooner. In 1967, he was comfortably alone in first place at the midpoint of the Interzonal Tournament—one of several tournament and match hurdles that championship aspirants must leap—when he withdrew in protest after the organizers insisted that he play a game on his sabbath. Most of us, I suspect, with the championship at stake, would have ignored the sabbath and played the game. But Fischer stuck to his principles, was disqualified from the tournament (which he almost certainly would have won), and had to begin the hard climb to the championship anew three years later.

Of course, we admire more those who risk more. That is why Barbara Fritchie is an American hero (at least to Yankees), whether or not, as legend has it, the ninety-five-year-old widow actually resisted Confederate General Stonewall Jackson's September 1862 invasion of Frederick, Maryland, with the words attributed to her by the poet John Greenleaf Whittier: "'Shoot, if you must, this old gray head, / But spare your country's flag,' she said."* Jackson supposedly responded: "Who touches a hair on yon gray head / Dies like a dog! March on!"

But whether or not the story of Barbara Fritchie (who was, at least, a real person) is true, our admiration for her is plainly admiration of her willingness to make the ultimate sacrifice for her beliefs. She was in that sense a thorough patriot, not in our deplorable modern sense of somebody who wants to escape the force of law while telling everybody else how to be a good American, but in the traditional sense of somebody who simply loves her country enough—or, as Whittier would have it, loves *our* country enough—that she will stand and die for its flag.

Like the first-century Jews who faced down Petronius, Antigone, too, offers the ultimate sacrifice—not for her city, perhaps, but for her family and her belief in the right. Certainly she meets McFall's test, for she is "willing to bear the consequences of her convictions, even . . . when the consequences are unpleasant." And Antigone's willingness to face death, even if the fact that it is suicide deprives it of some of its moral resonance, surely is a part of the reason why we admire her.

RIGHT AND WRONG

Now, one wants to be careful, to bear in mind Thoreau's famous observation that somebody's willingness to die for a cause does not make the

---

*This line is often misquoted, and thus misunderstood, as "spare *my* country's flag."

cause right. The soldiers of Hitler and Pol Pot marched bravely into battle, but they were wrong. Risking loss does not *prove* that one possesses integrity. But we are not, yet, arguing that Antigone was *right*; so far, we are arguing only that she acts with greater integrity than Creon. And certainly she has followed all the rules we have set down: she has been morally reflective, has acted on the basis of her discernment of right and wrong (even at significant personal risk), and has been willing to say quite openly what she is doing and why she is doing it.

Nevertheless, we cannot stop here and be satisfied; the reason I chose in chapter 1 to define *integrity* as beginning with discernment of *right and wrong* rather than of *our own beliefs* is, quite simply, that our own beliefs can lead us astray. Says Lynne McFall: "Suppose one's *principle* is 'Yield to temptation; it may not pass your way again.' "[18] Indeed, our own beliefs, no matter how cherished, can be unspeakably evil. The philosopher Stuart Hampshire puts the problem this way: "If a person has lived a blameless life 'according to his lights,' as the saying goes, the question always arises— 'Were his lights good enough, or could they have been better?' "[19]

The point is a crucial one. To admire somebody's integrity is not to say that he or she is right about the issue in question; we can, I hope, admire the virtue of integrity in people with whom we have sharp political and moral disagreements. Although, as I will argue (see chapter 14), there are surely some views of sufficiently obnoxious morality that one cannot hold them and remain a person of integrity, for the moment let it suffice to say that, having decided that a person is showing integrity, it is still for the observer to decide whether the underlying cause is a just one.

Sophocles plainly understands this. Despite the language of the Chorus, which criticizes Creon for his pride, the reason Creon becomes a villain and his niece a hero cannot be simply that he is unbending; Antigone is unbending, too, and the clash of their separate steadfastnesses breeds the tragedy. Yet Sophocles clearly does not think Antigone equally culpable with Creon. What, then, is Sophocles driving at?

The answer, surely, is that Sophocles means us to see Creon as unbending in *the wrong cause*. It is not enough, in other words, that he has integrity in the sense of pressing forward with what he believes to be right. Sophocles would have us inquire whether the cause he is pressing is actually right or not—and only then to decide how to measure his integrity. But here, perhaps, Sophocles slightly misses the mark, at least if he means us, in the classical fashion, to infer from Creon's distress the wrongness of his cause. As we have seen, the reason Creon lacks integrity is *not* that his judgment is wrong but rather that he did not do adequate work of discernment before reaching it. Still, by putting matters so starkly, Sophocles confronts us with a question that is crucial to the rest of our discussion: Can we admire the integrity of those we believe to be wrong?

I think the answer is clearly yes. Although I shall later argue that there are views to which discernment cannot lead a reasonable person, I think that universe relatively small and tightly bounded by our common experience. Thus I reject entirely our national polemical habit of dismissing our political opponents as craven moral creatures who cannot possibly possess any integrity. For too many of us who are deeply committed to our beliefs, all the integrity is on one side: our side. The other side doesn't have any. (If they did, they would agree with us.)

I remember as a teenager in Ithaca, New York, sitting in front of the television on a winter evening, watching a very popular and very conservative commentator and saying to myself that he had to be making it all up; he couldn't possibly believe what he was saying; he was only saying it to shock and thus to gain and hold an audience. In other words, he altogether lacked integrity. I was so sure that I was right that I went downstairs to tell my parents what I had figured out. But I had fallen, not for the last time, into a trap that most of us know all too well: the trap of assuming that all the arguments were on my side, so that anybody who disagreed was not only wrong but willfully blind to the plain truth of the matter.

We have to be wary in assuming that those who are not like us cannot possess integrity, although all of us do it: the well-heeled who believe that the poor are all lazy, the less well off who are certain that the rich are all corrupt. As the Lutheran theologian Paul Jersild has put it: "[T]he deviousness of the human heart leads both the 'haves' and the 'have-nots' to project the worst of human motivations upon each other."[20] Of course we do it—and we forget what should be obvious, that integrity in the sense of being discerning, of being forthright, of keeping one's commitments, is not the exclusive property of any part of the political spectrum.

DISCERNMENT REVISITED

Again and again in this chapter, we have seen how taking the time to reflect on right and wrong is crucial to integrity. To do so consumes resources—resources of emotion and of hours on the clock—but *not* to reflect on the right enhances the possibilities for doing the wrong. Whether one believes, with Aristotle, that we learn the habits of virtue through repetition, or, with Aquinas, that the God-given knowledge of the good rests within each of us, waiting for discovery, the fact remains that we cannot know what is right unless we think about it first.

For me as a Christian, a belief in discernment rests crucially on the belief in God and the duty of obedience to God's law. The great theologians saw this combination of discernment and obedience as a duty, not an option. Thus, John Wesley warned in a sermon that "the nature of the covenant of grace gives you no ground, no encouragement at all, to set aside any instance or degree of obedience."[21] According to Aquinas: "Granted that a person is not always bound to will the same thing God wills, he is bound to will what God wants him to will. Since the knowledge of what this is comes chiefly through the divine commandments, a person is obliged to obey these in all cases."[22] In a twelfth-century pamphlet, the Jewish philosopher Moses Maimonides put it this way: "Truly, people err when they dare to strike truth in the face and act against the clear and simple statements in the Bible."[23] So when the Book of Proverbs refers to the "integrity of the upright," it conveys a sense of uprightness as the capacity for discernment of God's will, but the reason it matters is that the duty to obey that will is absolute.

Moving once more from the realm of religion to the more general realm of ethics, we can say that we have a general duty to do the right rather than the wrong, a duty as absolute as the duty to follow God's will. We can further say that the upright individual—the person who lives an integral life—is not necessarily *better* at discerning right and wrong than others may be; rather, the upright individual is the person who will usually try. Skill in telling right from wrong obviously matters, but the willingness to attempt it ultimately matters more.

All of this rests simply on the notion that some beliefs and some acts are morally better than others—*and that it is possible to tell which are which.* In the Enlightenment tradition, one does this in part by reason. But one also listens for the voice of conscience, which incorporates a wealth of received social knowledge about what has, over time, been accepted as right or derided as wrong. And the conscience, argued Professor Tyler in the sermon we encountered in chapter 1, "is ever active and awake, passing judgment on every action and, according as it appears to be right or wrong, issuing its positive command or its stern prohibition."[24]

This notion of conscience proposes that the knowledge of right and wrong is there waiting to be discovered: either placed by God in Creation, or placed by a good society, as Aristotle would suggest, in the upbringing of its children. The philosopher Bernard Williams is very much in this spirit when he challenges the notion that has come down from Kant that a conviction that one course is right and another wrong must be a *decision*: "[E]thical conviction, like any other form of *being convinced*, must have some aspect of passivity to it, must in some sense come to you."[25] But Williams, arguing with Aristotle, also worries that ethical reflection may be more difficult if we work too hard to instill a sense of unwavering right and wrong in our children: in effect, they might grow into adults who will have difficulty reaching any moral conclusions other than the ones into which they have been trained. This might work well if the morality that society teaches is good—but if it is bad, where will we find our dissenting heroes, the next Martin Luther King, Jr., or Daw Aung San Suu Kyi?

Part of the answer to this concern is that we really have no adequate account of how societal mores change. We can *theorize* about why the same nation that countenanced slavery and segregation for three hundred years suddenly rejected that history in the 1960s—but we can never quite *know*. We do know, however, that people *do* change their minds, even about moral propositions.[26] They do it because somebody else convinces them, through argument or example; because they reason their way to a better moral answer; or simply because something mysterious and inspiring leads them to the God-given knowledge of the right that is buried deep within and masquerades as conscience. But the point is that they do it.

Nothing in my account turns on whether one sees the process of discernment as mostly reception or mostly reason; the point, rather, is that whichever view one endorses, we can hardly dispute the importance of reflection, of taking the time to separate the right from the wrong. In this way, the theologians and the philosophers agree, one's soul can find a bit of rest: "[T]he peace of the rational soul," wrote Augustine, "is the ordered agreement of knowledge and action."[27] Naturally. But that ordered agreement is possible only if one first takes time to seek the knowledge. Plato tells us in his dialogues that there were times when Socrates would quite literally *stop* to think—stop walking, stop his remarks—and we are surely meant to understand that Socrates is more admirable for this habit, that what he says after a suitable pause is deeply thought out and just as deeply meant.[28]

In today's polarized and mean-spirited politics, relatively few political activists or elected officials see the necessity for engaging in discernment prior to acting and speaking; the reason may be the near-religious fervor of infallibility that eventually seems to infect people who get involved in causes. But if we refuse to take the time for discernment, a discernment that might challenge cherished beliefs, then it is hard to see how we can ever construct a politics of integrity.

In our busy world, the instinctive response perhaps is to say that it is fine for Socrates or Augustine to stop and think, to take the time for discernment—What else did they have to do with their lives? And I know from hard experience how difficult it can be to find the time to be contemplative about moral questions; it is easier, and quicker, to follow our instincts or to follow the herd. The lack of time is an unfortunate characteristic of today's Americans, and volumes have been written about how it is hurting our children and our families, but it is hurting our morality just as much. For if we decide that we do not have time to stop and think about right and wrong, then we do not have time to figure out right from wrong, which means that we do not have time to live according to our model of right and wrong, which means, simply put, that we do not have time for lives of integrity.

(three)

Why Is Integrity Admirable?

I N the first chapter, I mentioned our disdain for the public figure who seems unable to be steadfast, who shifts ground with the political winds. A politician of that kind, I argued, shows a lack of integrity because the very first criterion is violated: if he is so swift to change, the chances are that his views are not well thought out in the first place. In other words, he cannot hope to live an integral public life because he has not engaged in the hard and deep discernment that makes integrity possible.

Although we rarely acknowledge the point, we like our leaders to be morally reflective people, individuals for whom a difficult problem is an occasion for careful thought. Or, rather, we like our leaders to *have been* people of this kind, probably for a very long time; for by the time they are ready to become leaders, they are in many respects fully formed. When a politician is elected to office or an executive is promoted to a senior position, we do not expect her now, for the first time, to begin to determine her views on the problems she faces. Her advancement presumably has come about largely because of the views she has held and acted on over time. And if we say that we expect leaders to be people of integrity, surely we mean, at minimum, that we expect them to act in ways that are consistent with what they said to us before gaining their positions.

Why do we expect this? Well, of course, we do not want to think that the leaders we have selected lied in order to gain their posts; but that is only a part of it. We also expect our leaders to do the things they said they would because we want to think that the things they said they would do resulted from careful reflection, rather than from reading the latest opinion polls. So in this sense, the *steadfastness* we expect of our leaders is evidence of their *reflective* character; and I believe it is that reflective character, more than the steadfastness, that we truly value. If Martin Luther King, Jr., and Abraham Lincoln are signal figures of American history, the reason is only in part that they persevered; the rest of the reason is that they persevered in just and glorious causes. And the ability to choose causes rightly stems from the ability to apply the discerning faculties.

In this chapter, by examining several qualities of leadership that we admire, we will see how they constantly relate back to the notion of discernment: of taking the time for genuine moral reflection in order to be sure that one is doing the right.

ADMIRING COMMITMENT

Any management seminar will teach that managers have to do what they say they are going to do: whether they promise reward for good work or punishment for bad, they must deliver. If they do not, they will lose the respect of their co-workers. "Integrity is the basis of *trust*," writes Warren Bennis, "which is not as much an ingredient of leadership as it is a product."[1] In other words, a reputation for integrity, which one must possess in order to be trusted by colleagues, must be earned.

Although we Americans tend to be cynical about our political leaders, the need for reliability is at least as great in politics as in business. Indeed, one very good reason to keep alive the possibility of finding and admiring integrity in those with whom we disagree is that that integrity in turn creates the trust that we need for ordinary social and political intercourse. In the previous chapter, I quoted the *New York Times* editorial holding that "the most important virtue in politics is integrity,"[2] and I think the *Times* was right.

I remember a fascinating moment in the debate over President Reagan's 1986 nomination of Daniel Manion to be a federal appellate judge. Everyone knew that the vote would be a close one, for Manion faced heated opposition, both from those who questioned his legal skills and from those who thought him too much the prisoner of ideology. After weeks of parliamentary maneuvering, the Democrats, believing they had the votes to defeat the nomination, surprised the Republicans with a request for an immediate roll call. The Republicans agreed to the proposal only after several Democratic members who opposed confirmation agreed, as is customary, to "pair" with absent Republican supporters, meaning that they would not vote.

But the Senate Republicans pulled two surprises of their own. First, Republican Slade Gorton, counted among Manion's opponents, voted in favor of confirmation. This still left the vote at 47 in favor and 48 against. Then Senator Nancy Kassebaum, who had already voted no, withdrew her vote, in order, she said, to balance the vote of Senator Barry Goldwater, who could not be found, but who was considered a possible vote by both sides. This left the vote at 47–47, which meant that Vice President Bush, who had rushed to the Hill, could break the tie. But before the Vice President could cast his vote, Democratic Senator Joseph Biden announced that he had changed his mind, that notwithstanding his previous agreement to pair with a Republican, he would now cast a vote and vote no (meaning Manion would lose). Moments later, evidently prompted by Senator Robert Byrd (also a Manion opponent), Biden changed his mind and once again withdrew his vote. I have always assumed that in the interim, Byrd reminded Biden of what, in the heat of battle, he briefly forgot: that it would be impossible to do business as a legislative body unless the members were able to rely on each other to keep their commitments.* Then Byrd himself, the master of Senate rules, changed his own vote from no to yes, which enabled him, as a member of what was now the winning side, to ask for a reconsideration, meaning that a new vote would be held on a later date.[3] (Manion was ultimately confirmed by a vote of 50–49.)

This aspect of integrity—the reliability of commitment—forms, along with the willingness to take risks for a cause, the foundation of our respect for the integrity of our opponents. Our faith that they mean what they say enables us to have conversation and, ultimately, to maintain civil society. That, perhaps, is yet another reason that we so dislike politicians who seem to change their positions with the winds: it is not simply that they cannot be trusted, but the forum in which they cannot be trusted is one in which trust is desperately needed. Politics without trust is simply war.

*This episode makes all the more poignant, and all the more hard-hitting, Byrd's 1995 criticism of Senator Robert Dole, the majority leader, for supposedly reneging on a deal to bring the Balanced Budget Amendment to vote on a particular day— a deal, said Byrd, that Dole abandoned when he could not find the votes to pass the amendment.

Our admiration for reliability, for keeping one's commitments, is connected not to rule 3, saying what we mean, but to rule 2, acting in accordance with what we have discerned. When we make commitments, the world assumes that we have thought them through, that we are not just running our mouths. For a commitment is not merely a statement, an exercise of the faculty of speech; it is quintessentially an act, and one on which others rely. If we did not believe that words that form a commitment are as much an act as they are speech, the First Amendment's protection of freedom of speech would make it impossible to enforce, for example, the law of contracts. Indeed, the law of contracts illustrates the notion of integrity with some precision, for the law generally assigns to the party who promises to do something the risk that it will be harder than she thought. This in turn encourages the rational individual to engage in deep reflection on whether to go forward with a contract. Our respect for contracts, as for other forms of commitment, surely rests on the belief that a person of integrity will do what she has promised, because it is her responsibility to weigh the risks before making the promise.

Lewis Smedes, an ordained minister who teaches at Fuller Theological Seminary, sees promises as a special form of human endeavor. In a beautiful sermon entitled *The Power of Promises*, he explains: "When a person makes a promise, he stretches himself out into circumstances that no one can control and controls at least one thing: he will be there no matter what the circumstances turn out to be."[4] A promise, in other words, is an open and unequivocal statement about how one intends to live; if sincerely made, it is also a claim of the importance of the particular choice that is promised. This is true whether the promise is to meet at noon tomorrow for lunch or to deliver a thousand bushels of wheat by next Monday. Now this is already an awesome responsibility to thrust upon anybody, but Smedes does not see it as in any way narrowing of the self. The ability to promise and then to keep the promise is an aspect not simply of liberty but of humanity: "A free self knows he becomes a genuine self by making commitments to other people—promises he intends to keep even when keeping them exacts a price."[5]

That, surely, is how promises of a special kind—we have been using the word *commitments*—differ from the promises that we make in our ordinary lives. Immanuel Kant notoriously argued for the psychologically impossible proposition that nobody should ever lie, and Augustine contended that any lie, and any promise not kept, was a sin against God's gift of speech. But, although we condemn most lies most of the time (see chapter 4) and most of us struggle to keep as many of our promises as we can, few of us would be able to live or to tolerate a life quite so constrained as Kant and Augustine would suggest. The modern law of contracts recognizes this, for it rests crucially on Oliver Wendell Holmes's famous dictum that the obligation created by a promise is simply the choice to perform a promise or pay damages for its breach. The legal scholar Anthony Kronman has argued that this ability to escape a commitment by paying damages—to "monetize" a relationship—is crucial to human freedom, for we might otherwise be forced to relate to others in ways that we find uncomfortable or even oppressive.[6]

Are some promises sufficiently distinctive that ordinary rules of contract law are, if not irrelevant, at least of diminished import? Surely the understanding of integrity we have developed suggests that the answer is yes. The most obvious example of an undertaking of this kind is the commitment involved in marriage. Although marriage is sufficiently important that I have made it the subject of two chapters (chapters 8 and 9), a few words should be said of it here, for the notion of fidelity in marriage can help illuminate the notion of fidelity in leadership.

Marriage, once treated in the law as a status in which the parties had well-defined roles, has over the years evolved in the legal understanding in the direction of contract.[7] In one sense, this has been a positive development, for it has freed married women from a legally enforced regime of expectations under which many chafed. Yet the model has obvious weaknesses. When marriage is only a contract, as the law nowadays treats it, one who decides to break it can in effect follow Holmes's dictum and buy his or her way out: paying damages instead of carrying out the promise. In fact, one can sometimes escape a marriage without paying a thing, because, under the "modern" laws enforced in most jurisdictions, divisions of marital property and obligations of support following divorce are in most circumstances awarded without regard to fault.

Yet consider the marriage vow itself. The form of words that is used in most Christian churches is a vow to remain faithfully married "until we are parted by death." This is not the stuff of the ordinary promise, like the promise to deliver a thousand bushels of wheat by next Monday, the sort of thing that must be monetizable to help us avoid personal relationships that we find awkward. In fact, only by reinterpreting the vow—by striving to make less of the words than what they very plainly state—can we reduce it to a promise of the usual kind. A respect for the integrity of the person who makes the vow requires us, however, to take it at face value; when it is said, it is meant.

And why do we believe that the vow is meant? Because its form requires such belief, and because the plain seriousness of the undertaking it represents suggests to us that it is not entered into lightly. Thus the person of integrity, before making a commitment on which others are expected to rely, will undertake a period of reflection, often a sustained one, in order to weigh the pros and cons and decide which course is best. And although all of us shoot from the hip from time to time, a person who does so consistently, especially in enunciating important commitments, is unlikely to be a person of true integrity, for acting on one's first impulse denies the possibility of that crucial sustained reflection.

This doubtless explains a good part of our open disdain for politicians who shift ground endlessly as the polls change around them. We say we like them to be steadfast, to believe in their principles. But *why* do we want them to believe in their principles? Just because they happen to have some? Surely not. Surely we want to believe that our politicians have come to their principles after careful and sustained thought, in some cases a career's worth; and if they jettison too quickly what we thought they believed, we have before us the evidence that they lack the first ingredient of integrity: the ability to think long and hard before making difficult moral decisions.

One saw a sign of this in 1976, when Richard Schweiker, a respected but maverick Republican senator from Pennsylvania, agreed to serve as vice-presidential running mate to Ronald Reagan, who was involved in what would prove an unsuccessful effort to oust Gerald Ford as the party's nominee for the presidency. Reagan and his advisers hit upon the rather audacious ploy of naming a running mate prior to the vote at the convention, probably in an effort to reassure delegates who feared that Reagan was a bit too far right for their taste. Schweiker was the antidote—and powerful medicine the Reagan people hoped he would be. It was not just that he disagreed with Reagan on such issues as abortion, where Reagan was adamantly pro-life. As *Newsweek* pointed out: "Ronald Reagan would appear to have been hard pressed to find a more liberal senator in either party."[8] To run with Reagan, Schweiker in effect had to jettison principles for which he had fought all his life—or, if not to toss them overboard, at least to admit to himself that they were less important than his own advancement in the party.

And Reagan, as a result of naming Schweiker, lost some of his conservative supporters (although they presumably returned to him in time for the 1980 landslide). To bolster Reagan's ideological core, his campaign staff let it be known that he and Schweiker had reached a rather remarkable agreement, under which, should Reagan be elected and die in office, Schweiker would govern according to Reagan's principles, not his own. (Speaking of integrity.) On the issue of Reagan's own integrity, no sooner did he

announce the Schweiker choice than his gleeful opponents began circu-
lating remarks the candidate had made just over two weeks before: "I don't
believe in the old tradition of picking someone at the opposite end of the
political spectrum because he can get some votes you can't get yourself."[9]
Except, when matters came down to the crunch, evidently he did.

The same has happened to many other politicians. There are liberals
who still have not forgiven the late Hubert Humphrey, once their champion, for his reluctance to distance himself from Lyndon Johnson's Vietnam
policy in 1968. George Bush took some hard shots in 1980 when he ran as
Vice President with a man (Reagan once more) whose fiscal policies he
had previously derided as "voodoo economics." And Bill Clinton has been
battered so hard by the media for a purported habit of changing his mind
that Garry Trudeau has begun portraying him in his *Doonesbury* comic
strips as a waffle—this even though some independent studies suggest that
the media's style of reporting, not anything Clinton has done or not done,
is responsible for his reputation.[10] (See chapter 6.)

Warren Bennis argues that Lyndon Johnson, Richard Nixon, and Jimmy
Carter, all of whom saw their presidencies collapse around them, "failed as
leaders." Why? Because "[e]ach was given to saying one thing and doing
another."[11] And although I think this quite an unfair indictment of Jimmy
Carter, who always struck me as too honest to be President, the more general point is useful: we want to know that we can rely on what our leaders
say.

Still, the nagging question remains: Why does a change of tune cause us
to admire our leaders less? The reason must be that when politicians are
able to change so thoroughly what they have claimed to stand for, we
begin to question whether their previously stated views were preceded by
anything like the degree of moral reflectiveness that is necessary for us to
have faith in what they say. Our leaders, in short, should be people of a
discerning nature, people who genuinely accept Socrates's admonition that
the unexamined life is not worth living.

ADMIRING FORTHRIGHTNESS

Closely connected to reliability of commitment is a second aspect of
integrity that we admire in our leaders. I have in mind forthrightness: we
can trust them to say what they truly think, even at risk to themselves. In
the previous chapter, I noted some of the reasons for our exaltation of such
leaders as Gandhi and King. Another reason, surely, is that they were forth-

right in the very special sense that civil disobedience often requires: not only did they break the law when conscience demanded it, but they stood up publicly and said they were breaking the law and accepted the punishment that their societies imposed. This they did out of the highest respect for their countries and their people, the belief that it would be possible, through the example of their open sacrifice, to inspire people to change the laws they saw as unjust. (I discuss civil disobedience in more detail in chapter 11.)

Antigone, whose case we visited in chapter 2, certainly shows a willingness to be forthright, without regard to the consequences of her actions. Indeed, she clearly has no intention of hiding what she is up to. When her irresolute sister, Ismene, promises to keep secret the burial of Polynieces, Antigone responds in disgust: "Dear God! Denounce me. I shall hate you more / if silent, not proclaiming this to all." Later, when arrested and brought before Creon for trial, she is just as clear: "I say I did it and I won't deny it." She *wants* everyone to know what she has done and why she has done it. When Creon will not budge and orders the sentence carried out, a defiant Antigone leaves the stage with a final thrust: "Look what I suffer, at whose command / because I respected the right."

Integrity will also require of leaders that they demonstrate forthrightness of another kind: they must shun our national habit of engaging in misdirection and instead simply tell us what they mean. Now, this is not easy to do, particularly in politics. For example, in early 1995, having voted to bundle a number of welfare programs into block grants to be returned to the states, the Republican-controlled House of Representatives exempted food stamps. The stated reason was that the federal government had to maintain a safety net, but nobody believed it, and it was difficult to see why the net should be that program rather than another. It turned out that the preservation of the federal-entitlement status of food stamps was being pushed by Representatives from farm states for whom the program provides a significant guaranteed purchase of food and therefore a significant subsidy. What a delight it would have been had the Republicans simply stood up and said so; the fact that they did not suggests that they thought indefensible the principle that seemed to be guiding their decisions.

One sees similar forces at work in the wonderful world of military procurement, where it often seems that every member of the Congress—including many Democrats who fancy themselves harsh critics of "unnecessary" military spending—is armed with an unimpeachable case for the military necessity of the particular weapons or vehicles or components made in his or her state. Some politicians are at last beginning to talk about military

spending in terms of jobs and local economies instead of defense. This political candor is a happy development—happy for integrity, that is.

True, there are times when perfect forthrightness by a leader will make
it difficult or impossible to gain the end in view, as, for example, when the
President is asked whether he has made up his mind to take a particular
military action. John Henry Cardinal Newman, in *Apologia Pro Vita Sua*
(1947), tells a story about St. Athanasius, who was being persecuted by
Julian, fled down the Nile on a boat, and found himself trapped. So he
turned to meet his pursuers, and when they asked him, "Have you seen
Athanasius?" he answered, "Yes, he is close to you." The searchers continued down the river, and Athanasius returned to Alexandria and hid.[12]

These examples have in common not only the aura of crisis, but also the
ability to meet a simple test: after the fact, there is no shame or dishonor in
admitting the deception publicly. Now, the test is far from ideal, and if it
truly excuses the leader from the duty of forthrightness, weak or unscrupulous leaders will be tempted to use it often. In her book *Lying*, Sissela Bok
warns that these seemingly good-faith lies are subject to "the dangers of
spread and mistake and deterioration of standards that accompany all
deception."[13] For just that reason, in all but the most extreme cases, leaders
will do well to recognize that the judgment on whether they possess
integrity will be based in part on whether they are willing to be forthright
in the face of risk—not on how skilled they are in the arts of deception and
evasion.

Corporations as well as individuals may earn reputations for integrity
through their willingness to be forthright in the face of risk. AT&T, for
example, won wide admiration in 1991 when, following a software failure
that shut down its long-distance services, the firm's chairman, Robert Allen,
at once accepted personal responsibility for the fiasco, and, by way of
apology, the company cut its long-distance charges on Valentine's Day.
And one of the reasons that recalls and even replacements of safe but
defective products are often appropriate, although expensive, is that they
signal the consumer that a firm is sufficiently forthright that it is willing to
admit its error and stand behind its product. Intel apparently overlooked
this fact in 1995, when it lost a measure of consumer goodwill by its refusal
for several weeks to replace defective Pentium microchips that would fail,
the firm insisted, in only a vanishingly small fraction of cases. But that was
not the point. Consumers simply did not want defective chips, and Intel,
buried by an avalanche of bad publicity (including some truly creative
jokes), at last gave in.

Indeed, the willingness to admit error is often an important part of forthrightness. Everybody's classic business example is the decision by the Coca-Cola Company to withdraw its "new" Coke from the market when its faithful public objected, demanding the return of the "old," now sold as Coke Classic. (New Coke has disappeared.) The new formula was developed as a result of taste tests suggesting that most people preferred it to the old, but the brand loyalty that gives trademarks their value is constructed of factors that no one fully understands. Brand loyalty, in fact, may be viewed as a kind of integrity, the fulfilling of a commitment to keep buying if the producer continues to produce at the same level of quality.[14] Coca-Cola, faced with a consumer revolt, showed a kind of integrity too, remembering its own side of the commitment: to give people what they want, not what some clever consultants say people will want.

ADMIRING STEADFASTNESS

Steadfastness, no less than forthrightness, is a part of the integrity of a leader, and for similar reasons: one who follows wants to believe that the leader has been reflective, has thought things out, and is certain that the course is right. Only a person who has done the hard work of discernment can stick to the course in the face of criticism and difficulty—only the person who has done that hard work, or a person of one other kind: the fanatic. Part of the point of integral leadership is surely to convince the people who look to you for inspiration that yours is the discerning rather than the fanatical kind of steadfastness.

Many of the leaders we most admire made the choice to stand fast in the face of criticism and risk. Martin Luther King, Jr., quite plainly exemplifies this aspect of integrity. So does Thurgood Marshall, who during his years of civil rights litigation often had to hide in out-of-the-way places or flee in the dead of night from people who hated him for his advocacy and who planned, quite seriously, to kill him. But he didn't stop. Indeed, a large part of what finally led America to turn its back on state-sanctioned racism was surely the steadfastness of the civil rights movement, not the leaders alone, but the marchers and boycotters, who braved whips and firehoses and dogs and guns and bombs and the noose in order to stand up and demand freedom.

The civil rights movement has become so solid a chapter of our history that we forget there was a time when most Americans derided it. One of the reasons America is able to forget is that the civil rights protesters, with their refusal to be turned away, earned a degree of respect that actually changed the way the nation thinks. Steadfastness in the face of criticism is therefore also an important part of leadership. Politicians in particular ought to have it: they rarely risk anything like what the civil rights marchers (or Antigone) faced, but they often face tidal waves of critique from people who dislike their decisions. And although I have always believed that we can learn from those who criticize us most harshly, an integrity based on discernment will not allow a retreat simply because the criticism is harsh. That is surely why our folklore celebrates Harry Truman's dictum "If you can't stand the heat, get out of the kitchen." We want our leaders, and especially our Presidents, to be able to stand the heat, and we often reward them if they do.

Data on Supreme Court appointments support this view. When a nomination encounters trouble in the Senate, the President may choose to make a fight of it or to back away. Although there are not many cases to study, the evidence suggests that when the President decides to fight, the nominee is almost always confirmed, even when outside observers believe the appointment is doomed.[15] The experience of the late 1980s and early 1990s, in which we were treated to three troubled nominations, is consistent with this thesis. One of the controversial nominees (Robert Bork, 1987) was defeated, a second (Douglas Ginsburg, 1987) was withdrawn, and a third (Clarence Thomas, 1991) was confirmed. Observers have offered all sorts of clever theories to explain the differences in the outcomes of the three, but one possibility is that the Presidents in question treated them differently. Ronald Reagan did not fight for Ginsburg at all and, by most accounts, decided not to fight hard for Bork either.[16] But George Bush fought very hard for Thomas, who faced charges of sexual harassment—potentially a far more serious offense than Bork (accused of writing dangerously radical stuff) or Ginsburg (accused of smoking marijuana as an adult)—and Thomas was confirmed, albeit by the narrowest margin in the nation's history.

Of course, presidential steadfastness, although important, cannot guarantee confirmation, especially when one moves beyond the Supreme Court and examines other offices that require Senate vote. Thus President Clinton, perhaps stung by charges that he had not fought hard enough for Lani Guinier, his controversial 1993 nominee to head the civil rights division of the Justice Department,[17] went down the line in 1995 for Dr. Henry Foster, his controversial nominee to serve as surgeon general. Foster, who had been honored by President Bush for his work to reduce teenage pregnancy, was accused during his confirmation fight of (among other things) being less than forthcoming about the number of abortions he performed while practicing medicine. But Clinton refused to back off, insisting that

Foster was the best person for the job. And, once having made that argument, Clinton would have sacrificed a measure of integrity had he withdrawn his support simply because controversy arose. But despite the presidential steadfastness, Foster was defeated anyway. (Clinton could have the satisfaction of knowing that a majority of senators were evidently prepared to vote to confirm Foster; but the Democrats could not muster the sixty votes needed to break a Republican filibuster.)

The Foster nomination, I should note, raised the integrity issue for many different people in different ways. Foster's opponents accused him of lacking it. Even the generally pro-choice *New York Times* came out against Foster, concluding that his "lack of candor" on the question of how many abortions he had performed "disqualifies him from serious consideration."[18] *The New Republic* disagreed, supporting Foster and presenting a dichotomy that became common among his supporters: "Either abortion is murder, in which case one is too many, or abortion is an often needed, if regrettable, procedure that should be legally and safely available."[19] In other words, if abortion is legal, it doesn't really matter how many Foster performed.

But this cannot be correct. The polls have made plain for more than two decades that although a majority of Americans would prefer to keep abortion legal in most circumstances, most Americans also consider abortion a moral wrong. In other words, the majority sentiment seems to be that although abortion should not be banned altogether, it raises significant and troubling moral issues.[20] Consequently, one could take the view—and I would bet that many do—that it is fine for physicians to perform abortions, but that they, too, should be morally troubled by it. If they are troubled, they will be forced to moral reflection about their conduct. And if reflective, they will understand the gravity of their act and may decide not to do it. Or, even if they go ahead and perform the abortion, it will not be just another surgical procedure; it will leave a strong impression on them. And if performing abortions leaves a strong impression, then the physician, by definition, will remember. Consequently, one could reason that if Foster was unable to recall, within an order of magnitude, the number of abortions he had performed, he was not morally troubled by the practice. And that would be an adequate (and integral) reason for objection to his confirmation.

It is no answer to say that Dr. Foster should not have been morally troubled by abortion because abortion is a constitutionally protected right. There are many constitutional rights that we must zealously protect but that may be exercised in morally thoughtless ways: freedom of speech is only the most obvious example. We would not say that because speech is constitutionally protected, we cannot criticize the moral character of the speech in which a nominee for public office has engaged. (Imagine how dull the confirmation hearings would become!)

This is not to say that the alarmist rhetoric of Foster's most vocal opponents was justified. Some pro-life leaders insisted that the American people would not accept a surgeon general who had performed any abortions at all. But this seems not quite correct. I think, as I have argued, that the American people would prefer a surgeon general who found the abortion dilemma a tough one—as most people do—rather than one for whom it was easy. There is some reason to think that Dr. Foster was that reflective man, as *The New Republic* editorial pointed out:

> He says he "abhors" abortion and considers performing one a sign of "failure." For this, he has been awarded the opprobrium of a group called the National Coalition of Abortion Providers, which brooks no acknowledgment of the real distress involved in having, or administering, an abortion.

Maybe, maybe not. Let it suffice to say that there is plenty of self-righteous silliness on both sides of the abortion issue, as there was plenty of it on both sides of the Foster debate.

Still, to return to the principal point, Clinton remained steadfast in his support for Foster despite the firestorm that raged around the nomination, and I suspect that his steadfastness helped Clinton's image with those in the middle more than it hurt his image with those who are committedly pro-life. Sometimes even a nominee who appears doomed is entitled to the full measure of the President's efforts. And there are cases—Foster was nearly one—in which that very presidential steadfastness can tip the balance.

In our politics, however, steadfastness is sometimes less popular than my glowing account would suggest is the ideal. When, shortly after his election, Bill Clinton kept his campaign promise to alter the rules on service in the armed forces by gays and lesbians, media commentators suggested that he was out of step with the American people. When he then acceded to changes in his proposals, media commentators complained that he was waffling. In short, not only do we criticize politicians for changing their minds (which makes them unprincipled); we also criticize them for *not* changing their minds (which makes them stubborn). That is probably why politicians go out of their way to explain why they are *not* defying public opinion: the survey you saw just didn't ask the question the right way! And the political activists who feed the media both the survey numbers and the ready criticisms are just as bad: the only reliable numbers are the ones that show that their side is right!

One sees this on such hot-button issues as abortion, where both sides will tell you that the numbers favor their positions; classroom prayer, where opponents insist that the survey questions are badly phrased; and gun control, which most Americans also favor, but where groups opposed to it contend, once more, that the data are misunderstood. Few of us, it seems, want to be counted as steadfast in a minority view.

In such treacherous waters, it is small wonder that cautious politicians think they can complete their political journeys more safely if they throw principles overboard. But one longs for politicians—or activists, or journalists—who, rather than trying to explain away polling data that show their views to be unpopular, are prepared to say, "So what? The majority is wrong on this!"

ADMIRING COMPASSION

We seem to want our leaders to show a steadfast devotion to principle but to temper it with something else . . . call it, for lack of a better word, *compassion*. It was a perceived lack of this tempering compassion that helped sink Michael Dukakis in 1988, when he was asked in the presidential debate whether he would alter his stance against the death penalty if his wife were murdered. Let us grant that the question was unfair and manipulative—still, I suspect that the television audience could scarcely believe its ears when Dukakis answered, with little evident emotion, by citing all the reasons for his opposition to the death penalty. What people wanted, I suspect, was for something in his answer—in his tone, in his *face*—to cry out, *My wife?!*[21]

This problem arises in the 1962 novel *Failsafe*, in which, at the height of the cold war, the United States accidentally launches four bombers on a nuclear strike against Moscow. When the Soviet Union is unable to stop the planes, the President of the United States, in order to forestall a war that would surely destroy both nations, orders American planes to drop the same number of hydrogen bombs on New York City. I raise this not to discuss whether the fictitious President was right or wrong, but to assess this matter of compassion. For we learn, just after the President announces his decision, that his wife is visiting New York City. And in what is doubtless meant by the authors as a demonstration of his integrity, the President makes no effort to warn or evacuate her, since he cannot do that for everybody.

I do not know many people—many people I like, at least—who could make that decision. Most of us in that situation, I suspect, would rescue our spouses, our children, our parents, and thus put the nation at risk. One sees the echo of this possibility every time the evening news tells us the story of a young person arrested for some horrible crime—and then offers images of his parents, who protest that he is a good boy who would never do such a thing. The family, after all, is our place of refuge from the wickedness of the world, and the first instinct of most of us is to see to the welfare of the members of our family before we turn our attention outward. Does this mean that we would lack integrity?

The philosopher Lynne McFall considers the question through the following example. Suppose that you are the captain of a ship. Your explicit duty is to "[g]uard the safety of all passengers equally."[22] Somewhere along the voyage, you spot your spouse drowning off the starboard side. Two other passengers are drowning off the port side. You have very little time. If you rescue your spouse, the other two passengers will drown; if you rescue them, your spouse will perish. What is the right action to take?

McFall's solution is a compromise: "Whatever choice I make . . . I would not be morally blameworthy." Why not? Because the captain owes two distinct duties, each of equal importance, and as it is impossible to satisfy both, we must allow the captain the moral freedom to choose one and to be forgiven the obligation to satisfy the other. Nor is it possible, McFall says, to structure a life in which such choices among duties need never be made: "By taking part in the wider community—through volunteer work, say, or even employment—we introduce the possibility of conflict, and the only way to avoid it would be to take up residence in our closets."[23]

INTEGRITY AND COMPROMISE

McFall's example of the ship captain leaves us with the problem of compromise. We ask of our leaders that they be forthright and steadfast, but does this mean that they can never compromise? Surely it does not. Let's see why.

A few years ago, I was invited to be a member of a televised panel discussion of the abortion question. I was seated near the middle of the group, listening to the drearily familiar and strident rhetoric from both sides and thinking all the while of Walter Murphy's observation that a reasonable person need only listen to a passionate argument from either side of the abortion debate to be convinced that the other side is right. All at once, a prominent pro-choice advocate brought me up sharp with the assertion that her pro-life opponents lack integrity (I do not remember whether she used the very word, but she certainly conveyed the idea) because of their willingness to compromise. If the pro-life side truly believed abortion to be murder, she seemed to be saying, then even one murder would be too many. So if pro-lifers accept legislation that allows any abortions to take place, she went on, they are compromising their central belief, and therefore lack integrity.

I suggested in answer that compromise is a necessary part of politics. Politics, after all, is the art of the possible, and every piece of legislation represents a deal in which each of the competing interest groups wound up with less than it would have preferred. This does not mean that they have abandoned their principles; it means that they got the most that they could. To the theorists of pluralism who dominated political science after the middle years of the century, this process of compromise was the glory of our democracy. And although we live in a harder-edged age, I believe that it still is.

The notion that compromise is inimical to integrity is as common as it is wrong. "The vocation of politics," writes Martin Benjamin, "requires a creative and complex blend of personal commitment and professional tolerance."[24] Of course. Integrity, especially on the part of a leader, should not be a recipe for going down to one glorious defeat after another. The philosopher Isaiah Berlin pointed out that it is not possible for an individual person, living a single life, to realize in that life all the positive values. Trade-offs and compromises are an inevitable part of living. True, all of us should be steadfast and uncompromising about *something*, but only the fanatic is steadfast and uncompromising about *everything*.

James O'Toole of the Aspen Institute, pondering the political compromises forced on Thomas Jefferson and Abraham Lincoln, both of whom he describes as unwaveringly antislavery, asks, "How can such pragmatism be labeled 'integrity'?" He answers that the integrity of the two Presidents "is evident from the fact that the long-term courses they adopted were based on what was morally right."[25] I do not take this to be an argument that the end justifies the means, which would, of course, be antithetical to the notion of integrity. Rather, in each case, the President in question was working in pursuit of more than one goal, and could move closer to one by temporarily postponing another; but if he tried to attain them in opposite order, he might lose them both.

Let us take Lincoln's views on slavery as our example. In an 1860 speech quoted by Garry Wills, Lincoln compares slavery to a venomous snake. One would have the right to kill it with a stick in the road, he says. But perhaps one would not have the same right to kill it if found in a bed where children are sleeping, because "I might hurt the children more than the snake," which is why slavery could continue for a while in the South. But not in the territories: "But if there was a bed newly made up, to which the children were to be taken, and it was proposed to take a batch of young snakes and put them there with them, I take it no man would say there was any question how I ought to decide."[26] As a piece of legal and political advocacy, this is a typical Lincoln masterpiece. But how does it measure up against the test of integrity that we have been examining?

First, consider the analogy as it stands. The compromise is apparent. Killing the snake is a value, but so is saving the lives of the children.* Lincoln's point is to avoid being so obsessed with the first that we overlook the second.

Next, consider Lincoln's approach to the problem of slavery itself. Take as a given what O'Toole assumes and what the President's biographers still squabble over: that Lincoln's antislavery sentiment was genuine and deep. If so, there is little doubt that he came to it as a result of genuine moral reflection. But it need not have been the only thing he valued. Preserving the Union was a value, too. Suppose, for the sake of argument, that preserving the Union was a lesser value than abolishing slavery. Still, one could argue that by making some compromises on the issue of slavery, Lincoln was able to accomplish both goals. But had he compromised instead on the issue of the Union, he would have accomplished neither.

A compromise can possess integrity provided that it meets a fairly simple test, which the Lincoln example suggests: the compromise must move you toward your goal rather than away from it. It must, in other words, be part of the strategy for attaining the end that discernment has taught to be good and right. And the individual of integrity, having agreed to compromise, must not pretend that the compromise is itself the end. Instead, he or she must be forthright in announcing that this is but one step along the road, and that the journey will continue.

---

*Lincoln may be mistaken on the merits of the analogy. He surely is just wrong when he says that we would not kill a venomous snake that we found in our children's bed. True, we might hurt the children in the process, and, as Lincoln himself points out, the snake might turn around and bite them; but if we *don't* try to kill it, it is likely to bite them anyway. The answer may be to coax the snake out of the bed, but if the snake won't come, sooner or later we have to get the stick.

Pope John Paul II recognized this point in his 1995 encyclical *Evangelium Vitae (The Gospel of Life)*. In answering the question of whether it is morally acceptable for pro-life politicians to support legislation that reduces the number of abortions but does not ban them, he says:

> "[W]hen it is not possible to overturn or completely abrogate a pro-abortion law, an elected official, whose absolute personal opposition to procured abortion was well known, could licitly support proposals aimed at limiting the harm done by such a law and at lessening its negative consequences at the level of general opinion and public morality. This does not in fact represent an illicit cooperation with an unjust law, but rather a legitimate and proper attempt to limit its evil aspects."[27]

In this, the pope is acknowledging human reality: rarely can any of us achieve our moral ends perfectly, or all at once. Integrity will at times require that we take what we can get.

True, there are people whose sense of integrity never allows them to compromise. We do not, however, think of them as people to admire, or as potential leaders of the nation or the world. We think of them as dangerous fanatics. And we are right.

ADMIRING CONSISTENCY

Finally, we have the right to expect the integral leader to display the virtue of consistency, for a moral understanding that has resulted from genuine reflection should certainly be applicable across very different cases—including application to friends and supporters of the leader. In the previous chapter, I quoted the theologian James M. Gustafson, who noted that the "word integrity would not come to mind as appropriate" for someone who "in similar circumstances . . . always did different things." By examining a handful of simple examples, we will see how hard it can be to live a life of integrity so understood.

Take the case of the National Rifle Association, which presents itself as defending, among other things, the right of individuals to own firearms that they need to defend themselves from those who would commit crimes of violence, then turns around and derides as "thugs" federal officers who are charged with enforcing laws that the N.R.A. happens to dislike. Of course, it may be that drug dealers and armed robbers also dislike the laws under which they happen to be punished. Maybe the officers who try to arrest them are thugs, too. (When pressed, the N.R.A. explains that it is referring to cases in which federal agents assault or even kill innocent citizens. This happens, tragically, in the enforcement of other criminal laws, too.)

Consistency does matter to the public, but perhaps less than an outsider would imagine. For example, the Clinton administration gained less approval than it probably hoped for its very public use of a 1994 federal law protecting abortion clinics to prosecute one Daniel Mathison for making death threats against employees of a pro-life counseling service. (Mathison pleaded guilty.)[28] But whether or not the public consistently values consistency, the student of integrity must value it, because only by the willingness to apply a principle consistently—in particular, to apply it when there is risk of criticism from friends and allies—can any one of us demonstrate the integrity that a leader must have.

Indeed, despite a volley of criticism in recent decades, most philosophers still hold the view that a principle, in order to *be* a principle, must be applied universally and impartially—that is, must actually be applied to all the cases that it fits, with no exceptions for partisan considerations. And even those of us who are not professional philosophers tend to think about principles this way, at least when we are criticizing others for inconsistency in applying them. Consistency is surely the very least that integrity demands. But when, in our partisan zeal, we are reluctant to act and criticize consistently, serious questions arise about whether we are principled at all.

Early in 1995, for example, liberals were understandably furious when Representative Dick Armey, the Republican leader of the House of Representatives, referred to Representative Barney Frank, who is gay, as "Barney Fag." (Armey at once apologized, insisting that the slur was inadvertent.) But when, a month or so later, Democrat Fortney Stark, a House member from California, called Republican Nancy Johnson of Connecticut a "whore for the insurance companies," the liberal silence was deafening.* (Stark, too, apologized.) Surely it is as despicable to call a woman a "whore" as to call a gay man a "fag." Party affiliation, in such a case, should be irrelevant.

Take another example. Early in 1995 many commentators pounded Senator Robert Dole for attacking by name violent films made by Democrats but omitting—and, in one case, praising by name—violent films made by or starring Republicans. Although Dole's rhetoric was overheated, he chose

---

*This was not Stark's first sexist insult to Johnson. In 1994, during the congressional debate over President Clinton's health care plan, Stark insisted that all of Johnson's information about health came through "pillow talk" with her husband, who is a physician.

a perfectly sensible target for his moral fervor. Gratuitous violence is rampant in Hollywood, and the film industry often seems to follow only a single ethical standard: if it makes money, it is worth doing. But Dole's many critics said he was being inconsistent, and their method—challenging him to generalize—is the method that integrity demands. If Dole was sincere, then he should have criticized films made by or starring Republicans as well. Moreover, the partisan character of his selections enabled critics to sidestep the force of his message—a message that was precisely on point.

To Dole's credit, when challenged on one of the Sunday-morning talk shows, he broadened his critique, although he seemed unable to move himself to an explicit condemnation of any of the work of the actor Arnold Schwarzenegger, a stalwart Republican campaigner, whose character in *The Terminator* massacred something on the order of two dozen police officers. (Imagine a "gansta rap" song about the killing of two dozen police officers. Imagine the public revulsion. Imagine the reaction by pro-family conservatives.) Schwarzenegger's 1994 film *True Lies* was, unfortunately, one of those singled out by Dole for special praise as a pro-family film— even though Schwarzenegger's character kidnaps and imprisons his wife for nearly having an affair; threatens to drop the man in question off a building if he does not leave town; stabs, shoots, and burns to death vast numbers of bad guys; and listens as his best friend pronounces: "Women. Can't live with 'em, can't kill 'em." All the elements for a successful shoot-'em-up, perhaps, but family entertainment? I wouldn't take my kids.

Or consider the many Democrats who quite understandably jumped all over Senator Jesse Helms for his comments early in 1995 that President Clinton was not qualified to serve as commander-in-chief and that Clinton's life might be at risk were he to visit a military base, at least in North Carolina. Helms was obviously talking nonsense. The Constitution makes plain that there is only a single qualification to serve as commander-in-chief, and that is to be the duly elected President. And the loyalty and discipline of America's service members should never be called into question, least of all by the chairman of the Senate Foreign Relations Committee.

But Helms's defenders pointed out that his Democratic critics were nowhere to be found a few years earlier when Democratic Senator Al Gore said, evidently meaning it as a joke, that in case something should happen to George Bush, the Secret Service was under orders to shoot Vice President Dan Quayle. The principle should be the same: the loyalty and discipline of members of the Secret Service should never be called into question. The comparison is not quite fair. Helms makes such outrageous comments regularly, whereas Gore's joke was an aberration. Still, perhaps Democrats should have wasted far less time and far fewer words on Helms's comments, recognizing that even Al Gore, whose integrity and fairness nobody questions, could slip into inappropriately morbid political jocularity.

Finally, let us consider a controversial action by a recent President: George Bush's 1992 pardons of several former Reagan administration officials who had been accused of wrongdoing in the Iran-Contra scandal. Democrats condemned the pardons as part of a cover-up, perhaps of Bush's own role in the arms-for-hostages deal. Republicans cheered because, they said, the "persecutions" had gone on long enough.

Two frequently offered justifications for what came to be called the Christmas pardons cannot pass the integrity test. The claim that Bush believed the statute under which special prosecutors are appointed to be unfair or unconstitutional would be persuasive if he had pardoned all individuals ever convicted by one. The claim that Caspar Weinberger, one of those pardoned, deserved a better ending to his long years of service to the nation would have been more persuasive had Bush also pardoned the estimable Clark Clifford, who did yeoman service for the nation, and who was at that time facing trial for purported financial manipulations.

That leaves the most attractive justification for the pardons: that they were part of an effort to heal the divisions over a hard-fought question of national policy. This is the explanation that one would most wish were true of these or any other pardons. On the same day as the Iran-Contra pardons, for example, President Bush pardoned two Jehovah's Witnesses—one from the World War II era, one from the Korean War era—each of whom had been convicted of refusing to register for the draft. The refusal in each case involved a religiously motivated understanding that war is wrong. (The law allows one to register and then claim conscientious-objector status, but not to refuse to register at all.) By expanding, as it were, our national tolerance of moral and religious visions outside the mainstream, the President sent a true message of healing.

Similarly, although it was politically wrenching at the time, President Ford, in retrospect, probably made the right decision in 1974 when he pardoned Richard Nixon just a month after Nixon's resignation as President. Although our national anger seemed to demand punishment for Nixon's crimes, Ford believed that in the long run, the national interest would be better served by enabling the ex-President to avoid prosecution, leaving him untouched by legal proceedings that would otherwise have kept alive our national obsession with Watergate, which, in retrospect, it was plainly time to put aside.

Do President Bush's Iran-Contra pardons fit this model? Maybe they do; maybe he should have justified them this way. But the analogy to the Nixon pardon is not perfect. For one thing, Nixon had just resigned in disgrace, and there was no longer any serious debate on whether he was guilty of a crime (although Nixon himself seemed to think he was not). Another important distinction is that Ford, unlike Bush, had to face the voters after his decision. Put otherwise, the "healing" rationale would have carried more weight had Bush handed down his pardons on the 1991 rather than the 1992 Christmas list, for he would then have confronted the judgment of the American people on his action. Indeed, the wrath or approbation of the voters is about the only existing check on the exercise of the pardon power. The only other check is the judgment of history. For that, we will have to wait.

(four)

Coda: The Insufficiency of Honesty

THE reader by now is probably wondering why I do not speak of plain *honesty:* Why describe a more complicated concept? Is it not honesty of which I speak?

The answer is no; although honesty is a virtue of importance, it is a different virtue than integrity. Let us, for simplicity, think of honesty as not lying; and let us further accept Sissela Bok's definition of a lie: "any intentionally deceptive message which is *stated.*"[1] Plainly, one cannot have integrity without being honest (although, as we shall see, the matter gets complicated), but one can certainly be honest and yet have little integrity. The definitional sources we discussed in chapter 2 seem to understand this, for in definitions of integrity, the word *honesty* often appears—but only as part of a list of the qualities a person of integrity must possess. So integrity itself must represent a different concept.

The first point to understand is that a person may be entirely honest without ever engaging in the hard work of discernment that integrity requires; she may tell us quite truthfully what she believes without ever taking the time to figure out whether what she believes is good and right and true. The problem may be as simple as someone foolishly saying something that hurts a friend's feelings; a few moments of thought would have revealed the likelihood of the hurt and the lack of necessity for the comment. Or the problem may be more complex, as when a man who is raised from birth in a society that preaches racism states his belief in racial inferiority as a fact, without ever stopping to think that perhaps this deeply held view is wrong. Certainly the racist is being honest—he is telling us what he actually does think—but his honesty does not add up to integrity.

In this chapter, we will try to understand why honesty alone is not a substitute for integrity; why there are areas of life in which we might prefer integrity without complete honesty; and how, at times, honesty without integrity can lead to moral disaster.

TELLING EVERYTHING YOU KNOW

A wonderful epigram attributed to the immortal filmmaker Sam Goldwyn goes like this: "The most important thing in acting is honesty; once you learn to fake that, you're in." (All right, it's borrowed from Thoreau.) The point is that honesty can be something one *seems* to have; without integrity, what passes for honesty often is nothing of the kind—it is *fake* honesty, or it is honest but irrelevant and perhaps even immoral. Consider the following.

Example 4-1. A man who has been married for fifty years confesses to his wife on his deathbed that he was unfaithful thirty-five years earlier. The dishonesty was killing his spirit, he says. Now he has cleared his conscience and is able to die in peace.

Observation 4-1(a). The husband has been honest—sort of. He has certainly unburdened himself. And he has probably made his wife (soon to be his widow) miserable in the process, because even if she forgives him, she will not be able to remember him with quite the vivid image of love and loyalty that she had hoped for. Arranging his own emotional affairs to ease his transition to death, he has shifted to his wife the burden of confusion and pain, perhaps for the rest of her life. Moreover, he has attempted his honesty at the one time in his life when it carries no risk: and, as we have seen, acting in accordance with what you think is right and risking no loss in the process is a rather thin and unadmirable form of integrity.

Observation 4-1(b). Besides, even though the husband has been honest in a sense, he has now been twice unfaithful to his wife: once thirty-five years ago when he had his affair, and now a second time as, nearing death, he decides that his own peace of mind is more important than hers. In trying to be honest, he has violated his marriage vow by acting toward his wife not with love but with naked and perhaps even cruel self-interest.

Observation 4-1(c). None of this means that the husband's thirty-five-year-old affair is a moral irrelevancy as he faces death. But if he treats his marriage vow with integrity, the question he should be asking himself is not, "Did I make full disclosure before I died?" but rather, "Did I make up for my wrong with the way I treated my wife for the remainder of our time together?" If he can answer yes to the second, he should still be able to die in relative peace.

The point is, as my mother used to say, you don't have to tell people everything you know. Lying and nondisclosure, as the law often recognizes, are not the same thing. Sometimes it is actually illegal to tell what you know, as, for example, in the disclosure of certain financial information by market insiders. Or it may be unethical, as when a lawyer reveals a confidence entrusted to her by a client. It may be simple bad manners, as in the case of a gratuitous comment to a colleague on his attire. And it may be subject to religious punishment, as when a Roman Catholic priest breaks the seal of the confessional, an offense that carries an automatic excommunication.[2]

In all the cases I just mentioned, the problem with telling everything you know is that somebody else is harmed. Harm may not be the intention, but it is certainly the effect. Honesty is most laudable when we risk harm to ourselves, but it becomes a good deal less admirable when we instead risk harm to others and there is no gain to anyone other than ourselves.* Integrity, in other words, may counsel keeping our secrets in order to spare the feelings of others. Sometimes, as in the example of the wayward husband, the reason we want to tell what we know is precisely to shift our pains onto somebody else, a course of action dictated less by integrity than by self-interest.

---

*This is one of the many reasons that a government official who leaks information, especially derogatory information, is rarely deserving of admiration for doing so. To leak with integrity—if such a concept is possible—would mean to come forward, sooner rather than later, and say, "Yes, I am the source." Doing so would likely ruin the leaker's career; he or she would never be trusted again. But that simply proves the point, for the leaker wants the best of both worlds: to be trusted by friends and colleagues and to harm, without risk, whomsoever he or she chooses.

Fortunately, integrity and self-interest often coincide, as when the criminal confesses in exchange for a lighter sentence or when we reward a politician of integrity with our votes. But often they do not, and it is at those moments that our integrity is truly tested.

Moreover, telling others what we know, like all the actions of a morally reflective individual, must be governed by a sense of proportionality. One should certainly go down the line for moral principle—that is what integrity requires!—but the practical question of how a principle is implemented should be answered in a way that does as little harm as possible. For example, suppose that a newspaper discovers where a former Mafioso, now in the federal witness-protection program, has been hidden by the government. Quite apart from the First Amendment issues, is there a sense in which the newspaper, if it publishes the information, commits an *immoral* act?

The answer is surely yes: yes, that is, if it is reasonably foreseeable that the witness will come to harm as a result of the publication. In morality, as in law, we should all be presumed to intend the reasonably foreseeable consequences of our actions; that rule would have the happy effect of encouraging discernment, for the newspaper (or anybody else), knowing that it will bear moral and perhaps even legal responsibility for the harm that is caused when it reveals a secret, will have a strong incentive to do the work of discernment. One of the great weaknesses of the mass media of the current era is precisely the refusal to exercise what used to be called news judgment, a part of which in the past was always a consideration of proportionality. (See chapter 6.)

The Supreme Court in its famous opinion in *Near v. Minnesota* (1931) even adapted the law of free speech to this proposition: "[N]o one would question but that a government might prevent actual obstruction to its recruiting service or the publication of the sailing dates of transports or the number and location of troops."[3] And although this language has had many critics, the justices have in recent decades shown a marked suspicion of the value of speech that, in their judgment, harms the nation's security in significant ways. In 1980, the Court imposed a constructive trust on the earnings from a book written by a former Central Intelligence Agency employee in breach of his employment agreement; the book's revelations, the agency claimed, made potential sources reluctant to work with it.[4] (A constructive trust means that the profits would go to the CIA rather than to the author.) The following year, the Court allowed the secretary of state to revoke the passport of a former CIA employee after the government presented evidence of "episodes of violence" against people or organizations that he had publicly linked to the agency.[5]

These decisions have their critics among civil libertarians and media lawyers, but their message resonates powerfully with the demands of integrity: Sometimes integrity is best served not by publishing but by keeping silent. In each of these cases, the justices plainly believed that the publication of the information would harm somebody else. Now, one might want to insist that the First Amendment applies even when a publication is reckless, in the sense that the writer or editor does not really care about the harm that he is doing.[6] Nevertheless, the decision to go ahead and publish without regard to the harm that might be caused is a moral decision and may be subjected to moral criticism. In short, the Court seems to think that my mother was right: you don't have to tell people everything you know, especially when you've agreed not to.

BARGAINING

Another weakness in conceiving integrity as mere honesty and conceiving honesty as telling all that you know is that it would make bargaining impossible. When we bargain, by definition we take positions that are not our final positions. I see a house that is listed for sale at $100,000. I wish to buy it and decide that I will pay the asking price if necessary, but my first offer is just $75,000. The owner responds, "I am sorry to say that I cannot take a dollar less than $95,000." I answer: "My absolute top is $80,000." Now, I am not telling the truth, and neither, I suspect, is the owner of the house, but we are not really being dishonest either, and we certainly are not acting without integrity.

There is a well-known Supreme Court case on this point, *Laidlaw v. Organ* (1817),[7] which I enjoy teaching to my first-year contracts class at Yale Law School. The case involved the purchase of tobacco in New Orleans at prices that were depressed because of the British blockade during the War of 1812. The buyer had evidently heard that the war was over, which meant that the price of tobacco was about to skyrocket. Communications being what they were, the seller didn't know, and the buyer was trying to take advantage of this momentary spread in the price. When the seller learned that the war was over, he took the tobacco back, and the buyer sued. The question that I ask my students is this: Did the buyer have an obligation to tell the seller that the war was over?

The effort to answer that question has generated a fairly sophisticated academic literature.[8] The Supreme Court said that the answer was no, there was no duty to speak, and most of the literature agrees. For present purposes, it is enough to make two points: first, if bargaining parties must tell each other everything they know, they will have less incentive to go out and get information; second, in the real world, we never tell the other party everything we know. That does not leave us free, either legally or morally, to commit fraud through active misrepresentations. And it does not mean that the government is wrong to require, in certain circumstances, that consumers be provided with sufficient information to make informed decisions on purchasing, borrowing, and investing. It does mean, however, that bargaining would be impossible if integrity demanded telling everything we know.[9]

ERROR

A third and very important reason that honesty alone is no substitute for integrity is that forthrightness, if not preceded by discernment, may result in the expression of an incorrect moral judgment. In other words, I may be honest about what I believe, but if I have never tested my beliefs, I may be wrong. And here I mean *wrong* in a particular sense: The proposition in question is wrong if, were I to subject my judgment to hard moral reflection, I would change my mind.

One example of this is Creon's decree in *Antigone*, which we discussed in chapter 2. Creon ordered that any Thebian who fought against the city must, if slain, be left in the sun to rot rather than being buried. Only after he ordered his own nephew to suffer this punishment and, one by one, the members of his household committed suicide did he begin to see his error. Far better, we concluded, for Creon to have undertaken more sustained moral reflection prior to issuing his decree.

In our turbulent political era, we are accustomed to hearing politicians render seat-of-the-pants judgments, which their staff members must later revise. One of the most depressing of these, for me both as an African American and simply as an American, was President Reagan's offhand comment at a press conference that it was too early to tell whether Martin Luther King, Jr., was under Communist influence during the civil rights movement. The White House backpedaled furiously, Reagan himself telephoned King's widow, Coretta Scott King, to apologize, and the incident was (more or less) closed—but how much better matters would have been had more thought gone into the initial comment. No doubt Reagan was saying what he thought, and so was being honest; but having failed to reflect on so important and controversial a matter, he made what was, by any definition, an error.

Or take the comment of Walter Mondale, the former Vice President who ran against Reagan in 1984 and who needed a snappy line to respond to Reagan's dismissal of several members of the Civil Rights Commission, which critics insisted was beyond the power of the President to do. Said Mondale: "I've got a plan. First, I'm going to fire everybody they've hired. And then I'm going to hire everybody they've fired." Unquestionably snappy, but it must have been said without much thought. The entire thrust of the criticism of Reagan was that the President did not have the authority to shape the commission as he liked, that a respect for its independence meant that he was stuck with the commission he got. Ideology, the critics insisted, had nothing to do with it. So Mondale, had he been elected, would have been in the same position as Reagan—and had he fired the commissioners Reagan had hired, Mondale would have been fairly subject to precisely the same criticism. Which is doubtless why Mondale, too, backed away from his comment.[10]

These, of course, are easy cases. A more significant problem arises when the speaker is being honest about his or her own moral beliefs and intends to act on them, but has never done the hard work of discernment. The rule is precisely the same: integrity grants no credit for being honest about your beliefs unless you have gone through a period of moral reflection, not just to be sure what your beliefs are but to be sure that your beliefs are right. Consider another example.

Example 4-2. Having been taught all his life that women are not as smart as men, a manager gives the women on his staff less challenging assignments than he gives the men. He does this, he believes, for their own benefit: he does not want the women on his staff to fail, and he believes that they will if he gives them the tougher assignments. Moreover, when one of the women does poor work, he does not berate her as harshly as he would a man, because he expects nothing more. And he claims to be acting with integrity because he is acting according to his own deepest beliefs.

Observation 4-2(a). The manager fails the most basic test of integrity. The question is not whether his actions are consistent with what he most deeply believes, but whether he has done the hard work of discerning whether what he most deeply believes is right. The manager has not taken this harder step.

Observation 4-2(b). Even within the universe that the manager has constructed for himself, he is not acting with integrity. Although he is obviously wrong to think that the women on his staff are not as good as the men, even were he right, that would not justify applying different standards to their work. By so doing, he betrays both his obligation to the institution that employs him and his duty as a manager to evaluate his employees. (For more on the problem of integrity and evaluation, see chapter 5.)

The problem the manager faces is an enormous one in our practical politics, where the dialogue that makes democracy work can seem impossible because of our tendency to cling to views we may not have examined. As the political philosopher Jean Bethke Elshtain has noted, our politics are so fractured and contentious that we too often cannot even reach *disagreement*.[11] Our refusal to look closely at our own most cherished principles is surely a large part of the reason. Socrates thought the unexamined life not worth living, and nobody has ever proved otherwise, except for what we do every day by example: the unhappy truth is that few of us have the time for constant reflection on our views on public or private morality. But examine them we must, or we will never know whether we might be wrong.

None of this should be taken to mean that integrity in the sense I have described presupposes a single correct truth; for example, if your integrity-guided search tells you that affirmative action is wrong and my integrity-guided search tells me that affirmative action is right, we need not conclude that one of us lacks integrity. As it happens, I believe both as a Christian and as a secular citizen who struggles toward moral understanding that some answers to our moral dilemmas *are* truer and better than others. But I do not pretend to have found very many of them, nor is an exposition of them the purpose of this book. For our present purposes, it is enough that we agree on the value—no, the necessity—of the search itself.

I mention the point just now for a reason. Vibrant democracy needs public dialogue, a dialogue among people of integrity who are ready and willing to argue for their competing visions of the right. Dialogue in turn requires openness: not just an effort to convince, but the willingness to open our minds and possibly be convinced. Too many of us, in our dialogues, listen to the other side's arguments only to work out refutations of them. (I confess that I do it all the time.) But to maintain a genuine and respectful dialogue among integral citizens, we must be careful to listen with our ears, not just with our mouths. If we listen closely and sympathetically to others, if we allow our views to be challenged, we are actually aided in the discernment that makes integrity possible.

But we Americans do public dialogue badly. I suspect that the principal

psychological difficulty that frustrates our national efforts to conduct public moral dialogues is not, as is sometimes asserted, that nobody believes
that there are right answers to our moral dilemmas; no, the American
problem is that we all believe that our own answers are the right ones. In
this sense, we are a land not of moral relativists, as is often charged, but
of moral objectivists: people who believe that there are universal moral
truths.

Our necessary if sometimes uncomfortable celebration of moral tolerance is a mark not of our relativism but of our objectivism; having learned
the lessons of history, we are trying in America to be morally cautious. It
is not that there are no right answers, but that, given human fallibility, we
need to be careful in assuming that we have found them. This point was
made famously by John Stuart Mill, and today the very variety of moral
truths in which different Americans wholeheartedly believe is proof of the
wisdom of tolerance.[12]

Tolerance is the reason that the most liberal Americans must accept hateful speech and the most conservative Americans must accept homosexuality. It is not that nobody could hold the view that one or the other is
morally wrong; it is rather that history has taught us to be careful about
enforcing our moral views as law. Obviously, we must enforce *some* of our
moral views. Today's political talk about how it is wrong for the government to enforce one person's morality on somebody else is just mindless
chatter. *Every law* enforces one person's morality on somebody else,
because law has only two functions: to tell people to do what they would
rather not or to forbid them from doing what they would.

And if the surveys can be believed, there is far more moral agreement in
America than we sometimes allow ourselves to think. One of the reasons
that character education for young people makes so much sense to so many
people is precisely because there seems to be a core set of moral understandings—we might call them the American Core—that most of us accept.
(See chapter 14.) Some of the virtues in this American Core are, one hopes,
relatively noncontroversial. Some three hundred American communities
have signed on to Michael Josephson's program to emphasize the "six pil-
lars" of good character: trustworthiness, respect, responsibility, caring, fairness, and citizenship. These virtues might lead to a similarly noncontroversial set of political values: respecting ourselves and others, for instance,
protecting freedom of thought and religious belief, serving our communities, and refusing to steal or commit murder. Other candidates doubtless
would stir some opposition, especially at the political fringes: support for
the right to private property, for example, or for the right of consenting

adults, in the privacy of their homes, to do pretty much as they please. The point is that without tolerance, we will not even be able to try.

But tolerance is only a tool for living together: Its hold on our national imagination is as much a mark of our pragmatism as anything else, for it is not as though most of us lack the instinct to punish those who do what we dislike. So tolerance is not, in itself, dictated by moral principle.* On the contrary, any moral system, even the most liberal, winds up with a set of rules and, eventually, tries to put the force of the state behind them. Even as we acknowledge our own fallibility, we must never make the mistake of substituting a principle of tolerance for moral judgment—or, still worse, of treating tolerance as an end in itself.

Indeed, tolerance necessarily has limits. Those limits are reached, in practical political terms, when the democratically elected legislature decides to outlaw something. (I am assuming the legislation is not unconstitutional.) In terms of integrity, one wants to preach tolerance because of the awful risk of moral error—but an integral citizen, having done the work of moral reflection, will nevertheless have convictions and will sooner or later have to decide whether to speak of them and act on them. The value of tolerance, in other words, is no excuse for a failure to exercise judgment lest we turn into those who, in the late Christopher Lasch's words, "cherish the ideal of the open mind (even if it turns out to be an empty mind)."[13] What integrity thus demands is not that the possibility of error paralyze us, but that we act with due respect for that possibility. And to take the first step along that road, we must avoid the trap of thinking that because we have been open and honest about what we believe, we have done all the work that integrity demands.

HONESTY AND COMPETING RESPONSIBILITIES

A further problem with too great an exaltation of honesty is that it may allow us to escape responsibilities that morality bids us bear. We admire people who are impelled by a sense of duty, an admiration that makes sense, in terms of integrity, if we believe that the sense of duty itself arises from an act of moral reflection. Great literature abounds with examples of self-sacrifice in the name of duty, from the warrior-heroes of the *Song of*

---

* I recognize that this point is controversial, but bear in mind what I have already said: I believe that there *are* true and universal moral propositions that, if we could but discover them, would properly guide all aspects of life.

Roland to the weary sailors of Joseph Conrad's wonderful story "Youth" (and the dedicated narrator of his more famous companion story, "Heart of Darkness") to the smokejumpers of Norman MacClean's classic *Young Men and Fire.* We do not admire those who shirk their duties too readily. But if honesty is substituted for integrity, we might say that if I tell you that I am not planning to fulfill a duty, I need not fulfill it. But it would be a peculiar morality indeed that granted us the right to avoid our moral responsibilities simply by stating our intention to ignore them, and integrity does not permit such an easy escape.

Consider an example. Before engaging in sex with a woman, her boyfriend tells her that if she gets pregnant, it will be her problem, not his. She says that she understands. In due course, they make love and the girlfriend does wind up pregnant. If we believe, as I hope we do, that the boyfriend would ordinarily hold a moral responsibility toward both the child he has helped bring into the world and the child's mother, the boyfriend's honest statement of what he intends does not spare him that responsibility.

This vision of responsibility assumes what I hope we can agree is true: not all moral obligations stem from consent or from a promise. The link of obligation to promise is a rather modern and perhaps uniquely Western way of looking at life, and perhaps a luxury that only the well-to-do can afford. As Fred and Shulamit Korn (a philosopher and an anthropologist) have pointed out, "if one looks at ethnographic accounts of other societies, one finds that, while obligations everywhere play a crucial role in social life, promising is not preeminent among the sources of obligation and is not even mentioned by anthropologists."[14] The Korns have made a study of Tonga, where promises are virtually unknown but the social order is remarkably stable. If life without any promises seems a bit extreme, we Americans sometimes go too far the other way, parsing not only our contracts but even our marriage vows in order to discover the absolute minimum obligation that we owe to one another as a result of our promises.

That some societies in the world have worked out evidently functional structures of obligation without the need for promise or consent does not tell us what *we* should do. But it should serve as a reminder of the basic proposition that our existence in civil society creates a set of mutual respon sibilities that philosophers used to capture in the fiction of the social contract. Nowadays, here in America, people seem to spend their time thinking of more and more clever ways to avoid their obligations instead of doing what integrity commands and fulfilling them. And all too often, honesty is the excuse.

The case of the reluctant boyfriend is, in its way, precisely like the cases of the tax protesters who insist that they do not owe any money to the U.S. government, usually because they believe that the internal revenue laws are unconstitutional. (Many of them insist that only the 1789 text of the Constitution and the first ten amendments count.) They therefore refuse to make any payments, even though, as residents,* they obviously receive some benefits from the national government.

To see the analogy, consider the form that their argument actually takes:

We will live in this country and accept its benefits. (I will make love to you.)

We are telling you in advance that we will not pay any taxes for the services we receive. (If a child results, it is your responsibility.)

So now that you are asking for taxes, we will not pay. (Oh, a child has been born? You're on your own.)

Now, of course, one might say that the cases are inapposite, that there is no moral responsibility for people who live in the United States to support it. One often heard that argument back in the sixties, from draft resisters. But although the argument has something of an honorable philosophical pedigree, it is no way to run a civil society.

HONESTY AND EVIL

The final reason to discourage the kind of *faux* integrity that arises from reliance on honesty alone is that it can lead to evil: the person who does not undertake the sustained moral reflection that is often needed to tell right from wrong is as likely to wind up doing wrong as doing right. Indeed, the possibility that a person of evil desires might claim, as a part of his integrity, the right to carry them out is one reason that the discernment I have been discussing is a discernment not of what we ourselves most deeply believe but of what is right and what is wrong. It is a discernment, in other words, that does not yield to our passions or prejudices, but actively challenges them.

The philosopher Jonathan Lear, who, in a fascinating commentary on

---

*I use the word *residents* rather than *citizens* because many tax protesters are members of the Constitutionalist movement, which does not accept the concept of national citizenship.

Aristotle, warns that "reflective endorsement [of one's own character] must be something more than a desire urging itself forward," offers the following hypothetical:

Example 4-3. "Compare, by way of an extreme example, a reflective Nazi torturer who became the insensitive, cruel man that he is by a process of intimidation, brutalization, and bullying in SS training camp. As he is about to turn on the gas, he reflects that he is glad to be the person he is in the position he is in: for the Jews, he reasons, are not really human, but parasites which weaken and degrade the human race. In ridding the world of them, he is helping man to achieve his highest nature."[15]

Observation 4-3(a). The first and most obvious point is that the Nazi torturer has not engaged in any discernment at all; he has certainly done his duty as he understands it, and has even taken some perverse pleasure in doing so, but it is a duty that could not survive even the mildest moral inquiry. The guard's efforts at reflection, as Lear points out, are "manifestation[s]" of his *un*freedom" because "his character is a product of coercion and his reasoning is bogus, a product of ideology and propaganda."[16]

Observation 4-3(b). This is plainly one of those rare examples (as I mentioned in chapter 3 and will take up once more in chapter 13) in which the moral understanding in question is sufficiently obnoxious that no amount of discernment would make a consideration of its moral rightness even plausible. Thus, even if my first observation is wrong and the torturer *has* engaged in discernment, he still is not acting with integrity.

Observation 4-3(c). Finally, if the torturer had to make the decision today rather than half a century ago, given the history and the world's virtually unanimous condemnation of genocide, he would have an additional important reason to pause and think. Of course, the fact that nearly everyone else in the world is on the same side of an issue does not prove the moral truth of that side—the whole world once practiced slavery—but if, as I believe, humanity tends toward moral progress, the consensus that a course of action is morally wrong is at least a datum worth taking into account.

The short of the matter is that honesty and consistency about one's principles are insufficient to show integrity when we can see that the principles themselves are evil. I suspect that few of us would be willing to forgive the Nazi torturer on the ground that he has done his best to figure out the right, given the training with which he has been saddled. In other words, we are reluctant to concede that the fact that one has been raised in a murderous society is a justification for doing murder. What is the reason for that reluctance?

Part of it, I suspect, is that despite all the hard work of the Enlightenment effort to enshrine human reason as the font of moral understanding, most of us believe in a universal right and wrong that is available deep inside us whether we are raised to it or not. We believe, in other words, in conscience. Many of the great theologians shared the view that the knowledge of good and evil is somehow innate, so that if we can learn the right way to look for it, we can find the moral truth that too often eludes us.

Indeed, Aquinas, struggling to resolve the problem of evil, proposed that people who do evil are simply blind to the good. Evil, viewed this way, is not necessarily the result of a *willed* blindness to a revealed moral truth. The blindness may come about instead through a failure of discernment—a failure not in the will to discern but in the development of that faculty, or even in the knowledge that discernment is possible.

Here I am put in mind of a newspaper story that my wife and I read some years ago in which a New York subway motorman talked about the difference between what happened when he was a child and did wrong and what happens when many of today's children do wrong. The difference, he said, is that when children of his generation (my generation, too) did wrong, they knew it was wrong. Today's kids, he said, do not. But if they do not, it may not be because they lack the capacity to choose between good and evil; it may be because they lack the knowledge of the possibility of choice. For this, one can only fault the societal institutions that should, one hopes, facilitate and improve this discerning faculty.

Aquinas, following Aristotle, put the point this way: "[M]an has a natural aptitude for virtue; but the perfection of virtue must be acquired by man by means of some kind of training."[17] Lear's example of the Nazi torturer thus reminds us that even if we believe in the existence of this thing called conscience—even if the knowledge of good and evil is innate, perhaps God-given—the ability to discover that inner knowledge is developed only through education: as good a case as one could make for serious attention to using all the institutions of society to teach our children, by word, habit, and example, the elements of good character.

But in order to set examples for our children, we must decide what it would mean for the institutions of our society to conduct themselves with integrity and for we ourselves to do the same in our daily lives. Those problems are the subject of part II.

(ii)

Applications

[W]alk before me, as David your father walked,
with integrity of heart and uprightness,
doing according to all that I have commanded you,
and keeping my statutes and my ordinances.
                                        —1 Kings 9:4

(five)

The Best Student Ever

W HEN we talk of life, we talk of what we have experienced. So as I turn to the practical side of integrity, I will begin with an activity with which I am intimately familiar. I refer to writing letters to potential employers, evaluating the work of my students. Here, the reader may well suppose, is one arena of life in which the rules of integrity that we developed in the first part of the book should apply with precision. But as it turns out, the rules of this particular game—performance evaluations—make it all but impossible to act with integrity, not only for me as a law professor but for employers and managers and many others besides.

QUALIFICATION INFLATION

At the Yale Law School, I occasionally teach a seminar on "Law, Secrets, and Lying." A few years ago, I asked the class about letters of recommendation that professors often write to help their students gain the judicial clerkships that so many budding lawyers crave. (A clerkship is the chance to spend a year as an assistant to a federal judge.) I observed that the letters—much like letters of recommendation for students seeking admission to law school—are awash in hyperbole: "Mr. X has one of the keenest intellects I have ever encountered." "Ms. Y is as brilliant a student as I have ever known." Nobody is ever just pretty good or even in the top 20 percent: Every student earns superlatives. Every one of them is one of the best.

When letters of recommendation read this way, the reader has trouble sorting them out. The purpose of a reference is to assist a potential employer (or college or professional school) in making the often difficult decisions on hiring (or admission). If all the letters are the same, however, they are effectively useless. And nowadays, more and more, all the letters are the same.

You might suppose that the concept of integrity developed in this book would apply in a rather straightforward way to letters of recommendation: the writer should reach an honest evaluation of the applicant and should write a letter reflecting that evaluation. If the writer is unable to do so, then the letter should state explicitly the reasons for his or her reluctance. And if the writer is uneasy writing a positive recommendation, perhaps he or she should tell the student. But that is not what happens. It seems as though everybody deserves a letter and everybody deserves a powerful one.

As we discussed whether anything might be wrong with this practice, I told the students a story from the year that I was privileged to spend serving as a law clerk to the late, great Thurgood Marshall at the U.S. Supreme Court. One of the tasks of the clerks was to help the justice sort through applications from law students hoping to clerk for him in the following term of the Court. That year, we received two different letters from a very prominent law professor endorsing two different students for clerkships, and referring to each as the brightest student in his particular law school's graduating class. As this was obviously impossible, the only rational option was to discount both letters entirely.

One thinks here of Hannah Arendt's prediction that although a liar "may get away with any number of single falsehoods," it will be "impossible to get away with lying on principle."[1] For at least one of the letters *must* be a lie, if one conceives of a lie as an intentional misstatement of the truth. Obviously, the case is an extreme one—but the problem of lying in recommendation letters is pervasive. Would not both applicants and potential employers be better served, I asked my seminar, if their professors made more of a stab at honesty?

My students had an interesting take on the matter. The genie, they argued, will not go back into the bottle. Now that the market has set a pattern of letters so drenched with hyperbole that they are effectively useless, everyone who writes a letter must follow that model. If a letter of recommendation calls a student anything less than brilliant, the reader, comparing it with others, will assume that the student is somehow deficient. "She's very bright" simply will not do—not when the reader has become accustomed to learning that everybody else is "one of my best students ever."

Letters of reference, the students told me, are written in a special language, a language in which there are only a few gradations: *brilliant, one of the best,* or *the best.* Once the reader understands this, the terms can be translated: for *brilliant,* read "okay," for *one of the best,* read "pretty good," for *the best,* read "outstanding." Consider the obvious analogy to the phenomenon of grade inflation: just drop every grade a few points, and you should know what a transcript really means. Nowadays, a grade of C, which once indicated average work, is treated like a failure; similarly, a letter stating that a student is "average" would be taken to mean that the student is a disaster.

Thus, in my students' analysis, even the professor who wrote the two letters for two students, each of them his best, was not actually lying; in the special language of recommendation letters, he was not even engaging in hyperbole. He was simply saying, in that peculiar language, what was true. The worst sin he committed, then, was to forget what he had written in one letter when he sat down to write the other. And perhaps he did not even forget. Perhaps the reader was meant to translate the special language of recommendation into ordinary language and conclude that neither student was actually the best but both were very good.

I suppose I understand my students' point. After all, there are other areas of life in which we talk this way. The lover's confident if muddled declaration, "I would do anything for you," is meant to be taken seriously but not to be taken literally: by stating it, the lover signals something else, an allegiance, a certain depth of love. But *not* to say it—to declare instead what is likely true, "I would do many things for you"—somehow loses romantic effect.

For the sake of such effects, we have done terrible violence to—may I say the word?—the integrity of our language. As we spin toward hyperbole, it is harder and harder to trust (or even to understand) the literal meaning of what we say to each other. In our politics, this is particularly true. It is hard to believe that anyone actually considers the 70 percent or so of American adults who favor classroom prayer in the public schools a dangerous fringe, but that is how antiprayer forces often describe them.[2] And the legal scholar Ronald Dworkin, in his book on abortion, counsels pro-choice activists not to take literally the frequent pro-life rhetoric that accuses them of murder: they do not, says Dworkin, really mean it.[3]

Well, maybe they do and maybe they don't. Integrity might seem to require that we be more accurate in our labeling, of both our students and our opponents. But what is clear about our politics, as about our letters of recommendation, is that we have reached the point where hyperbole is often the price of admission.

PUFFERY AND ITS COUSINS

In the law of advertising, there is a word for this strange language of hyperbole. The word is *puffery*. Puffery—the form of words one uses, in the jargon, to "puff" a product—is defined as an advertising claim that is favorable to a product but that nobody would ever believe. The concept is most easily understood by example. Imagine that an automaker markets its new model as THE BEST CAR IN THE WORLD. Does the potential buyer understand this literally? Does she assume that the car is in fact the best in the world, that somebody has tested it, that it holds a specific rank, that it has gained some official stamp of approval? Does she assume that the automaker stands behind it, that if another car turns out be somehow better, she will get her money back? The law of puffery says *no*.

This *no* matters. Suppose that a reasonable potential buyer, on seeing the advertisement, *would* believe the claim to be true. In that case, if the claim is false, the automaker risks liability for false advertising. But the courts have said that there is no liability for puffing a product, because puffery, by definition, involves a claim that will not be believed.[4]

If, however, nobody believes the claims that are made when products are puffed, then why do advertisers do it? Why do they use words like *best* and *most?* And if, as the courts say, nobody believes the claims, why don't consumers get angry at the terrific lies told in the commercials for the puffed products?

The answer is the same here as in the case of the impossibly glowing recommendation letters. The market has evolved a special puffing language, a set of claims that, as the courts say, no buyer believes, but that, as marketers know, every buyer expects. If a firm fails to puff its product, it at once arouses the consumer's suspicion—assuming that the firm is able to gain the consumer's attention at all. In other words, the consumer, perhaps without being aware of it, wonders *why* the automaker is reluctant to call its car the best in the world, or why a soft-drink maker promises only that the buyer will *like* the soft drink, not that the buyer will *love* it. (Is it any wonder that the experiment with a lemon-lime drink called Like, intended to compete with Seven-Up and armed with the lackluster slogan "You like it, it likes you," was an abysmal failure?) I suspect that is why, even though it sticks in the memory of anyone over the age of about thirty, the WE'RE NUMBER TWO, WE TRY HARDER campaign that Avis ran for years always left me a bit put off. Yes, I always wanted to respond, you might be number two, but you needn't be so proud of it.

In the language of the market, one wants, or at least expects, every company to make the bold proclamation that it is the absolute best. It does not matter whether it actually *is* the best or, indeed, whether a means of measurement even exists. What matters is that the company show the confidence (perhaps brashness is a better word) to *say* that it is the best. In the language in which products are puffed, to claim for one's company anything less is really to stop trying. So the reason that every car rental firm— or every deodorant or every dentist—will claim to be the best is not that every one really *is* the best, or even that every one *believes* itself to be the best, but rather that consumers expect the claim. To be the best is in that sense the *minimum* claim; one must present at least that much to get the consumer's attention so that the rest of the message can get through.

Indeed, grabbing and holding the consumer's attention has grown more and more difficult, and the devices for accomplishing it have grown more and more sophisticated. There are probably not many people left in America who are fooled by those big manila envelopes bearing legends like SWEEPSTAKES PRIZE NOTIFICATION and CONGRATULATIONS, YOU ARE AN OFFICIAL WINNER of a contest you did not even enter. But there are other methods. Lots of direct-mail solicitations are now designed to resemble official government forms or even checks. Not long ago, I received in the mail from one of my credit card issuers an envelope bearing on the outside the phrase CREDIT ENHANCEMENT NOTIFICATION, which seemed nice, except that in the past, increases in my credit line had been presented in more subtle envelopes. And, sure enough, the "enhancement" was not an increase in my credit line but some special service that the bank wanted me to purchase.

Trying to fool the customer with such schemes might be clever marketing, but it seems to lack integrity in the most basic sense: the advertisement that is disguised as something else does not meet the third criterion of integrity, because the firm does not say what it is doing and why. In fact, the pretense is like the Trojan horse, intended to mislead, which means that the firm is disobeying the third criterion quite flagrantly: not only does it not say what it is doing; it claims to be doing something else.

It is easy to imagine, however, the firm's reply: the advertisement that arrives in a disguise is no more than puffery of a very sophisticated kind. Consumers expect it. The day is long past when direct-mail solicitations can be honest about themselves, can look like what they are, because consumers will simply throw them away. In order to grab consumer attention, even for the briefest of instants, they must instead look like something else. The consumer, through experience, fully understands this, which is why so many of the formerly successful schemes—envelopes that vaguely resemble government documents, or little clear windows that seem to show a check nestled inside—no longer work as well as they once did. When an envelope arrives in the mail without any outward signs that it is an advertisement, the consumer in effect must guess whether it is or is not, and thus whether to open it or not. And if the consumer decides to open it, and if the material inside is flashy enough to catch the consumer's attention, then it has done its work.[5]

Something similar is happening in the increasingly wild world of direct-mail fund-raising, where the left and the right both are sacrificing accuracy for the sake of gaining attention. One group I have supported with contributions in the past probably will never get another penny of my money because of its shameful opportunistic efforts to capitalize on the April 1995 Oklahoma City bombing: Not an envelope arrives now without the word *militia* somewhere in the return address. (I suppose that integrity requires me to write and say *why* I have stopped giving.) But my being offended is unimportant. An analysis in the *New York Times* reached this depressing conclusion: "fund-raising letters, whether for causes of the right or the left, are designed to reach the gut, not the brain. They are written that way for one reason: it works."[6]

RELUCTANCE TO JUDGE

It works: That explains the seeming lack of integrity in advertising and fund-raising, perhaps. It cannot quite explain what is going on in this strange, puffing language of recommendations. I fear that the refusal of so many professors to write accurate letters of reference is part of a larger problem in academia today and, from what I understand, in other professions as well: the reluctance, not to say refusal, to judge the performance of others. One sees it in the phenomenon of grade inflation on campus (a phenomenon that some elite universities have finally started to address) and in the routine and utterly useless "He-worked-here-and-caused-no-trouble" letters of reference nowadays supplied by ex-employers. It is as though those of us who are actually charged with evaluating the work of other people would rather not have the responsibility.

Once, during my brief period of private law practice, I was all set to recommend that we hire a particular person who had interviewed well and whose reference letter from the previous job was fine. And then her last boss told me—on the phone, not in writing—that the applicant had been dismissed because of poor work habits and might have been stealing from the firm. Now, you might think that problems of that sort should be part of the reference, that even a minimal integrity would require one employer to warn the next; but you would evidently be wrong. I was fortunate to get the information I did; lots of employers would not have provided it, even on the telephone. As a 1992 study in the *American Business Law Journal* noted, "Most employers today either give no employment reference information, or merely confirm that the (former) employee worked for the employer during specified dates and at a specified rank or position."[7]

Why? A fear of litigation is presumably part of the reason, for lawsuits against former employers for their negative references are said to be on the upswing. Putting aside cases alleging discrimination, which will often, although of course not always, involve allegations that deserve to be taken seriously, a growing number of lawsuits charge former employers with breach of contract, wrongful interference with business relations, or even *defamation* for revealing the reason for an employee's discharge. A 1993 article in the *Wall Street Journal* warned that more and more courts were applying a bizarre variant of defamation called "compelled self-publication," in which the employee claims that because the ex-employer is going to reveal to potential employers the official reason for the discharge, the employee must reveal it first.[8]

It all sounds very scary. But the *American Business Law Journal* study, which compared reported court decisions in the periods 1965–70 and 1985–90, concluded that the fears of employers are generally unfounded. The authors found "that the relative frequency of such litigation probably has not increased, that defamation law still privileges employers so that (former) employees seldom win any award, and that the size of awards has declined over time." The authors speculated that employers who were reluctant to report the true reasons for the discharge of employees were basing their behavior on media reports of jury verdicts awarding damages "in a few atypical cases."

And although everybody hears about lawsuits employing such bizarre theories as "bad-faith grading" by a college professor who awarded a low grade or infliction of emotional distress by an employer who gave a poor performance review, what is less frequently reported is that such cases are usually dismissed.[9] True, employers will want to avoid the cost and bad publicity attending even lawsuits they expect to win, but over time, if employers keep winning, one would expect the number of suits filed to drop. (Moreover, litigation may run the other way: sometimes, the new employer sues the old one for failure to warn that the employee in question is violent or prone to steal.) In short, there is good reason to be skeptical of the claim that the still rare case in which a teacher or an employer is successfully sued for writing the wrong words can quite explain our growing hesitation to evaluate with integrity.

I do not mean to insist that litigation has no effect on how we hire, promote, and fire. In the field with which I am most familiar, the academic world, we are already facing a crisis of confidentiality. Academic tenure debates are traditionally carried on behind closed doors, in the hope that professors will be open in their evaluation of their junior colleagues' work. But this has been growing harder for years. At one well-known law school, a junior member of the faculty up for promotion was given the confidential file of written comments from senior colleagues. Given the file by whom? Probably a senior colleague. At Yale Law School, an account of one closed faculty meeting wound up in the local paper. The account was in important respects inaccurate, but that is not the issue; the problem is that the leak could only have come from a member of the faculty, who deemed the end he or she was seeking far more important than the tradition of confidentiality. (Nope, no points for either leaker's integrity in breaking tradition, because neither one ever came forward and said openly, "I did it and here's why.") In both cases, the effect is to chill the honesty and depth that evaluation of scholarship demands.

Litigation has only complicated matters. The Supreme Court has held that neither the First Amendment nor any special evidentiary privilege allows universities that are facing employment discrimination claims to withhold reviews written by outside evaluators of the candidate's work.[10] One can hardly expect anything else: a university, in the eyes of the law, is simply an employer, and when it faces a lawsuit, it has the same obligation as other employers to open its internal deliberations. At the same time, one can scarcely miss the effect this rule will have—is already having, I suspect— on outside reviewers. The pressure to be less than honest increases with the likelihood that one's comments will become known, because fewer and fewer academics seem to have the integrity to stand behind their criticisms of their colleagues. University officials have complained that the court decisions allowing tenure files to be opened will make it harder and harder to obtain the written evaluations that tenure deliberations have traditionally demanded.[11]

Here again, I make no claim to exemplary behavior. Although I do sometimes agree to write evaluation letters for professors up for tenure at other schools, I rarely do so unless I am comfortably enthusiastic. I do not relish the thought of being at the center of a public battle of the sort that too often breaks out nowadays when tenure is denied. And if my motives seem self-interested and unintegral, well, I suppose I must plead guilty; but I have better things to do with my time. I am far from alone in this. I have colleagues who, citing a fear of publicity, will not write the letters at all. So the integrity of one important process—the adjudication of discrimination complaints—seems to be on the way to destroying the integrity of another—peer review for academic tenure. Probably that is inevitable: we must sometimes establish priorities among our integrities. But we can weep for the demise of the old system even as we try to work out how to build a new one to meet the demands of a new age.

That is what everybody is doing now: working out new ways to perform the evaluations that are necessary in both the workplace and the campus. We need to do this because people are simply less willing than in the past to put the truth to paper—at least when the truth might hurt someone's career. I continue to harbor doubts, however, that litigation is the principal cause. What else might be the source of this unfortunate reluctance to judge others, especially students?

Conservatives sometimes lay the blame for the problem squarely at the door of such fashionable academic theories as deconstruction and multiculturalism, which, because they question established hierarchies, are said to call the authority to evaluate into question. Perhaps there is *something* to the charge—I recall, for example, my conversation a few years ago with a respected white sociologist who told me all the reasons that he graded his black students more leniently than his white students. But the claim that left faddism has somehow done in our standards of judgment is a gross overstatement of the sort that has become common in this era that has linked the fate of the public intellectual to the ability to command television time, which in turn is linked to the ability to shock. There are causes aplenty for the decline of standards, if we would only look.

For example, the old-boy network, under siege but still stumbling along, has created vast spaces for mediocrities who happen to be white and male to move ahead, unjudged, as has the fawning relationship between members of Congress and the PACs that more or less purchase their votes in exchange for favors that those who fund the PACs have not earned. In law enforcement, the notorious "blue wall of silence"—the tradition that police officers do not turn one another in—renders any serious investigation of police incompetence or even corruption extraordinarily difficult, with the rare exception of very public malfeasance (preferably captured on video-tape). Across the country, union seniority and work rules often make it impossible for firms to reward their best people with the highest salaries. The problem has become particularly acute on Wall Street, where corpo-rations bring considerable pressure to bear on analysts not to downgrade their stocks. The pressure may include anything from refusing to give infor-mation (so that the analysts are at a competitive disadvantage) to refusing to invite them to corporate events. The result, according to the *Wall Street Journal*, is that many savvy traders have come to take stock recommenda-tions as necessarily exaggerations: so *buy* means *hold*, and *hold* means *sell*.[12] In short, we are all a little bit dirty on this one.

So, rather than place blame for our reluctance to judge, let us be satis-fied with pointing out that it is antithetical to integrity to give someone an evaluation, a letter, a grade that he or she has not earned. We might have a lively discussion of what it means to earn an evaluation, but my concern is with the teacher or manager who *consciously* decides to avoid trouble by ranking somebody higher than the ranker actually thinks justified; or who refuses to do the work of figuring out where students or employees rank; or who decides not to get involved in evaluation at all. Such acts of unintegrity are corrupting: not only do they ease the path of the doer away from integrity, but they send quite unfortunate signals to those who look to their teachers or managers for models of behavior.

Now let us consider a simple example.

Example 5-1. A college professor receives a telephone call about one of her students from a firm that is thinking of hiring him. The professor never agreed to serve as a reference, and the student did not list her as one. But the employer, suspicious of the glowing tone of the formal ref-erence letters, is making random calls to other faculty members whose names appear on the student's transcript. The student received a B in her course, based on a very fine paper that would have been an easy A, except that it was turned in several weeks late. If the professor decides to tell the employer the truth, which may cost the student a chance at the job because of his poor work habits, will she be acting with integrity?

Observation 5-1(a). The easy answer is yes. She should tell the truth or decline to comment, because to do anything else would be actively misleading. But if she declines to comment, even if she states that it is her policy, the employer might well take it as a negative reference anyway, assuming—in this case, correctly—that she does not want to say anything because she cannot say anything nice.

Observation 5-1(b). The potentially difficult point for the professor is that the student never asked her to serve as a reference. However, it is quite unclear why that decision on the student's part should bind the professor to say nothing about him. We might question the professor's integrity were she to conduct a campaign against the student, contacting potential employers before they even ask, in order to harm his job prospects: a vendetta almost always will lack an integral justification.

I said that the example is simple, and it is. But there is a complicating factor. Were the professor to follow the course of action I propose—the course that integrity demands—she might very well hear from the student. The employer, deciding not to give him the job, might let slip the reason. And even a sanitized version ("We had questions about your work habits") might supply a sufficient clue for the student to figure out who provided the derogatory information. Litigation, of course, might follow, or worse: There are cases of physical assault upon, and even murder of, faculty members by disgruntled students. But even if none of these horrors occurs, the professor, in today's world, might well be thrown on the defensive by the student, who would complain that she had, through telling the truth, ruined his life. I have heard that very cry from students who were dissatisfied with their grades. I once had an agonized telephone call from the assistant dean at another school, one of whose students I had allowed into a seminar: Would I please raise the young man's grade, because he otherwise would be unable to graduate? The premise of these complaints is fascinating: if the student gets a bad grade or a bad reference, it is the fault of the professor, not the student.

GRADE INFLATION

Although I am loath to be too critical of colleagues I admire, I believe that the grade inflation about which so many people get so exercised rests on a similar refusal by faculty members to behave like adults, that is, like people with enough integrity to disappoint other people. It is as though some professors want to believe that everybody deserves to be first. But everybody doesn't.

A good deal of grade inflation probably stems from the desire of professors to avoid the guilty feelings that honest grading might generate, as well as a fear of being disliked by students, or perhaps simply a fear of arguing with them. The net effect is that the grades that students work so hard to earn matter a good deal less. During my undergraduate years at Stanford in the 1970s, graduate students in at least some departments, as I recall, were not permitted to count grades of C toward their degrees. That meant that many mathematics and science courses in which both graduate and undergraduate students enrolled were graded essentially on an A/B curve: except for cases of utter disaster, instructors were loath to award C's, because too much time was spent arguing with students desperate to raise their grades and avoid repeating the class.

Grade inflation is a signal that professors are no longer treating grades as though they matter. But faculty members who are unwilling to say this are participating wholesale in a breach of our rule 3. And, as with most breaches of integrity, they are causing great harm. Obviously, grade inflation is bad for potential employers, who may be unable to evaluate transcripts. It is also unfair to those students who achieve genuinely outstanding work but are tossed into the vast pool of A averages, not all of which are actually earned. One of my Yale colleagues, upon hearing that a candidate for a teaching position had nearly straight-A's from Harvard Law School, grumbled: "Yeah, but who did he have? I mean, do those grades really count?" Thus we move from the raw data of the transcript to the use of informal sources of information—always a dangerous practice, because of the bias and intense subjectivity that we automatically import.

Indeed, the collapse of grading as a serious enterprise, by forcing potential employers to rely on faculty contacts and other informal sources rather than grades to obtain reliable information, could severely retard the cause of racial justice. Working harder in the classroom and thus earning better grades than the white kids has always been one of the things that minority students have been counseled to do: only by being better, we have told each other for a generation and more, can we hope to avoid the pernicious effects of the old-boy network and other informal means of hiring that have traditionally been closed to us. (And even with better grades there is no guarantee.) But if every student gets the same high grades without doing the hard work, the informal contacts become even more important and the old-boy network is back in business.[13]

But perhaps most important, as one would expect from so patent a breach of integrity, grade inflation is bad for the students who receive inflated grades, because the meaningless grades leave them incapable of

judging *their own* performances. I remember receiving an A in an acceler-
ated undergraduate physics course in which I had understood little of what
went on. But I did not realize how little I had understood until I tried to
apply my "knowledge" in a more advanced course in the subsequent term.
Had I received the grade I deserved—perhaps a B, probably a C—I would
have worked harder (because I would have known that I was in trouble)
or perhaps abandoned the field of physics a good deal sooner. Either one
would have been an improvement.

But instead of providing accurate evaluations, we indulge this almost
willed refusal to judge our students. So, rather than turn down requests
from weaker students for letters of recommendation, we have developed
this peculiar language in which so-so students become great and good students become brilliant and no words are left over to describe the truly
exceptional students. And the students themselves understand and take
advantage of the dilemma in which our own reluctance to appear mean
has left us. I have heard more than one student argue quite seriously that
faculty members are *obliged* to write letters for any student who asks, as
though we are an employment agency—but then, some faculty members
behave as though we are, pulling out all the stops, calling in favors all over
the country and generally making great nuisances of themselves to get jobs
for the students they like the best—using these informal methods because
the grades and letters are largely fungible. (Again, let me emphasize for the
reader that this practice can have serious racial exclusionary effects.)

I admit that I do not act like an employment counselor. I turn down
some of the students who ask me for letters, unless I actually have something interesting to say. I generally limit my endorsements to two categories: the student whom I have supervised in writing a major paper and
the student who has served as one of my research assistants. Then, even
if I am in principle willing to write a letter, I always explain to the student
asking for one that I write long and quite complicated letters, pointing out
weaknesses as well as strengths. I point out that some judges or other
potential employers might think that since I eschew the usual language in
which letters of recommendation are written, I am trying to warn them
off—that is, by writing an honest letter instead of lying, I must mean that
the student is not good enough to hire.

This prospect saddens me, for I harbor no wish to make more difficult
the task of finding a job, but I simply am not capable of writing the dreary
succession of "best-student-in-a-decade" letters that so many law faculty
members churn out. Some of my students are less saddened than angry, or
perhaps offended, for many of them behave as though glowing letters of

recommendation are theirs as of right. I cannot really blame them. Years of higher education have trained them to believe it. But I also cannot indulge them. The long and complicated letter, with all its risks, is the only kind I am able comfortably to write.

I do not want to say that professors (or employers) who make a different choice lack integrity, and, indeed, that is not what I believe. I would rather say that they are fluent in a strange but obviously useful language that I am far too old to learn.

(six)

All the News That's Fit

L ANGUAGE, language! If there is an institution in America that should care deeply about language—its possibilities, its ambiguities, and ultimately its integrity—that institution is surely the press. Words make news reporting possible; and the choice of words makes news reporting accurate or inaccurate, fair or unfair, integral or unintegral. Ordinary mortals, such as law professors who are called upon to write letters of recommendation, may stumble and struggle to be inoffensive, may even prevaricate to avoid argument, but journalists, shielded as they are by the First Amendment and heirs to a proud tradition of freedom that stretches back through time, from Reston to Lippman to Riis to Garrison to Franklin to Zenger, must surely be built of sterner stuff.

Or must they?

Most of the journalists I know are dedicated and sincere professionals who do indeed want to inform the electorate—to tell the people, as the old saw has it, what they need to know. But 'twixt cup and lip comes there many a slip, and doing the job of reporting with integrity is not as easy as truthfully writing that X said this or that Y was accused of that. In this chapter, I will speculate on what integral reporting might look like and how some common journalistic practices get in the way.

MAKING THE FACTS FIT THE STORY

A few years ago, a reporter at a prominent newspaper called me to discuss affirmative action. He wanted to know about the views of beneficiaries of the programs, a problem about which I had written. Choosing my words with care, I said approximately this: "A lot of the beneficiaries hate it, but that isn't my own view." Perhaps I should not have been surprised to discover that when he wrote his article, he left out everything after the comma, leaving the impression that I, too, hated it.

Such an omission could be put down to accident or editorial error, but I doubt it, because it happens too often, and not only to me. I would put the omission down instead to the desire on the reporter's part to document controversy. I think he had made up his mind before he called me what he expected (perhaps wanted) me to say, and was determined to write that I had said it. And, had I challenged him, he could have produced his notes to show that I did, indeed, say precisely what he quoted me as saying— even if what he quoted me as saying was (obviously) not what I meant.

This is, unfortunately, not a unique occurrence, not in a world in which controversy is what makes the story. Very often, by the time a reporter actually gets around to interviewing people, the story is all but written; all that remains is to get the right quotes to fill it out. And the quotes must not be complex, because there is no space for complexity: so the quotes are simplified to make the point that the sides on a particular issue are hopelessly divided.

In discussing very controversial subjects with journalists, I have experienced this often. A reporter will ask: "What do you think about X?" I will say, "Well, the good outweighs the bad." I will go on to list the many good points and the few bad ones, and the enterprising journalist, for whom controversy trumps accuracy, will then write—or broadcast—a story that mentions only the bad things I mentioned. If challenged, the journalist will respond, truthfully, that everything in the story is in his notes.

It's scary.

I hasten to add that I am not one of those who waxes furious upon discovering that the reporter's recollection of an interview differs from mine. (As I have warned many a disgusted colleague or friend, people who are prepared to be angry when misquoted should not bother granting interviews.) And there is little point in complaining: editors routinely state that they stand behind their reporters, whether sincerely or not. This editorial judgment is commercially unsurprising—no news organization could survive if it consistently undercut its staff—but it is also more than a little arrogant, to say nothing of unrealistic. Many reporters do not bother to use tape recorders, relying instead on their own ears and the speed of their own pens, and thus writing down only bits and pieces of what is said. I have gone half mad in interviews, watching the journalist's pen scratch, stop scratching, scratch, stop scratching, often stopping, perhaps to rest aching fingers, just when I am trying to explain a crucial point. I once said to a reporter, "Please write this part down," and she looked at me with that special First Amendment arrogance that every journalist can do at the drop of a hat, not deigning to reply with what she was obviously thinking: *Don't you dare tell me how to do my job.*

She was right: I had no business telling her what to write down and what to ignore. On the other hand, had I complained of the way I was quoted in the story she wound up writing, she would have had no basis for insisting that she could not possibly be in error, and her boss would have no basis for backing her up. No basis, that is, except for the essential clubbiness of the fourth estate itself.

Perhaps the trend is new; perhaps it has been ever thus. In either case, journalistic integrity is being harmed by the need to make the facts fit the story rather than making the story fit the facts. All too often, having made up their minds that the story has a certain ending, reporters and editors are disdainful of evidence that the ending is wrong.

In 1994, I was invited to appear on one of the Sunday-morning network talk shows for a panel discussion about public school classroom prayer. (I declined, not least because the panel was scheduled for Easter morning, when some people have plans with their families.) Out of curiosity, I asked who was lined up for the show. The producer told me that on the pro–school prayer side, they had tentatively decided on the Reverend Pat Robertson, founder of the Christian Coalition. Although I range from a skeptic to an opponent on school prayer,* I must confess that I was taken aback. I feared that the pro–school prayer side would not get its fair shot on the show, and I said so.

The producer asked why. I told her that Robertson has very high negative ratings in the public eye and that if he were the principal spokesman for the cause, the cause would have no fair shot at convincing anybody, at least on that particular Sunday morning.

Unfazed, she asked me whom I would recommend instead.

*My concern about classroom prayer is a profamily one: that the practice inevitably will interfere with the fundamental right of families to raise their children in their chosen religions, a right that is older than government and with which government has no authority to interfere.

I argued that she should be trying to tell the public a story it might not already know. For example, I pointed out, support for classroom prayer is higher among African Americans than in just about any other demographic group; certainly it runs high among the worst-off among us, and the inner cities are hotbeds of support. Why not, I asked her, give the movement a more complicated face, presenting a black supporter? I suggested, for example, Sharon Pratt Kelley, at that time the mayor of Washington, D.C., and a classroom-prayer supporter.

The producer was openly skeptical. Perhaps, she said, if the subject were urban affairs. But Kelley was not a "name" in the school prayer movement, meaning, I suppose, that Kelley's was not the name she wanted. She had her story already—classroom prayer was supported only by the most conservative forces of evangelical Christianity—and she would not be swayed by the facts. Such as the fact that classroom prayer is supported by more than two-thirds of American adults,[1] hardly a fringe, the great majority of them not members of the Christian Coalition.

Indeed, the media has little interest in unmasking the complexities of the stories it reports. When was the last time you saw an abortion story in which the pro-life side was represented by the Prolife Alliance of Gays & Lesbians (PLAGAL), which because of its political complexity has managed to become an outcast from both left and right? Or a story about the economy that noted that the strongest supporters of redistributive policies tend to be the purportedly conservative Christian evangelicals and Roman Catholics?

What the media love instead is a caricature, and nowhere is this truer than in media coverage of religion. Consider what non-Catholics hear about the Roman Catholic Church. Thanks to news reporting, the entire nation understands (or thinks it understands) the position of the Roman Catholic Church on abortion. But how many Americans know anything at all about the Church's position on issues of social and economic justice? Many well-educated Americans have heard of *Humanae Vitae*, Pope Paul VI's encyclical on artificial means of birth control, and perhaps of *Evangelium Vitae*, Pope John Paul II's 1995 encyclical on abortion. But how many know that *Evangelium Vitae* also attacks the death penalty? How many know anything at all about *Sollicitudo Rei Socialis*, John Paul II's powerful assault on consumerism and the culture of possession and gratification—and who, upon reading it, would classify the author as a conservative? That the National Conference of Catholic Bishops has been active in the battle against abortion is a fact of which even schoolchildren seem aware;

that the bishops have fought for a more equitable distribution of the nation's wealth is a fact of which even many well-educated Americans seem unaware.

But the media love to paint some religionists as conservative and others as liberal, and because the dividing line is almost always the uniquely difficult issue of abortion, we wind up with a terribly skewed portrait of American religion. For example, analysis of General Social Survey data from the 1980s shows that among Christians, biblical literalists—the more "conservative" grouping, according to the media—are significantly more liberal on economic issues than are most other Protestants. The theologically "modernist" denominations, such as the United Church of Christ and the Episcopal Church (my own), even though often identified in the press as liberal, turn out to be much more conservative on economic issues than other Protestants are. And Roman Catholics are, on average, more strongly liberal on these issues than are Protestants.[2]

The media's obsession with such social issues as abortion, gay rights, and classroom prayer (on all of which traditionalists tend toward the traditional) blinds us to the complexities of the Christian community. Because so many conservative leaders endorse traditional Christian teachings on these causes, we assume that everyone who agrees with the traditional positions must be conservative on other issues as well. But it isn't so; the world is full of pro-life, pro–classroom prayer, pro-union households, many of which are black, which is why one wag has said that the unbeatable presidential candidate would be a New Deal liberal who opposed abortion and supported school prayer. Here again, our assumptions mislead us, and the data exist to prove it. People who are pro-life are far more likely than people who are pro-choice (41.2 percent to 31.9 percent) to hold a strong position in favor of government assistance to the unemployed.

Of course, the figures I have been discussing are influenced by the economic liberalism of black evangelicals, but this fact simply illustrates another media failing: the refusal to take the religiosity of African Americans seriously. For those same African American evangelicals who support "liberal" economic justice positions are more "conservative" than the national norm (or the norm among Christians) on such social issues as abortion, classroom prayer, and the role of women. Indeed, the Reverend Jesse Jackson, before he became a presidential candidate, preached strongly against abortion.

In the abortion battle itself, the pro-life side is often portrayed through coverage of Operation Rescue, the activist group that tries to interfere with the functioning of abortion clinics. In truth, the pro-life movement itself is hotly divided over the tactics of Operation Rescue, but when journalists report on the abortion battle, they often speak as though all abortion foes are one. They aren't. For example, during the 1992 "siege," as it was called, of Buffalo abortion clinics, the pastor of one Baptist church said this: "The religious community is largely opposed to abortion. But we are also opposed to Operation Rescue's attempts to violently close legally operating clinics."[3] Several churches in the South, where the question of civil disobedience was fully fleshed out during the years of the civil rights movement, have adopted a sauce-for-the-gander attitude, displaying some integrity of their own: if we opposed Dr. King's disobedience in a cause he believed in, they explain, we must oppose Randall Terry's as well.

I mentioned PLAGAL earlier, but there are other pro-life groups that the media chooses to ignore. Pro-life feminists gave rise to a memorable bumper sticker back in the seventies: I'M PRO-LIFE AND PRO-ERA. Daniel Berrigan—yes, *that* Daniel Berrigan—crusades against abortion. One might think that the very existence of these and other groups would be a fascinating story for a nation that has overdosed on the same old abortion stories. Evidently, one would be wrong. They do not fit the mold, a member of PLAGAL said to me, and so they are invisible.

Still, all of this could be avoided if the journalist who seeks to report with integrity would just take the time to follow the rules: think about the good and fair and true way to say it, and then say it that way. Make the story fit the facts instead of the other way around. Sometimes, following the basic lessons of journalism school is all the integrity one needs.

INTO ATTACK MODE

Abortion is far from the only area in which some journalists make up their minds first and get the facts later. Let us consider for a moment a fact of American political life that just about everybody knows because just about everybody has read it in the newspaper or heard it on the radio and seen it on television, over and over again. That fact is that the President of the United States, Bill Clinton, changes his mind a lot. We know it like we know the day of the week; and should we forget, commentators, political opponents, and the regular news columns are there to remind us. We may not recall the particular set of issues on which he is supposed to have waffled, but we know that he has been doing it, and doing it more than other Presidents, because . . . well, because it keeps getting reported as a fact.

But suppose it isn't true. Suppose the media have gotten the story wrong. How would we know that?

Consider: According to a study by the Center for Media and Public Affairs, news coverage during the first six months of his presidency was overwhelmingly negative. The coverage of Clinton, says the center, has been far harsher than coverage of his predecessor, George Bush—and many observers pointed to what seemed to them the mean-spiritedness of the Bush coverage.[4] So when readers or viewers come to the news about Clinton, the chances are that what they will read or here will be bad.

So why the negative coverage? The view of a growing number of media critics, including the political scientist Thomas Patterson, who studies news coverage of Presidents, as well as such distinguished journalists as Morton Kondracke, is that something has changed radically in the way the media cover the presidency. What has changed is variously described as a cynical or hypercritical attitude, and there is truth to that. But, more, journalists thirst for controversy, and they have found out a good way to get it. Instead of reporting what the President said, report what the President's opponents say about what the President said. And, presto! Now all at once there is manufactured controversy—and the spin goes from neutral to negative. It has, say the critics, been happening since the mid-1980s. It happened to Reagan in the last years of his presidency. It happened to Bush for nearly his entire presidency. And it is happening to Clinton.

Yes, but what about those broken promises? Patterson, whose 1993 book *Out of Order* argues that reporters now cover the White House the way they used to cover political campaigns, has written that "Clinton's record is the profile of a president who easily could have acquired a reputation for keeping his promises."[5] Patterson wrote in 1994 that Clinton "has fulfilled or is pursuing most of his major commitments," listing, among others, "a tax increase on higher incomes, the abortion-counseling ban, family-leave legislation, the North American Free Trade Agreement, and the Brady law." He did not achieve national health care, but even his opponents would not say it was for lack of trying. Unfortunately, says Patterson, a promise kept is not deemed newsworthy; but a promise broken is news for months.

Not only did Clinton try to keep most of his campaign promises, Patterson argued, but he worked well with Congress (at least when it was run by Democrats). How well? "Congress backed Clinton's position on 88% of contested votes in 1993, a level exceeded only twice in 40 years—by Dwight Eisenhower with 89% in 1953 and by Lyndon Johnson with 93% in 1965." And, yes, says Patterson, Clinton has sometimes abandoned his prior positions, most notably on the question of the Haitian boat people.

But no more than other Presidents. (And in the long run, Patterson notes, his Haitian policy worked.) And while we are on the subject of the Congress, the journalist Howard Kurtz points out that congressional leaders back off promises and change their minds constantly, but somehow the label of waffling never seems to stick to them.[6] Why not? Because that isn't the story. The story is that Clinton is a man who dithers and backs off. Once the story has been selected, it takes on, as they say, a life of its own.

There is, however, a story about Republicans too, and that is the story that they are bad people. According to a study by the same Center for Media and Public Affairs that found the spin on Clinton stories overwhelmingly negative, the coverage of the GOP-controlled Congress was mostly negative too[7]—slightly more so on the television news programs than in the pages of the newspapers.

If, as nearly everybody seems to think, journalists have strong political biases, why is it that the Democratic President and the Republican Congress both receive sharply negative news coverage? Patterson's answer is that a culture of negativity has replaced the older and healthier culture of skepticism that once governed journalistic coverage of politics. This negativity has a far more powerful hold on the media than any ideology. The point seems to be that every politician is a liar and a rascal, and the only distinction is between the ones who have been caught and the ones who have not.

You might suppose that journalistic integrity would require letting the facts, in effect, speak for themselves. But more and more of the language in today's news stories is editorializing. Sometimes it is quite blatant, as when a network news anchor stated that the Republican budget agenda would "demolish government aid programs, many of them designed to help children and the poor."[8] As it happens, that is precisely my view of much of the Republican budget agenda, but I do not pretend that it is anything other than a personal opinion. What has happened to modern journalism, says Patterson, is that the dividing line does not exist.

What makes this tendency so tragic is that not so long ago, genuine investigative journalism was one of the nation's glories. In the era of Watergate, journalists did two things that nowadays seem almost quaint: they did the legwork on the stories themselves, rather than relying on canned responses from the opponents of whomever they were covering, and they did not think an unconfirmed leak from a single source by itself constituted news. In the contemporary effort to make every story look like a scandal, the press has so inured the public to political outrage that when something truly terrible does occur—like the selling of arms to people responsible for slaughtering American troops—reporters have available no language with which to make clear that this story is different from the others. Instead, it is just another headline, and the perpetrators are able to portray themselves as heroes.

But let a politician *say* any of this—let a President or a Speaker of the House complain about his press coverage—and you can predict with absolute accuracy that somewhere in the dismissive statement by the criticized newspaper or network defending its journalistic integrity, two key words will appear. One of the words is *First*. The other is *Amendment*. Which brings us, I suppose, to the heart of the matter.

FIRST AMENDMENT ETHICS (I)

The unfortunate habit of journalists who are charged with acting irresponsibly is to trot out the First Amendment, which protects freedom of the press, as though it is a shield against criticism. But not only is the Constitution no shield; it isn't even relevant. As the media critic Ken Auletta has pointed out, the First Amendment is not a code of ethics. The amendment tells reporters what they have the right to do, but it does not tell them what they ought to do. What we have seen in the earlier chapters is particularly true here: the fact that one operates under the protection of the Constitution does not mean that one operates with integrity.

Consider the case of Faye Resnick, a friend of Nicole Brown Simpson who wrote a book purporting to offer details of Simpson's relationship with her husband. Judge Lance Ito, presiding over O. J. Simpson's trial for his ex-wife's murder, begged the media not to give the book too much coverage prior to the completion of jury selection; the judge was worried, he said, about preserving the possibility of a fair trial. Some editors complied with Ito's requests, but others ignored them. In particular, CBS aired an interview of Resnick by the reporter Connie Chung, responding to critics with a bland recital of its First Amendment privileges. The network added that the broadcast was "consistent with responsible journalism"; one critic responded that it was "consistent with ratings journalism."[9]

It is said that some potential witnesses in the case were never called because, having sold their stories for significant sums of money, they might be too easily impeached. A depressing account in *The New Yorker* detailed the enormous energy that journalists—principally, but not exclusively, from the tabloids—expended in order to track down witnesses and offer them cash. If challenged, presumably, these reporters, too, would say that ensuring a fair trial was not their responsibility.

But one wonders exactly what this can mean. Do journalists have *less* civic responsibility than other citizens? This cannot be so. The strictures of integrity should apply to everyone, which means that a journalist, just like any other citizen, must engage in genuine moral reflection before making a difficult decision. Of course, it may be that the decision to air an interview that a judge said would interfere with a fair trial was not a difficult decision. But that fact, if true, is a problem in itself. And it has nothing to do with the First Amendment.

A funny thing happened to the First Amendment during America's transition from an agrarian nation stretched thinly along the east coast of the continent to the dominant economic and military power on earth. The freedom of speech lost its core as a vital component of self-governance— the ability of citizens to discuss politics and, in particular, to criticize their government without fear of reprisal—and grew into an apologetic leviathan, able to shield from community scrutiny everything from violent pornography to tabloid rumor-mongering to hurling racial epithets to burning the American flag. I would not want to say that any of these activities should be entirely without the protection of the First Amendment; but I do fear that we are rapidly losing sight of the political understanding at the amendment's heart. The First Amendment is not an accident. The Framers did not add it to the Constitution by happenstance. They did it out of the most profound deliberation, because they knew we were going to need it. They could not have dreamed, however, of what it would ultimately become.

A few years ago, I was on a panel with some journalists and lawyers to talk about free speech and free press. The moderator asked us to consider the hypothetical case of a book that described a horrible murder in such luridly compelling terms that it caused a young man to go out and duplicate the crime.

Now, problems of this kind pose a genuine challenge for defenders of press freedom, among whom, despite what I have said about bias, I certainly count myself. The challenge they pose is whether one is genuinely willing to defend the worst cases in order to save the best ones. Simply put, if we give the government the power to outlaw violent and exploitative pornography, we risk also giving it the power to outlaw anything else it doesn't like, such as publication of its embarrassing secrets. And that, I thought, would be the answer the journalists on the panel would offer: something on the same theme, but of course more elegantly put.

I was wrong. Among the panelists was one of the nation's most respected newspaper editors, and he chose a tactic that infuriates moderators all over the world: challenging the hypothetical rather than answering it. The case was impossible, he said. It could never occur. It could never occur because books do not cause people to do bad things. People may choose to do bad things, but a book could never be the cause.

Now, this is a surprising view for a journalist to have. Did he also believe, I wanted the moderator to ask, that books could never cause people to do *good* things? Was writing useless? Did Sinclair and Riis and Garrison and Stowe accomplish nothing with the prose that, most of us were taught, moved people to try to make the world better? Was writing as a means to press for social change a waste of time? (The answer to this question would indeed have been fascinating, given that the sponsor of the panel was PEN, the writers' group.)

Of course he believed none of these things. I prefer to think that the hypothetical was hard for him because it challenged, in the end, his faith: his faith that words are good, that putting them together to tell a story is a virtuous calling, and that if some unscrupulous writer put the words together wrong, to describe something that didn't happen, to propose something horrific, why, the way to fix that was to rearrange the words until the truth came shining through. When somebody says that a book made somebody commit a terrible crime, that logic is shattered: it is too late, then, to reassemble the evil words into something benign.

It is part of our tradition that the cure for bad speech is more and better speech. When waxing poetic, defenders of free speech and press like to quote John Milton's 1644 argument for press freedom, the *Areopagitica*: "And though all the winds of doctrine were let loose to play upon the earth, so Truth be in the field, we do injuriously, by licensing and prohibiting, to misdoubt her strength. Let her and Falsehood grapple; who ever knew Truth put to the worst, in a free and open encounter?"

Now, if the truth is told, Milton was not talking about press freedom as we think of it today. His argument was addressed to the question of whether free *publishing* should be allowed—that is, whether books should be printable without a government license, for the licensing system was, from the time the printing press was invented, a powerful tool for protecting monopoly profits in the private sector and giving the Crown considerable power over what could be printed. But Milton certainly was not arguing (and not even the Framers believed) that words, once published, could not form the basis of a legal action.

Even though we would not want today (I hope) to return to an era when the government enjoyed broad powers of censorship, I emphasize the limited argument Milton was making because there is a lesson in it. Milton thought that if lots of people published, one of them was bound to get the story right, no matter how many others got it wrong. He argued that truth would win out; he did not contend that nobody would get hurt in the process.

This is a point that press freedom advocates do not like to admit, and that hate speech rules (although I am a skeptic of them) tend to reflect: words *do* wound, and wounds do fester, and not all of those wounds are healed by more speech. Some of those wounds will never be healed at all. Such is the raw power of language.

The point of the First Amendment's protection of free speech and free press is that the government is dangerous, and, if it held the power to censor, it could not be trusted to use that power with any wisdom. Why not? Because *we* are the government, and we cannot trust ourselves. The point is *not* that we can trust editors and publishers more than we can trust government officials; indeed, I have met many editors and publishers whom I would trust a good deal less. The problem is that the power to tell others what to write and publish is sufficiently dangerous that it is likely to corrupt whomever holds it.

This suggests that the same power to determine what will and will not be published can corrupt editors and publishers who, after all, can tell others what to write and publish. That it can corrupt producers who decide what will go on the air. And often it does. Integrity, as we have seen, fades fast as one moves beyond risk. The First Amendment, in its current guise as an excuse for everything, makes decisions on what to publish or broadcast virtually risk-free, and thus, almost inevitably, corrupting as well. The genius of our First Amendment traditions, and of Milton, is the recognition that we are better off with lots of differently corrupt entities that might cancel one another out than with one big one.

NEWS MISJUDGMENT

That is not to say that the American news media are corrupt, at least not yet, but the freedom to write or broadcast without challenge has led to decisions that do not seem much driven by a ranking of the relative news value of competing stories.

Early in 1995, after one guest on a television talk show was arrested for the murder of another, supposedly because, while the show was being taped, the victim had confessed homosexual yearnings for the accused killer, commentators (and talk-show hosts) fell over one another to ask the question that *TV Guide* screamed on its cover: "Have the talk shows gone too far?" A nice question, but a little late; of course they have, and they did so a long time ago, but to pin on them the responsibility for a murder is ridiculous. One need not, however, excuse the act of murder, which is vicious and immoral and deserving of harsh retribution, to realize that the talk shows (which are incredibly profitable) bear some responsibility. In the desire to shock, they deliberately create provocative situations, knowing—indeed, I suspect, hoping—that some guests, and some viewers, will fly into the paroxysms of anger, sorrow, pain, guilt, joy, whatever, that make such fabulous television. ("How did you feel when you watched them drag your dead nine-month-old out of the wreckage?" a reporter with the common sense and moral sensibility of a gnat will ask while broadcasting live from the scene of a train wreck.) We may call it journalism and we may say that the First Amendment protects it, but what it really is, is emotional pornography. And the media industry understands perfectly well that emotional pornography is where the money is.

Remember the hearings on Anita Hill's charges that she had been sexually harassed by Clarence Thomas? Just about everybody seemed to watch at least part of the proceedings, which all the television networks broadcast live and at extraordinary length—the sort of treatment usually accorded presidential funerals and major wars. And given our national addiction to this kind of emotional pornography, it is easy to see why the sexual harassment charges would gain a large audience. But a press that loudly proclaims its own integrity has no obligation to pander to that audience. The charges were obviously important and, today, more than half of Americans believe that they were true.[10] But at the end of the day, Justice Thomas has only one vote—the same vote as, to take the two most recent examples, Stephen Breyer or Ruth Bader Ginsburg, neither one of whose hearings attracted the television coverage of Thomas's.*

Again, the Simpson trial is a case in point. I continue to be astonished

---

*Since the Thomas hearings, many observers have insisted that their true importance came in making sexual harassment real to America; and with fresh awareness, there is a fresh possibility of getting it under control. I hope this is true. But this does not explain the news judgment exercised at the time of the hearings, unless, of course, editors and producers now wish to claim that they covered the hearings so heavily not because the public wanted to know but because the press knew, just *knew*, that the hearings would spark a fresh and important interest in the harassment problem. In this scenario, the press just wanted to be part of a movement for social change.

at the number of otherwise competent journalists who insist on calling it "the trial of the century," even though some of us learned in school that the trial of the century took place at Nuremberg in 1946. But that is less a problem than the shameless pandering by a journalistic establishment that continues to claim that it is exercising news judgment. One radio station in New York City *advertised* itself during the Simpson trial as offering more frequent updates on the proceedings than any other. Now, this is not a judgment about what is important; this is a judgment about what will make money. And how absurd has that judgment made the news? In the first three months of 1995, the network television newscasts ran more stories about the Simpson trial than they did about the President of the United States.[11]

Let me be very clear: I have enormous sympathy for the families and friends of Nicole Brown Simpson and Ronald Goldman, but not *more* sympathy than I have for the families and friends of countless other murder victims. Other than its value as emotional pornography, there was nothing about the Simpson trial that made it a more *important* story than the tale of other trials of other accused murderers. Unless, of course, the importance of a story is judged by how many members of the public would like to have the story reported.

The exercise of news judgment, then, can mean telling the American people what the editors think they should know or telling the American people what the editors think they want to know, but these are not the same thing and pursuing both simultaneously is impossible. The second, moreover, does not involve any judgment, or at least any professional journalistic judgment; it requires only a guess about the tastes of the audience. So good journalists pursue the first—telling the people what the people *should* know. And this seems to me precisely right. Making judgments about what is useful and useless, what it is good to report and what should be ignored, is a central part of the free speech mission. If this is what the media are up to, however, we should hear a good deal less about the people's "right to know," since it turns out to be a right to know only what professional journalists see fit to tell them.

Exercising news judgment with integrity is like doing anything else with integrity: it requires both time and contemplation. Consider, for example, a journalist who discovers that a prominent politician has had a string of extramarital affairs. Once upon a time, the story would not have been reported, which probably constituted a bit too much of a nod and a wink. One can scarcely deny, after all, that the way a politician treats his or her spouse gives us a bit of information about the way the politician treats relationships of trust.*

But that does not mean the story should be run. First, a problem of proportionality arises. Will the fire generated by the story consume all other issues? This is a point that an editor who believes that integrity in the news business implies the exercise of judgment must contemplate. Even if a candidate's fidelity matters, as I think it does, that does not mean that a newspaper, knowing the public's taste for voyeurism, acts with true integrity when it publishes a story that will, for a time, make it difficult to concentrate on any of the important issues over which the electoral battle is presumably joined. This is what happened, for example, in the course of the media's rather relentless pursuit of Gary Hart in 1988. Even if it was true that he in some sense invited the press to track down rumors of his marital infidelity, the focus on verifying those rumors soon made it pretty much impossible to discuss anything else about his presidential bid. For that reason, if no other, Hart was wise to step aside when he did.

Second, there is the problem of equivalence. When all is said and done, the newspaper considering whether to run the story must ask whether it would run the same story were its subject not a politician but a famous columnist or commentator—for example, one who writes for the newspaper in question. (Who said that the only sacred cow the press respects is itself?) If the paper really believes that marital fidelity gives us information about trust, then it is plainly as relevant to the public's evaluation of the straying columnist as to the public's evaluation of the straying politician, for journalists, too, hold a public trust that they must repeatedly earn. Should the newspaper decide that the story would be unimportant if it concerned a journalist, it must face the possibility—no, the likelihood—that it is not exercising news judgment at all, but simply playing to the public taste for sexual scandal on the one hand and, on the other, protecting its own. That is not the course of integrity.

Finally, there is a question of privacy—not the privacy of the candidate

---

*Many journalists have advanced the argument that stories about the personal lives of politicians are more relevant when the politicians themselves campaign on such issues as "family values"; the point being, apparently, that the press is doing the vital work of ferreting out hypocrisy. But this argument makes the decision on running the story begin to sound like the decision on whether to punish; and the rationale is convincing only if the newspaper also runs stories about the personal lives of the journalists who ferret out the "hypocrisy" of others.

but the privacy of the candidate's spouse and family. The family in such cases is always humiliated and often shattered. Of course, news judgment might demand that the story run anyway. But the newspaper should not be so self-righteous as to pretend that its actions are without consequences. The editors should not hide behind the shield of buck-passing: "Well, it's really Senator So-and-so who is responsible for this pain to his family." No, it isn't. It is the newspaper that decides to run the story. The paper has made a judgment: this much news is worth that much pain. Certainly the First Amendment makes the press free to make that decision, and certainly nobody can or should try to interfere with the news judgment of a paper's editors. But the editors also have a responsibility, thrust upon them as much by integrity as by the Constitution, not to pretend that their precious freedoms are without cost to anybody else.

FIRST AMENDMENT ETHICS (II)

Since we are talking about integrity, let us take the matter down to basics. Is it moral for journalists to lie in order to get a story? Consider the following example, which is drawn from a case decided by the Supreme Court in 1991. (It is not a literal account of the case.)

Example 6-1. A newspaper reporter, in order to get a story he wants, approaches a state employee and offers him anonymity in return for information. The employee agrees and supplies the reporter with the information he needs. On further checking, the reporter decides that the source's information is mainly accurate, but that the source has misled him in some respects. The newspaper then publishes the story, but names the source and also explains how the source slightly misled the reporter.

Observation 6-1(a). The newspaper would appear to be acting without integrity, for it made and broke a commitment. The only justification for its action would be if it had issued a prior warning to the source that his name would be used if his information proved inaccurate.

Observation 6-1(b). The legal aspect of the case that came before the Supreme Court *(Cohen v. Cowles Media Co.)*[12] was whether the source could sue the newspaper for breach of contract. He did so, and won damages of $200,000, which the Court upheld against a First Amendment challenge. Laws that apply to everybody, the majority wrote, "do not offend the First Amendment simply because their enforcement against the press has incidental effects on its ability to gather and report the news." Which is another way of saying that the source kept his commitment and was entitled to expect that the newspaper—at least, an *integral* newspaper—would keep its own.

Indeed, to suggest a constitutional right to beguile would be bizarre. Consider the following example. Suppose that in my capacity as a law professor, I come to suspect one of my students of cheating, perhaps of copying a paper from some other source. I call the poor fellow to my office and I say to him: "I have reason to think you plagiarized your term paper. Just tell me the truth and I promise I won't tell a soul. You won't be punished. You'll just have to do another paper." Faced with this combination of implied threats and explicit promises, the student confesses. Yes, he did it. No, it won't happen again. He does not know what got into him. And so on and so on. I console him all the way to the door. Then, no sooner is he out of my office than I waltz down the stairs to the office of the dean of students and insist that the cheater be tossed out. Surely I have broken my promise, and surely—whether or not one believes I have breached a legally binding contract—I have done the student a moral wrong. I have misled him to obtain information and then harmed him by disclosing it when I promised I would not. This is not an action backed up by integrity.

Or, if one thinks that I lack the constitutional privilege that a newspaper might have, suppose that I do not after all go to the dean of students. I go to the campus paper with a juicy story. (Perhaps the student's mother or father is somebody famous.) Or I simply post the student's name and deed on the door of my office: publishing it, at least within the relatively narrow community of the law school. In either case, if, as I believe, the student has a legitimate gripe against me (morally, and perhaps legally), then the source whose name was exposed has a legitimate gripe against the newspaper. That this is so is probably obvious to the reader; indeed, only a journalist or an undercover spy would imagine for a moment that there is nothing morally bankrupt about lying or breaking one's word in order to obtain information.

When reporters and editors rely on the First Amendment as a putative shield in such cases as this one, they are making a serious error in analysis. They behave as though the freedom-of-the-press clause is there as a coincidence; or as though the real intention of those who wrote it was to ensure the maximum profits for media conglomerates: "Congress shall make no law . . . abridging the freedom . . . of the press *to make money*," they would have the amendment read.

The point is that journalists, no less than others, have moral responsibilities, and, as Auletta points out, they cannot resolve their ethical questions by pointing to the First Amendment. The First Amendment grants many freedoms, but it gives not a clue as to their good and proper use. Surely we would want to specify, as a bare minimum, that they must be used with integrity.

But what does that mean? Well, we might say that *Branzburg v. Hayes*, a much-criticized 1972 decision in which the Supreme Court held that the freedom of the press does not include a constitutional right of reporters to refuse to divulge to the grand jury the identities of their sources, struck a blow for integrity. Wrote Justice White for the majority:

> [W]e cannot seriously entertain the notion that the First Amendment protects a newsman's agreement to conceal the criminal conduct of his source, or evidence thereof, on the theory that it is better to write about the crime than to do something about it. Insofar as any reporter in these cases undertook not to reveal or testify about the crime he witnessed, his claim of privilege under the First Amendment presents no substantial question. The crimes of news sources are no less reprehensible and threatening to the public interest when witnessed by a reporter than when they are not.[13]

Now, one could distinguish the actual individuals involved in the cases before the Court—one had witnessed drug dealing, the other two had witnessed meetings of the Black Panthers—but to quarrel with the justices on whether the grand juries looking into the Panthers were really investigating a crime could cause us to miss the force of Justice White's argument. The presence of a reporter does not create any immunity for the perpetrator of the crime; so why should the accident that the witness is a reporter instead of someone in another walk of life mean that the crime should go unpunished?

Moreover, even had *Branzburg* been decided the other way (and some states have adopted by statute limited "shield" laws in an effort to reduce its scope), the Supreme Court would only have crafted a *right* of reporters to refuse to divulge their sources. It would not have invested them with a *responsibility* to refuse to do so. Whether to do it and when would remain a moral question for each journalist to answer.

Precisely because the question is a moral one, we can admire the integrity of reporters who, having made the commitment to keep their sources confidential, go to jail rather than break their word. (Again, reflect on the unintegral character of the newspaper's actions in *Cohen*.) On the other hand, we must not forget the point we saw in chapter 4, that simply stating one's intention not to fulfill a moral commitment does not excuse its nonfulfillment: so that if there is a duty to come forward and report a crime, a reporter's promise not to do it may not be morally binding. (However, given the understandable but depressing data on the reluctance of witnesses to come forward, it does not appear that we as a society believe that we share a moral responsibility to report crimes.)[14]

What other moral responsibilities does integrity impose upon the news media? Recall from chapter 4 the example of the newspaper that learns where a famous Mafioso, now in the witness-protection program, is being hidden by the federal government. My point, which I hope will not need explication, was that to reveal the witness's whereabouts, whether legally punishable or not, would be not a victory for the First Amendment but an offense against morality.

Consider the following example, which readers who are not too vain to read the occasional work of popular fiction may recognize as derived from a novel by Tom Clancy:

> **Example 6-2.** Following an armed attack on a territory of the United States, the government decides on a massive deception, hoping to convince the enemy that a particular aircraft carrier is in dry dock, still undergoing repairs, when in fact it is on its way to war. In order to make the deception effective, the government asks the television networks to broadcast pictures of the ship in dry dock. The government is not simply asking the networks not to reveal the secret truth, an enterprise in which, to their credit, they frequently cooperate; it is asking them to help spread the lie. In Mr. Clancy's fantasy land, the networks, after a bit of grumbling, agree that to do what he says is their patriotic duty. But let us assume that in our real world, at least one network refuses to be partner to the deception, and eventually even tells the real story—while the ship is on its way to war. Has the network acted with integrity?

> **Observation 6-2(a).** The first and easy answer is that if the network has made its decision after appropriate soul-searching (as opposed to simply a knee-jerk "We-have-the-story-and-we're-going-with-it" attitude), it could well be said to be acting with integrity. Of course, we would want the consideration of what action is appropriate to take into account the problem of proportionality: American service members might die because of its decision.

> **Observation 6-2(b).** The second and more difficult point is that even if, as Clancy proposes, a network that cooperates might in the short run gain kudos from the American public for its patriotism, it might also, in the long run, lose a degree of that respect. The integrity of its stories might

be called into question, as readers and watchers wondered in the future whether this or that story was true or was the result of a government plant. This corrosive effect of too much coziness is common in societies that have government controlled, or government connected, news outlets.

Observation 6-2(c). Moreover, there is risk of another kind in encouraging cooperation of this sort between the apparatus of the federal government and the apparatus of the news media. The reason is not so much that reporters are watchdogs and so must maintain their independence—as we have seen, that is rarely an accurate description of the function of the modern media—as that the government and the press each possess so much power that the two of them working in combination might overwhelm democracy. I do not say that every cooperative act is a threat to democracy; but there is a slippery slope, and we must watch our step. (Indeed, we have already stumbled a good way down, given the social hobnobbing between media and government folks in Washington.)

Observation 6-2(d). Finally, note that the First Amendment has nothing to do with the outcome. The fact that the network has a constitutional right to refuse to cooperate says nothing about what it *should* do.

The point is that the First Amendment contains no *shoulds*; the press has to supply those itself. Consider once more our earlier discussion on whether journalists covering the Simpson case had a responsibility to minimize conduct that might interfere with the ability of the judge to conduct a fair trial. If the reporters in question wished to act with integrity, the answer must be an unequivocal yes.

I mention all this not because I believe that the freedom of the press will be respected only if it is used with a degree of integrity. I do not think that the Framers assumed that it would always be used with integrity, but it is certainly true that they recognized that the freedom of the press—like all the liberties in which they believed—would be of the greatest use to democracy if used with integrity. The Sedition Acts of the early Republic, which punished false speech about the government, should have been ruled unconstitutional and certainly must have chilled legitimate criticism, but they had at their core an understanding that seems to me exactly correct: the freedom of the press should ideally be used in a way that is responsible, by those who want to tell the truth and are willing to stand behind and support what they say, as against its use by those who will say anything to get their way. The Federalists who supported the Sedition Acts erred only in supposing that legislation was the proper way to get people to use their liberties morally. But if that supposition was a mistake, the Federalists were hardly the only group in our history to make it. More to the point, the freedom of the press was protected for a reason, and nowadays, in our rush toward tabloid voyeurism and other forms of emotional pornography, we act as though there wasn't one.

The press nowadays justifies its own conduct according to what is sometimes called "the people's right to know," and although this right appears nowhere in the Constitution, it can be derived from natural law, if one is so inclined. The philosopher John Finnis, in his 1980 book *Natural Law and Natural Rights*, argues that in our culture, the pursuit of knowledge for its own sake is a given—nobody feels the need to justify it—and he defends this axiom as a fundamental aspect of human flourishing. The people who run the contemporary communications media would doubtless agree.

And although it is unclear whether the Framers of the First Amendment shared this natural law view, it is today sufficiently institutionalized that we speak freely of the press in the terms it long ago adopted for itself: as the fourth estate, holding a special place in society, checking the government with its simple yet relentless drive to discover, to illuminate, to *know and make known*. Despite its natural law moorings, this vision is in one sense highly instrumental, the product of our shared skepticism (which politicians sometimes forget) about the power of the central government. The institutional role of the press in a free society, then, is to check and balance a state apparatus that might, left to itself, run rampant. The trouble is that an institution that holds that much power—and the checking function is an exercise of genuine power, let us make no mistake—needs the scrutiny that, in our society, is applied only by . . . um . . . the press.

DOUBLE STANDARDS AND SACRED COWS

This leads us to the issue that should concern the student of integrity the most: the vigorous refusal of the press to apply to itself as an institution the standards that it insists on applying to everybody else.

In early 1993, shortly before President Clinton withdrew his star-crossed nomination of Zoe Baird to be attorney general, I had a conversation with an editor at an influential American magazine that had just run an editorial calling for Baird to step aside. Baird, you will recall, was pilloried for hiring an undocumented alien as a nanny. The editor, who had voted for the editorial, confessed to me that she had the same problem. When I expressed some consternation (I am biased here—I know Zoe Baird and admire her), the editor explained that unlike the attorney general of the United States, she had no responsibility to enforce the law. What was unacceptable, she said, was to put a person who had broken the law in the position of chief law enforcement officer.

Let me confess that I remain as puzzled now as I was then. I understand the *logic* of the distinction; I simply am not sure that I understand the *morality* of it. The person who must enforce the law must not have broken it—all right, I understand that much of the argument, whether or not I entirely agree with it. But what about the people whose institution plays so important a role (as the institution itself would insist) in checking the power of the attorney general and other government officials? Are there not standards for them as well? John Howard of the *Wall Street Journal* has put it this way: "Given the impact the media have on public policy discussions, we should be willing to subject ourselves to more scrutiny."[15] To the student of integrity, the point might seem obvious—but it seems not to be obvious to most journalists.

Consider the question of whether journalists should accept speaking fees from organizations whose interests may be at stake in the stories they report: Should a reporter covering the health care debate accept an honorarium to address a convention of health insurers? Should a columnist who writes about securities regulation accept an honorarium from an association of brokerage houses?

Some reporters do not accept honoraria, and some publications do not allow their staffers to take them or require them to follow special rules. In a 1994 *New Yorker* article by Ken Auletta, some journalists who do accept honoraria suggested a possible distinction between themselves and government officials: one group is paid with tax dollars and the other is not.[16] But that distinction is specious. The question is not how federal funds are being spent. The question is whether the potential for conflict of interest exists. If journalists report on issues directly related to the interests of groups that are also paying them to speak, the potential is obviously present. And the test is a simple one. If a reader or viewer, upon learning of the honorarium arrangement, would wonder about the reporter's biases, then the appearance of impropriety exists, for the very quality the journalist seeks to market—objectivity—is called into question.*

*Concerned about this public perception, some publications and television networks—including, in one recent instance, ABC News—have moved to restrict the honoraria that reporters may earn from groups they cover or may cover. Another possibility is to require disclosure, publishing the amounts once a year, as federal employees do. But even better than regulation of the practice is for the press to reconsider the holier-than-thou attitude with which it reports purported conflicts of interest by government officials.

Many journalists reject the notion that the viewer's perception or desires are crucial. But when one thinks in terms of integrity, this test is obviously the right one. Think for a moment about the question of acceptance of honoraria by members of Congress. Why is there a problem in terms of integrity? There is a problem because the elected representative is, in effect, marketing himself or herself to voters as the protector of their interests. If the representative is receiving significant funds from other interest groups, however, that marketing claim may be called into question. The problem is not that the claim becomes false, that the representative becomes "bought"; the problem is that the voters might *suspect* that this is so, that their elected representative is not after all what he or she is claiming to be, which would be a violation of rule 3.

When a journalist accepts an honorarium from a group with an interest in the stories that he or she reports, the problem is a precise analogy. The journalist markets himself or herself to the audience as either (1) an objective reporter of facts, or (2) a thoughtful individual who has reasoned out an opinion worth hearing. Were the journalist's audience aware that he or she was receiving speaking fees from organizations whose interests might be affected by the way the stories come out, the audience might question either one of the marketing claims. Thus the audience might *suspect* the existence of bias where previously it was willing to accept the journalist's claim.

As members of the news media have rushed to cover this story about their own, several journalists have protested their innocence—or, perhaps, their integrity—insisting that they would never bias a story because of an honorarium. Journalists, by and large, are honorable people, and I am willing to take them at their word; but then I only hope that they will be willing to take at their word the government officials whom they excoriate for accepting money from interest groups. If journalists can take the cash and remain free of the taint of bias because their characters are pure, there is no particular reason to suppose that government officials will do worse—unless one assumes that government officials are, as a group, people whose characters are inferior to those of the reporters who cover them.

None of this should be taken to mean that journalists should be forbidden to accept honoraria from groups they cover. Nor does it necessarily mean that all honoraria should be disclosed to the always curious public. It does mean, however, that the many journalists who raise questions about the integrity of public officials for alleged conflicts of interest should be a bit more attentive to the beams in their own eyes; that if they think it is possible for reporters to take money and retain their objectivity, they should think at least as highly of government officials. But what it really means is the simple lesson of this chapter: integrity in journalism requires that the press apply to itself the same standards it applies to everybody else. Only in that way might it be possible after all to realize Milton's dream.

(seven)

And Nothing But the Truth

NO account of integrity would be complete without a few words
about the role of law and the role of lawyers. For better or worse, we
Americans rely on law as a principal guarantor of our national integrity,
and lawyers, despite the ill repute in which they are held (some of it for
good reason), remain the guardians who make law work. Moreover, in the
strange complex of rules that govern the conduct of trials, we can learn
useful lessons about what we *really* think of integrity—that is, what we
really think about *each other's* integrity. Perhaps that is the place to begin.

THE GREAT WAGER

In my role as law professor, the course I most enjoy teaching is Contracts,
which all students take at the outset of their legal education. I find that few
aspects of the course perplex beginning law students more than the reve-
lation that there was a time under the English common law when one
could defend against a suit to collect a debt by what was known as the
wager of law. The defendant who chose, as the courts then put it, to wage
his law would get his friends and neighbors to swear alongside him in the
name of God that no money was owed; if these oaths were duly sworn,

the court would give judgment for the defendant, and the plaintiff could not collect the debt.[1]

In an earlier age, the defendant was allowed to choose the *wager of battel.* He could fight the plaintiff, or acquire a champion to do the fighting on his behalf—and God would grant victory to the one whose lawsuit was just. Even after the Lateran Council banned ordeals in 1215, which was supposed to end the direct invocation of God as the force that would choose among competing earthly truths, England did not abandon the wager of battel. Indeed, as a formally available choice, it continued into the early decades of the nineteenth century.

Somehow law students never have any trouble understanding the wager of battel, with its dramatic imagery of glistening armor and swirling swords and somebody left for dead. In the wager of battel, after all, something is at risk: real harm will ensue. The wager of law, however, evokes puzzlement. Swinging a sword is one thing; everyone recognizes that it wouldn't be easy. But to get up on the witness stand and swear in God's name to tell the truth and then lie—why, that's a fairly simple matter! In the many years that I have been teaching Contracts, this history has always evoked the same response: How could this practice have existed? Why wouldn't people just lie?

Why, indeed? In the cynicism of our age, nobody assumes that simply because an individual swears by God to tell the truth that the person thereby *is* telling the truth. Indeed, hardly anybody seems to think that an individual who swears by God to tell the truth is *probably* telling the truth. The fact that an oath has been sworn raises no presumption of credibility. An oath, whether before a congressional committee or on the witness stand at a trial, is seen as a silly little formality, like the stamping of a passport with a visa in the form of some elaborate seal, one of those bizarre traditions that must be dealt with before one can get to where one wants to go. The oath is the price of admission, but it is the chance to tell the story that matters. And that the price has been paid is evidence, for many people, only of the witness's eagerness to speak—not of the witness's veracity. Of course the defendant's neighbors would just lie; *a fortiori* the defendant himself will just lie; the wager of law, seen by today's standards, seems silly.

It would seem less silly, of course, to one who earnestly believes that there is a God sitting somewhere beyond human ken, prepared to mete out all sorts of interesting punishments on those who swear falsely in His name.[2] In an earlier age, when religious devotion was more common, no laws against perjury existed because everybody assumed that God would take His own measures against false swearing.[3] An excellent deterrent, obviously: A witness who is certain that eternal damnation will follow a false oath is hardly likely to get up on the witness stand and call on God and then lie. So the fact that so many people evidently *do* get up on the stand and lie, and that nobody expects anything different, is evidence, if any is needed, that few people actually believe that anything bad will happen (from supernatural causes, at least) to those who do it. Which is, perhaps, another way of saying that despite consistent polling data to the contrary,[4] most Americans probably harbor some doubt about God's existence—or at least about the likelihood of divine retribution for bearing false witness.

I wonder how many of us would lie under oath for a friend's sake—an oath, let us say, sworn by God. Swearing by God, and believing what one swears, suggests an oath resting on a stronger bond than in normal discourse, for there is, if one is lying, the possibility of punishment, not in this natural realm, but in one more supernatural. Or so the Anglo-American tradition once believed.

At first blush, the understanding of integrity developed in earlier chapters would seem to suggest that lying to save a friend from debt, or even from prison, is not permissible, unless one is willing to say openly that one has this bias, to say something like, "My friendship is so strong that I would lie." To make that part of one's testimony would of course cause the testimony to be ignored, but, as we have seen, integrity is not about winning but about playing by the rules. And sometimes playing by the rules makes it impossible to win.

The notion of "playing by the rules" plainly helped the defense in the 1995 trial of football star O. J. Simpson for the murder of his ex-wife and an acquaintance. Whatever one thinks of Simpson's acquittal, he plainly benefited from the requirement that the prosecution prove its case beyond a reasonable doubt—a standard under which, inevitably, the guilty sometimes go free. The idea that criminals might remain unpunished is not, perhaps, an entirely pleasant one, but it has existed, in one form or another, as long as there have been juries.

Juries once had a freedom to roam that our modern ideal of the "impartial" jury denies. Indeed, our ideal of impartiality is not much justified by the institution's history. Other than a requirement that jurors lack a personal stake in the outcome, the common-law jury was not supposed to be impartial in the modern sense of the term. In the early thirteenth century, when the English criminal jury was in its earliest stage of evolution, its function was to present the guilty party (an early form of indictment) for trial by ordeal, such as drowning. If the suspect survived the ordeal, the

jury could still, if it desired, effectively exile him from England by reporting to the court that, even if innocent of this particular offense, he possessed a "villainous reputation" in his community—a fact of which the
jurors were expected to be aware because they lived in the community
with him.[5] And, just as the jury could rid the community of defendants
found innocent, it could also, and frequently did, embrace individuals who
had plainly committed the crime, by declaring an individual to be "not sus-
pected." Impartiality had nothing to do with it. The original criminal jury
was a body of considerable discretion, to which it was entitled precisely
because of its knowledge of the defendant.

Why is it so important to us that the jury be impartial? Surely the answer
lies in the collapse of the assumption that God is present in the courtroom.
The common-law jury could be very different from our model and still be
fair for a simple reason: *the oath was thought to mean something.* The
jurors took an oath to do justice, and they still do. They were promising to
put aside their prejudices, and they still do. It is simply that we do not
believe them anymore. The sharp distinction between those who have
positions in the matter in question and those who must decide the facts is
needed only in a society that believes that its citizens are prepared to lie
and manipulate under oath. Plainly, we are such a society. But if we think
so little of the people who sit on a jury that we distrust their oath to do
justice, one marvels that we trust them with the verdict.

Many commentators attributed Simpson's acquittal, at least in part, to
race: Simpson is black, as were most of the jurors. This analysis, even if
accurate, provides a depressing reminder of our national cynicism toward
the justice system.[*] Trial by jury is constitutionally guaranteed, but has
become so manipulated, in both criminal and civil cases, that hardly anybody seems to believe in its basic fairness. We tell each other fantastic stories—some of them even true—about verdicts by "runaway" juries in civil
cases. (At this writing, the Alabama Supreme Court has *reduced* to a mere
$2 million the punitive damages awarded to a man who bought a new
BMW, only to discover later that the manufacturer had failed to disclose
that the car had been repainted.)

[*]The close attention to demographics was especially pernicious, representing
media reinforcement of the race-, gender-, or class-based essentialism that has in
recent decades so diverted efforts to build a genuinely pluralistic civic life. White
people think this way, we are told, and black people quite differently. Women
believe one thing, men another. The rich want one thing, the poor want something
else. Integrity would suggest that "experts" who make such assertions should at
least provide some basis for their certainty.

If we have little respect for jurors, we have even less for witnesses. Witnesses are cross-examined by lawyers bent on poking holes in their stories, their backgrounds are scrutinized, their veracity is constantly challenged—and all of this is well within the rules. The reason we allow all of this can only be that we think the possibility that witnesses are lying is very great. But the labyrinth of fair procedures that we therefore lay down should be seen as a cost, not a benefit, of living in a society that thinks so little of its people and of their capacity for telling the truth. Does this mean that our processes lack integrity? No; it means that we assume that our people do.

THE EXPEDIENT LIE

If oaths mean less than they did, a system that was designed for a society in which the truth was valued begins to lose both its purpose and its common sense. If a witness's tale is inconvenient for our side, we simply assume that the witness is lying. The fact that the witness is under oath is beside the point. As the heated public debates over the veracity of testimony in the Simpson trial make clear, we obviously do not think that taking an oath makes somebody more likely to tell the truth. In fact, a more or less respectable body of scholarship proposes that the defendant in a criminal case should have the *right* to lie under oath—that for the defendant to swear "I didn't do it" should not be prosecutable as perjury. No court has yet bought that argument. A few federal courts, however, have created an exception to the federal False Statement Statute for defendants who lie to investigators in order to protect themselves.[6]

The False Statement Statue allows imprisonment for up to five years or fines of up to $10,000 for anyone who "willfully" makes "any false, fictitious or fraudulent statements or representations" to "any department or agency of the United States."[7] Courts have carved out a special exception, known as the doctrine of the "exculpatory no," to allow people who are under investigation to deny their guilt. The doctrine is sometimes defended as part of the constitutional protection against self-incrimination, which is found in the Fifth Amendment, and is usually interpreted to cover only specific denials of guilt (or of the elements of a crime, such as receiving a particular check or meeting a particular person at a particular place). So the doctrine does not allow, for example, a suspect to try to cast guilt upon somebody else. But it does allow a suspect to lie.

Now, this is a remarkable proposition for the student of integrity. Not only is our system constructed on the assumption that witnesses (and jurors) will lie; it appears, in some cases, to be prepared to reward them for doing so. Rewards of this kind create a tremendous temptation toward acts of unintegrity. (So do other rewards, such as book contracts for convicted felons.) And they symbolize our national abandonment of the civic ideal (see chapter 11) that even lawbreakers, as a signal of their personal integrity, their wholeness of being, should be willing to stand punishment for their crimes instead of using every device at hand to escape. Instead, through the exculpatory no doctrine, we reward them for denying their crimes.

Sissela Bok, in her book *Lying*, classes a lie of this kind as a lie of "self-defense," intended to avoid "harm to oneself."[8] Most people probably understand what leads those under threat to lie to avoid harm to themselves, and with that empathy often comes a kind of societal permission. Bok warns that "[s]elf-defensive lies can permeate all one does, so that life turns into 'living a lie.'"[9] But the expedient lie, the lie to get us more smoothly where we want to go, is as much a part of our traditions as claiming to value truth. And, like all of our traditions, its very ubiquitousness is part of its difficulty, for expediency, like justice, comes in many guises.

Often we recognize the lie and still reward it. Recall that in chapter 1, I lamented the celebration of the football player who cheats—lies, really—in order to win. Political scientists have explained how our national cognitive dissonance combines with our choice for "rational ignorance" to practically beg political candidates to lie to us in order to get our votes.[10] And the rules sometimes actually encourage the expedient lie. Again, consider the conduct of a criminal trial. In cross-examination, a lawyer will try to make even a witness he knows to be telling the truth appear to be at best confused and at worst a liar. In a system that relies on the adversity of the parties to discover the truth, a lawyer can do nothing else. Still, this conveying of a false impression—trying, in effect, to fool the jury into disbelieving a truthful witness—is nothing but an expedient lie.

The sociologist Orlando Patterson, whose very fine book *Freedom* won the 1993 National Book Award, has argued that even if Clarence Thomas lied to the Senate Judiciary Committee in 1991 in denying Anita Hill's charges of harassment, he was justified in lying, because his objectionable conduct and words arose in a context that could not be understood in the cold light of the hearing room.[11] In effect, says Patterson, the high political cost of literal truth created a moral justification for Thomas to lie. More precisely, if Thomas was lying, he was doing so, Patterson says, because of the vast cultural differences that would render his conduct incomprehensible to his judges.

The gist of Patterson's point—and he is hardly alone in believing it—is that Thomas, if he lied, was justified in doing so because the punishment for telling the truth would not fit the offense. Well, maybe. Perhaps this is why the wager of law died out as a defense of the action for debt, not so much because defendants were willing to lie under oath but because they were able to convince themselves that justice—not fact, but justice—would best be served by a denial. Nor would the denial be a lie, if justice required it; for the defendants, using the argument that Patterson sets forth, could reason instead that the truth would not be served by an admission of facts out of the context that provides justice.

Ah, but how would the defendant obtain the oaths of friends, needed to wage his law successfully? Especially, how would the defendant find them in an age when oaths were thought to be a serious undertaking? The answer, perhaps, is that he would appeal to their sense of justice, convincing them, in Patterson's terms, that the facts would not be correctly understood in the context of the courtroom. And why not? One traditional, if controversial, understanding of the role of jury in Anglo-American jurisprudence has been that the jury is a democratic force, empowered if the case so requires to mete out justice in spite of the law as the judge might have explained it. This notion, called "jury nullification," holds that the jury, in the interest of justice, can interpose itself between the state, seeking to prosecute, and the individual who claims a moral justification for his or her wrongful act, or who, perhaps, insists that she has already suffered enough. And since, at common law, the jury, too, was bound by its oath before God (and was liable for perjury for a false verdict), the risk of a runaway jury was small.

Jury nullification, as the constitutional theorist Akhil Amar has argued, appeals to an often forgotten ideal of democracy—the people *against* the state, in the service of a higher law.[12] The doctrine of jury nullification was all that stood between Jon Peter Zenger and prison for seditious libel. Civil rights protesters tried it, too, with modest success, because juries were not sympathetic. Nowadays, it is relied on by everyone from the anti-abortion protesters of Operation Rescue to parents who face criminal charges in the death of children not properly restrained in automobiles. *Even if our clients violated the law in some technical sense*, the lawyers argue, often explicitly, *you, the jury, should set them free*. We know from interviews with jurors that some of this went on during deliberations over the fate of Marion Barry as well as, two decades earlier, in the Chicago Seven trial.[13]

Was the Simpson jury up to something similar? Many observers evidently thought so, arguing that the jury was punishing the prosecution for its reliance on a racist police detective as a key witness. Whether or not this is what happened—and whether or not, if it happened, it was justified—the point is that it would not have been unusual. On the contrary: the nullifying jury, as we have seen, has a rich pedigree and a healthy provenance. And, bearing in mind that the jury historically was under oath, the democratic jury, able to undo the command of the sovereign, is not a bad idea. The Framers of the American Constitution, in guaranteeing the right to trial by jury, seem to have had in mind a bulwark against government oppression.[14] The Sixth Amendment's guarantee of a jury trial can be seen as a means of preventing the legislature, which promulgates the laws, and the executive, which prosecutes their breach, from combining to keep the people in thrall. The trial by democratic jury, then, can be seen as a branch of popular sovereignty, another of the many checks and balances on excessive government power. And like all checks and balances, this one may be used for ill as well as for good.

Nowadays, judges often instruct juries that they are not to be swayed by the litigants' appeals to principles of morality and justice. But this is a mistake, not only in its lack of fidelity to history, but in its inattention to possibilities of injustice. On the other hand, it is not clear that juries should actually *ignore* the judge's instructions. If, believing the defendant to be guilty, the jurors nevertheless set him free, pretending that he is not guilty but meaning that they are pursuing a higher ideal than the law, have they somehow broken their oath?

Maybe not. The line of argument that allows one to pursue a higher goal by seeming to lie about another state of facts is not exactly unknown in Western history. The historian Gerd Tellenbach reminds us that during the medieval dispute over the royal right to invest bishops—the so-called investiture controversy—forgers at the imperial court at Ravenna drew up what purported to be papal documents taking the side of the emperor against the pope. The forgers, Professor Tellenbach says, comforted themselves with the knowledge that they "were in no way guilty of falsifying the law, but were merely constructing impressive documents which would be of great use for polemical purposes."[15] The forgers were convinced, in other words, that the law was as their forged documents proclaimed it; the forgery itself was simply the most efficacious way of proving their case, which otherwise might not be believed

Like the forgers at Ravenna, the nullifying jury, content that it is doing the right thing, nevertheless lies about what it is up to. It does not announce in its verdict, "Yes, we think the protesters committed the acts they are charged with, but we will apply a higher law and release them."

It announces instead the simple words "Not guilty." The ordinary under-standing of those words is that the defendant did not commit the acts charged. Since we know the defendant did commit them, this verdict seems to be a lie. Still, perhaps there is no lie, because it is perfectly well understood by the parties to such a case—and by other observers as well—that nullification has occurred. A lie, we might say, is no lie if everyone recognizes it as such. So perhaps—I emphasize the conditional—perhaps the jurors are therefore not lying, and thus are keeping their oaths.

Thus, we might conclude that some lies, like those told by the nullify-ing jury, speak their names. At times, as in the case of the Ravenna forg-ers, a lie is deemed necessary to bring the truth to light. The forgers were sure that ecclesiastical law granted the right of investiture of bishops to the crown. The documents they forged were simply by way of trying to prove it to a skeptical world. And if that seems like an awfully shoddy case for avoiding the honesty that integrity would seem to demand, it simply is more evidence, if we need any, that the expedient lie, part of our tradi-tions or not, is a terribly corrupting thing.

Moreover, if the demands of integrity are avoided—or, rather, ful-filled—through the appeal to "justice" as an excuse for a lie, then the def-inition we have been using is left in tatters. It is one thing to say, as Orlando Patterson does, that Clarence Thomas may lie because the truth would result in punishment disproportionate to the harm; but unless Thomas is willing, somehow, to signal that this is what he is doing, then he is not following the third rule of the integral life. He is not saying what he knows is so and, moreover, is not saying that he is not saying what he knows is so.

At the same time, the Thomas example shows how integrity may actually be promoted by the Fifth Amendment's privilege against self-incrimination. The courts held long ago that this privilege means not only that the accused in a criminal case cannot be forced to answer questions about the alleged deed, but that he may not be forced to take the stand if he prefers not to. If the defendant never takes the stand, he need never confront the problem of what to do when one is under oath and has committed a crime; he need never go through the complicated and implausible analysis of the Ravenna forgers or, for that matter, of Patterson's defense of Clarence Thomas. And he need never weigh the consequences of admitting his deed against the consequences of breaking his oath. This means that his integrity is never tested—remember that true integrity must involve risk of loss—but it also means he never lies.

FIRST THING WE DO . . .

I have managed to avoid so far any explicit discussion of lawyers, but I can do so, I think, no longer.

There is an old joke about a fabulously rich man who, as he lies dying, summons to his bedside his three most trusted friends: his doctor, his priest, and his lawyer. When the three are assembled, he tells them, "I know they say you can't take it with you, but I'm going to try." He then distributes three identical and very thick packages, each of which turns out to contain ten million dollars in cash. "I want all of you to come to my funeral," he says, "and when they put me in the ground, throw the envelopes in after me! Promise!" Each friend in turn promises that he will do it.

In due course, the rich man dies, his three friends attend the funeral, and, at the cemetery, each tosses the thick package into the grave. Then, as they begin the walk back to their cars, the doctor says, "My friends, I have a confession to make. Last night, I was sitting in my office with the package, and I got to thinking about the new wing for sick children that the hospital is trying to build, and I thought, Well, this ten million dollars could do a lot of good instead of ending up covered with dirt. I knew that our dear friend, if in his right mind, would have preferred this charitable use. So I took the money out and gave it to the hospital for the new wing. The envelope I put in the grave was stuffed with old newspapers."

The lawyer rounds on him in a fury. The money, he says, was given in trust. The doctor was a trustee. By converting the money to his own use, or even to the use of a charity, he has violated a sacred legal duty, and maybe has committed a felony besides. The lawyer is still in full cry when the priest says, "Not so fast, my son," and then proceeds to tell his own story, for he, too, has a confession to make. He was sitting in the rectory last night, thinking about the church's efforts to raise enough money to endow the soup kitchen and homeless shelter it has been running. And he, too, finally decided that it was better to put the money to good use than to bury it in the ground. (He quotes the parable of the talents.) So he gave the money to the soup kitchen and homeless shelter and he, too, stuffed the envelope with newspaper.

Now the lawyer is nearly apoplectic. He reads both men the riot act: as an officer of the court, he says, he may well have to report this breach of fiduciary duty. And apart from the law, he says, there is friendship to be considered. They disobeyed the dying wish of their closest friend. "You should have done what I did," he concludes. "In order to be absolutely certain that I carried out our friend's request with the most meticulous care, I put the cash in my office safe. And it's still there, safe from harm. Then I wrote a check for ten million dollars, and that's what's in the grave!"

There are so many of these stories, and they never leave the legal profession looking heroic. Surely we would all be better off if the image of lawyers matched what Anthony Kronman, the dean of the Yale Law School, has said it should: that lawyers should be people "possessed of great practical wisdom" who are "devoted to the public good but keenly aware of the limitations of human beings and their political arrangements."[16] According to Kronman, the legal profession has been suffering through a profound crisis of identity, and if his glasses are a bit too rosily colored as he examines the stated ideals of the past, he has unquestionably hit upon what would be a useful "ideal," as he calls it, for the present.

But there is the ideal and then there is the reality. Stephen Gillers, who teaches legal ethics at New York University Law School, illustrated the problem of the image of lawyers with a hypothetical situation based on the O. J. Simpson trial:

> Can the public ever understand how a lawyer, in court, can be suggesting a massive police conspiracy to plant Simpson's blood and create false evidence, while in the same evening, out of court, the same lawyer is acknowledging to opposing counsel that the blood is his client's, that his client "did it," and that the only question is the deal?[17]

Gillers's point is that what the lawyer says in open court, what we read about in the papers or see on television, may not be what the lawyer actually believes. Sounds moderately unintegral. Lawyers arguing in court, says Sissela Bok, "sincerely believe that they manipulate the facts in order to convey a 'truer picture.'"[18] But she is perhaps being a bit generous. Sometimes the lawyers are just dissembling. Thus, Gillers goes on to ponder:

> What is the leverage for that defense lawyer? "I'll be able to persuade the jury that your evidence is junk because the DNA tests were botched and because your officers are evil"—all the while knowing it's not true.[19]

"All the while knowing it's not true": that, in a nutshell, is what scares people about lawyers. Lawyers, I believe, want to be statesmen; Kronman argues that they *should* be statesmen.[20] But instead they are condemned as ambulance chasers and regulation producers, and they are blamed, occasionally with reason, for many of the nation's problems. (Although it must be said, when one looks at the two-million-dollar BMW verdict, that it is juries of the people who grant these awards; lawyers can only ask.) Our lack of respect for the lawyers who try the great criminal and civil cases of our day is compounded in the often topsy-turvy world of legal ethics, where the rules, although they carry a certain degree of internal coherence, often seem to the lay observer like so much gobbledygook.

The rules, it must be said, if not gobbledygook, sometimes *are* slightly nutty. Among the most important of the rules (important to lawyers, I mean) is Rule 1.6 of the American Bar Association's Model Rules of Professional Conduct. Rule 1.6 prohibits a lawyer from revealing client confidences, but with two important exceptions. First, the lawyer may reveal what the client has told her in order "to prevent the client from committing a criminal act that the lawyer believes is likely to result in imminent death or substantial bodily harm." Second, the lawyer may reveal a confidence "to establish a claim or defense on behalf of the lawyer in a controversy between the lawyer and the client."

This all requires some explanation. The lawyer may not go to the authorities to prevent her client from committing an ordinary crime—burglary of Tiffany's, say, or a hundred-million-dollar securities fraud—but only to prevent physical harm. If this rule seems silly, it gets even worse. According to the official commentary, the lawyer need only try to "persuade" her client not to do the deed. But the rule does not *require* any "preventive action" at all. Thus, every nonlawyer's nightmare: "Counsel, tomorrow I'm going to murder my boss." "Fine. That will be one thousand dollars, please."

And then there is the tantalizing matter of the second exception. The lawyer may not tell anybody that her client is about to defraud the securities markets, but in a controversy with the client—for example, litigation over the quality of the lawyer's representation—the lawyer can bring up any relevant confidences. In other words, Rule 1.6 of the Model Rules does virtually nothing to protect the public from evil clients, but it bends over backward to protect the bar.

Oh, yes, one more thing. If the client plans to break the law in a way that will implicate the lawyer's services, the lawyer is supposed to make a "noisy" withdrawal—to cease representation and openly disaffirm any opinion or document that might assist the client in this illegality.[21] Sounds good, but sounds strange. In the first place, if the potential lawbreaking is so important, why not let the lawyer disclose it directly, rather than signaling it by withdrawing from representation? In the second place, why is the exception limited to the *use of the lawyer's services* to commit fraud? The answer, again, is that the exceptions are drawn for the protection of lawyers.

Legal ethics, making a fetish of self-protection and a hash of public protection, would thus seem to come up a bit short in the integrity department. The Rule stands on its head Martin Luther's stricture that the godly
man must "suffer every evil and injustice without avenging himself" but
"[o]n behalf of others . . . he may and should seek vengeance, justice, protection, and help, and do as much as he can to achieve it." [22] And yet there
is method even to this seeming madness.

Except in the movies, where all their clients are unjustly accused, criminal defense lawyers have a tough time convincing the public of the morality of their work. But their work is obviously necessary. Under the rules, a
lawyer is required to be a "zealous" advocate for her client, but always
within the bounds of the law. How zealous? Every criminal procedure
teacher uses the same joke to illustrate what lawyers call "arguing in the
alternative": "I wasn't there and anyway it was self-defense." This, of
course, is Gillers's very point.

But here we may have the germ of an idea. A few years ago, I watched
a televised discussion among a group of criminal lawyers. The moderator
eventually got around to asking them how they could justify . . . well,
doing what they did. Most of them went through the automatic answers,
as though by rote: "My job is not to decide if my client is innocent or guilty
but to make sure that the prosecution crosses all the t's and dots all the i's
before it takes somebody's freedom away." Or: "It's better that a thousand
of the guilty go free than that one innocent be punished." And of course:
"Everybody deserves a lawyer." (That last one always rankles. Everybody
is certainly entitled to a lawyer, but not everybody deserves one.)

But one well-respected lawyer had a different take altogether. I cannot
recall it word for word, but the gist of it went like this: "When you are
accused of a crime, everyone is against you. The entire weight of the government is against you. Your friends turn on you, sometimes your family.
You lose your job. And you have no idea whether there is anyone you can
trust, trust not to judge you, trust to keep your secrets. In this world, everybody needs a friend, somebody to talk to. And at that moment, when you
stand accused of a crime, your lawyer is the only friend you have. And so
that friendship, your only friendship, has to be secure and absolute."

All right, maybe the reader is unconvinced; maybe I do not convey it
well. But here, nevertheless, is a rationale. The lawyer-client relationship
turns out to be like . . . a marriage! Not only do spouses often stick together
when one of them falls into trouble but, in the best marriages, the partners
know they can share just about anything with each other and not have it
repeated. And the marriage analogy also would explain the way the rules

release the lawyer from her obligation of confidentiality if and only if the client is somehow abusing the lawyer's trust: a spouse's betrayal often excuses the other spouse from continuing the commitment.

The only thing it does not explain is the smoothness and, at times, the glee with which a lawyer can stand up and say one thing in the courtroom in the afternoon and then, later in the evening, say something else altogether when talking lawyer to lawyer. Or the related matter of cross-examination intended to damage the credibility of a witness who is under oath and whom the lawyer knows to be telling the truth. Perhaps the courtroom lawyer is the modern descendant of the Ravenna forgers, manufacturing evidence to prove what might be made to be true, if only enough evidence can be created. Not, perhaps, terribly persuasive. But then, there has to be some reason left for the public to hate the legal profession.

Besides, the fact that we can work out clever reasons why lawyers should (must?) be allowed to behave as they do does not mean that we lawyers should expect the public to admire us. On the contrary, the lies we are forced to tell, and the convoluted arguments we must offer to justify them, virtually ensure that lawyers will be not only disliked but distrusted. Among ourselves, we lawyers may share a vision of integrity; but the shared vision is sufficiently unattractive that we must excuse our fellow citizens for dismissing it as bunk.

THE ROYAL FORGERS REVISITED

Oh, and by the way, whatever happened to those forgers at Ravenna, the ones who believed in false documents in service of the true cause? Their fate history does not record. But those who have not totally abandoned as Eurocentric an education about the history of the West will surely recall the story surrounding the resolution of the investiture controversy: how poor Henry IV, the Holy Roman Emperor, threatened with excommunication and deposition both, rushed to Canossa, then the Holy See, where he stood in the snow for three days, so it is said, before Pope Gregory VII would grant him audience and accept the surrender that allowed Henry to keep his throne. Maybe Henry stood in the snow, or maybe, as many think, that story, too, was manufactured by Henry's busy royal forgers; the point is, he kept his throne and he gave up the power of investiture—at least for the time being. The forged papal documents, when faced with real power relations in the world, turned out to do no good in proving the truth. But the pope's victory did not turn on the fact that the forgers lied.

The pope won because, at that moment of history, he commanded the support of more political and military leaders than Henry did; or, as Stalin would have been surprised to learn, Gregory won because he had more divisions.

In a political world, power is the ultimate test of truth, for what matters is not what happened but what vision of the past can be enforced. If Henry had been able to muster more armies than the pope—had Gregory not been able to strip him of two-thirds of his soldiers by a few cleverly chosen words to German clerics on whose good will Henry relied—well, very likely the ecclesiastical verdict would ultimately have been in Henry's favor, that is, that the royal prerogative had always existed, just as the forgers said. But since the emperor turned out to command fewer troops than the pope, the truth came to be that the royal right of investiture had never existed.

Nowadays, we have lots of royal forgers. They are at work every day, in politics, in law, in public relations, in advertising, and in the countless simple manipulations of everyday living. They tell us not what is true, or even what is nearly true, but what will help them (or nowadays their clients) get to where they would like to be. What matters is not veracity but verisimilitude; it is less important for something to be true than for it to seem to be true. So in our politics, one side calls its platform a "contract," knowing full well that it has no intention of paying a penalty for breaching it, and the other insists that the same "contract" will "cut" various programs, knowing full well that it will simply slow the rate at which they increase. And, according to our own strange predilections, we reward with our votes not the side whose story is most probably true but the side whose story sounds the best.

Perhaps what integrity demands is that we at least spend greater efforts than we sometimes do searching out the expedient lies of everyday life and making plain that we will not stand for them. We can punish instead of reward people we believe to be telling us untruths. In this way, we can push American society toward greater integrity and, by happy coincidence, put our many royal forgers out of business.

(eight)

Until We Are Parted

ALL this talk of oaths and fidelity leads us to what is, for millions of Americans, perhaps the most important promise they make: the marriage vow. In an era when so many marriages end, often quickly, in divorce, it may seem awkward or a bit old-fashioned to discuss the integrity of the commitment that a marriage involves.

Yet marriage obviously matters. The majority of Americans will be married for some part of their lives, and most of those who are married actually stay that way. Some 78 percent of American family households are the households of married couples.[1] And even though the divorce rate has lately been about half of the marriage rate, we have a long way to go before we can say that those numbers are set in stone. After all, nine out of ten married people tell pollsters they would marry the same person again.[2]

But serious scholars rarely write about marriage any longer, except to analyze its failings or to score larger political points; so scholars on the left tell us all the ways that it is oppressive and scholars on the right warn us of all the dire threats that it faces. And like so much serious scholarship, work of this kind is a useful bore.

My starting point is different. Marriage is an institution of enormous beauty, even if that beauty is too often marred by human fallibility.

Whether one believes, as I do, that the institution is God-given and state-encouraged, or whether one believes that it is a human invention that has been functional over time, one can scarcely avoid the simple fact that the great majority of Americans cling to the ideal of marriage with an almost romantic affection. Surely we cry at weddings because we can scarcely bear the beauty of the union we are witnessing—and also because hard experience has taught us of its fragility. We marry out of hope, or fear, or desire, or desperation, and certainly out of love; and yet I believe that in every marriage, no matter how begun, there is that kernel of possibility that *this* is the one for the ages.

That, at least, is how most people think most of the time. It is not, sadly, the vision of marriage in the academy. Given the central importance of the institution of marriage in American life, it is alarming to reflect upon the volumes of contemporary moral and political philosophy that are written without any mention of marriage or family and, in particular, without any discussion of marital commitment.

Clearly, a book on integrity would not be complete without a consideration of the issue. We have previously defined living with integrity—the *integral life*—as including three elements: (1) doing the hard work of discerning right from wrong; (2) acting on what one discerns, even at personal cost; and (3) saying what one is doing and why. Using these three elements, it is possible to construct a vision of a marriage lived with integrity, or what might be called an *integral marriage*.

To understand the notion of integral marriage, it will be useful to divide our discussion into two parts: the integrity of the underlying marital commitment and the problem of what happens when the commitment becomes impossible to fulfill.

MARRIAGE AND ROMANCE

The connection between marriage and romantic love is of fairly recent vintage. In medieval Europe, for example, romantic love was love at a distance, love in a chaste sense, unpursued and generally unpursuable—precisely because marriage, which was entered into for other reasons, family or social obligation, made the pursuit of one's love impossible. The dreamily unattainable quality of the object of one's romantic love generated some wonderful literature, from Andreas Capellanus's *Art of Courtly Love* to Dante's *La Vita Nuova*. Indeed, the modern ideal of the "companionate marriage"—the union between two people who actually like and respect each other, as against the union between two people who for familial or economic or social reasons make a good pair—is largely a development that took root in the middle of the twentieth century. As the philosopher Michael Walzer has pointed out, what has changed is that "marriages are taken out of the hands of parents and their agents (matchmakers, for example) and delivered into the hands of children." We have moved from arranged or customary marriages to marriages based on an ideal of romantic love, says Walzer, and "[t]he distributive principle of romantic love is free choice."[3]

Plainly, the move from marriages made out of obligation to marriages made out of freedom is a wonderful development in any theory of human flourishing that values the individual. It has the virtue of liberating men and women alike from the older tradition of being forced by circumstance to spend their lives with people to whom they made a less than loving commitment in the first place. But it also carries a significant and often unremarked cost. If people believe that they are marrying out of love and free choice rather than out of duty, they are more likely to decide, if love should die, that the free choice to join together is no more significant than the free choice to part, and to look for love elsewhere; those married out of duty expect less love to begin with, and what duty has brought together, duty may keep together.

The data support this point: in societies where arranged marriages are still the norm, divorce rates are relatively low. But not only are divorce rates higher in the United States than in many other countries; our young people are more likely than most others to insist that a marriage be based on love and to believe that when love ends, a marriage should end too.[4] And what our young people tell the pollsters they can only be learning from the behavior of their elders.*

Do not misunderstand the point: I do not favor the dutiful marriage over the companionate marriage, and I do not believe that marriage, companionate or traditional, should be a prison. I do worry that the high divorce rate may be linked, in uncomfortable ways, with the sense of hyperoptimism that

---

*I am here discussing only monogamous marriage. Polygamy (the precise term is actually *polygyny* if, as in most places, it involves a single husband with multiple wives) is still practiced by some traditional cultures, although in the West it is generally seen as oppressive to women. But in Islam, for example, limited polygyny (the Quran permits four wives) has been defended as *improving* the status of women, who might otherwise remain widows or unmarried in a war-torn society. See John L. Esposito, *Islam: The Straight Path* (New York: Oxford, 1991), pp. 94–96.

freedom of choice in the matter of love may often generate, with the result that people who marry may do so without any thought to the possibilities that their love may change or die—and thus without any thought to whether their marriage entails some set of duties that will enable it to survive the loss of the joyful giddiness in which it began. And I worry further that in making divorce so much easier to obtain, we may be tempting people whose marriages are troubled in the direction of an easy but undiscerned choice to leave; or, worse, that we may actually be tempting into unintegral marriages people who might hesitate, were divorces harder to secure.

In a tongue-in-cheek but nevertheless thought-provoking essay entitled "Restatement of Love," which gently lampoons the summaries of law produced by the American Law Institute, the lawyers Gretchen Craft Rubin and Jamie D. Heller attempt a definition of love: "Parties in 'love' are those parties to a relationship who consider themselves engaged in the highest level of emotional intimacy attainable and who generally presume that such state will continue indefinitely."[5]

This mocking definition is an effort to capture the occasionally delirious quality of love, especially new love, a delirium without which fewer couples would probably exercise their "free choice," as Walzer has it, to marry. Even if it is true, as some studies have suggested, that "love" is principally a luxury of the well-to-do,[6] it is also true that marriage is for most of us the most substantial commitment of our lives. To do so not out of a sense of duty to family or tradition but out of a freely willed choice is—or should be—rather awe-inspiring. That it often does not inspire awe, but proceeds instead out of a degree of giddiness, tells us that here, as so often, we are not stopping to think. Couples who are in love, say Rubin and Heller, not only are delirious but "generally presume that such state will continue indefinitely." With a bit less hysteria and a bit more hard-headedness, any number of couples might turn away.

A study of recently engaged couples found a striking tendency toward underestimation of the chances of divorce generally, as well as of many of the painful consequences of divorce.[7] Not only did the newly affianced underestimate the likelihood of any marriage ending, they even further minimized the likelihood that their own marriages would end. We could debate long and hard over whether these mistaken estimates are in some sense rational, but it is difficult to deny the authors' conclusion that they are functional. Were the estimates of marital success closer to our society's depressing norms, many couples would probably decide that marriage is not worth the effort. In short, the self-deceptive character of the couple's estimation of success may be crucial to the survival of the marriage institution.

Most institutional religions, well aware of both the delirium and the poor risk assessment that freedom has wrought, require couples considering marriage to attend counseling sessions, to prepare them for the many realities—spiritual, emotional, even economic—of the choice they are in the process of exercising. This process is consistent with the first rule of integrity, that we must take the time to stop and think, even when stopping and thinking brings a note of sobriety to our delirium. Indeed, in order to give serious content to the vows—in order for the vows to be said to have meaning—the couple exchanging them *must* in some fashion pursue the path of discernment. If they do not, they will not be able to marry with integrity.

Another way to encourage people to take the time to stop and think, to understand the importance and delicacy of the enterprise upon which they are entering, is by surrounding the marriage moment with ritual. And so we do. Everything about the marriage vow shows its special seriousness: the peculiar yet powerful language, the pomp and circumstance of the setting (even when the setting is the office of the justice of the peace), and, for most, the religious atmosphere in which the vow is taken. For a wedding vow, according to tradition, is a promise before God, and is made in the name of God. To be sure, although most weddings continue to be performed in houses of worship, a growing number are not. But even if, as society grows sadly more secularized, vows in other forms are used, their genesis, and their unspoken model, remains the oath in the name of God.

This is true even of the so-called common-law marriage. The law has long recognized common-law marriages, but it is not widely understood that such a marriage also requires ceremony of a kind: either the couple must exchange words intended to symbolize a marriage bond or they must, for a period of years, live openly as husband and wife.[8] In short, regardless of the process through which a marriage is entered into, it is accompanied by formalities that demonstrate its uniqueness among promises and, indeed, among human experiences.

And among the ways in which marriage is unique is this: we treat the marital commitment as sufficiently strong that, even though it is often broken, our society shares a general sense that breaking it without a very good reason is wrong. For the student of integrity, it is important to understand *why* we have that sense, and what it entails for the notion of integral marriage.

MARITAL COMMITMENT

I was reading not long ago about how some evolutionary biologists have concluded that men, unlike women, are in effect genetically coded for promiscuity. The reasoning is straightforward and, in its way, quite clever. In prehistorical times, males with a genetic tendency toward having sex frequently, and with multiple partners, would indulge these tendencies and would thus produce more offspring than men with what we might call weaker sexual inclinations. (The inclinations of women were less crucial genetically because women, no matter what their tendencies, face an absolute limit of about one child a year.) Over time, then, the male genes that tend toward more frequent sex with multiple partners would obviously reproduce themselves more often and would therefore crowd out the others. So today's men, the product of hundreds of centuries of this breeding, would be well supplied with genes that would demand frequent sex with multiple partners.[9]

Now, I confess that I find all this a bit much to stomach, but let us suppose for the moment that it is true: that nature has coded men to have lots of sexual partners. Does this mean that traditional marriage, in which a man bonds to a single partner for life, is a bad idea? Or that men who are unable to be true to their wives, who have frequent affairs, should be forgiven because it is just "in their genes"? Or, indeed, that we should perhaps *encourage* men to follow their genes into rampant promiscuity and frequent reproduction with multiple partners? I would suggest not, which seems to be the mainstream view.

In placing a moral construction on what some would argue is the following of natural instincts, the American people are taking a view of marriage that is at once very old-fashioned and remarkably durable. Marriage is a civilizing institution, a means of curbing desires or inclinations that might otherwise make social stability impossible. The device through which marriage performs this crucial function is the notion of *fidelity*.

Fidelity, loosely understood as simply not having affairs, is actually a more complex bundle of ideas. The wedding vow, after all, typically involves a number of promises of several different kinds. In the Episcopal Church, where my wife and I were married, the standard vow is a promise "to have and to hold from this day forward, for better for worse, for richer for poorer, in sickness and in health, to love and to cherish, until we are parted by death." This is more than a promise not to cheat. It is a promise to stay, to care, to treat with a most profound affection: "to love and to cherish." And at its heart is a central notion of integrity: fidelity means keeping your word.

The moral force of this commitment does not depend on the sacramental nature of the ceremony. For example, in Judaism, where marriage is not a sacrament and "there is no need for priestly or rabbinic sanction," the marriage relationship is nevertheless surrounded by a formal network of mutual and balancing obligations—including, of course, the commandment against adultery.[10] In Islam, marriage is "a sacred contract or covenant, but not a sacrament." Again, duties are imposed on both spouses, and the formality of the occasion embodies the expectation that the duties will be fulfilled.[11]

In ordinary language, infidelity—literally, a lack of faithfulness—refers to adultery, but in the context of the marriage vow, it plainly refers to the breach of any one of the several promises. This is a point we frequently miss. A husband says to his wife, "I am leaving you because I no longer love you, but I want you to know I have never been unfaithful to you." The statement is a self-serving lie. The husband means that he has not had any sexual involvement outside of marriage. But his choice to cease acting with love toward his wife is a choice for infidelity. And of course the decision to leave the marriage altogether is the ultimate act of infidelity. It may, in some circumstances, be justified, but not as a part of fidelity.

Let me here make plain what the following discussion may at times obscure: I am not arguing, and do not believe, that every person who breaks a promise, even a marriage vow, acts without integrity or is in some way immoral.[12] I do fear, however, that we as a society too often fail to take our marital commitments as seriously as we should, and that the end of marriage too often comes without the aid of the discernment—not about ourselves alone but about right and wrong—that makes integrity possible. Marriage is unique among human institutions, and discerning what is right when one has the need or desire to break the vow is thus not like discernment of any other kind.*

Lewis Smedes of Fuller Theological Seminary sees the marriage vow as a specific case of a more general presumption in favor of promise keeping. Says Smedes, with punch: "if you have a ship you will not desert, if you have people you will not forsake, if you have causes you will not abandon, then *you are like God.*"[13] Smedes's point of reference is God's

---

*I should note that the approach of the Western religions to marriage has been historically complex. Judaism has always celebrated marriage and family life. Christianity in its early years was much like traditional Buddhism, exalting celibacy and often questioning marriage. (Some Christian sects, believing that the Second Coming was imminent, preached against marriage.) Even Islam, in which marriage is considered a duty, has included movements that preach celibacy.

answer to Moses' question at the burning bush. Moses asked the voice for its name. The answer is commonly rendered in English as "I am who I am." But Smedes argues that in context, a better translation of the relevant Hebrew is "I Am the One Who Will Be There With You"—not God's name, but God's identity.

Following this track, Smedes characterizes the marriage vow this way: "When two people get married, they take on two new identities. Each of them says to the other what God said to Moses: 'I am the one who will be there for you.'"[14] The traditional Christian vow captures this sense: "for better for worse, for richer for poorer." Too many people, says Smedes, misunderstand the vow, and believe that they are saying instead: "I will be there for you as long as you provide me with all the satisfaction I have coming." Says Smedes: "This is not a promise; it is a contract." He adds, quoting Stanley Hauerwas, that the power of a promise is "the power to stick with what we are stuck with."[15]

The line from Hauerwas is useful, because it captures what, for many, a lengthy marriage becomes: an experience in being "stuck with" somebody else. In the days when marriages were made on the basis of duty or social position, this concern could perhaps be camouflaged. "He is a good husband," the wife's relatives would tell her if she shared the pain of no-longer-loving. "She is a good wife," the husband's friends would assure him. And, in both cases, the adjective *good* implied far more than *good to you*; it carried some sense of a Platonic essence of spouse, the ideal, a person that anyone should be happy to have.

In the welcome era of freer choice, however, being "stuck with" the wrong person is inestimably more painful, for there is always the sense that one *could have chosen somebody else*—or, indeed, that if there were a divorce, one still could. Now to be stuck is to be wounded, perhaps deeply. In any other arena of life—a job, a school, a neighborhood, the performance of just about any other obligation—one would not put up with such pain had one the resources to go elsewhere. So what is the reason to put up with it in marriage? The answer, if there is one, must come in a richer understanding of the nature of the promise that one makes when entering a marriage.

COMMITMENT AND PROMISE

To understand marital commitment one must discover the proper blend of the traditional notion of duty and the modern notion of free choice, a combination of the old and the new; in that way, one can get a sense of what has been promised in a marriage and what obligations the promise entails. And to begin that investigation, it is useful to return to Lewis Smedes.

In chapter 4, the reader may recall, we quoted Smedes on the essence of promising: "When a person makes a promise, he stretches himself out into circumstances that no one can control and controls at least one thing: he will be there no matter what the circumstances turn out to be."[16] The marriage vow with which most Americans are familiar, includes, in some form, a promise to remain faithfully married "until we are parted by death." Religious implications aside, this is, if one thinks about it, a remarkable form of words. A promise is made that is explicitly intended to be lifelong. Even though we live in a society that more and more treats the marriage vow like any other, the words of the promise, and our respect for the integrity of the person who makes such a promise, require us to treat it differently. It simply is not like any other promise. The interesting question for the student of integrity is just how it is different.

One difference between the marriage vow and other promises is that in the Christian tradition, marriage is a sacrament; most other promises are not. The Christian understanding of marriage as a sacrament rests crucially on each spouse's freely assumed intention of keeping the vow. According to the Jesuit theologian Karl Rahner, a marriage between baptized Christians is a moment of "self-actualization"—not for the newly wed couple but for "the church as such." The people who make the free choice to marry, says Rahner, "manifest clearly the sign of love in which there becomes manifest *that* love which unites God and man."[17] That status as a sign of God's love is what produces the sacramental character of the marriage. Plainly, if the spouses take their vows with mental reservations, the sacramental character is lost. God's love is without reservation, as Smedes reminds us, and so should the couple's be.

Again, this point is not limited to the Christian marriage. It can be equally true in traditions where marriage is not a sacrament and in marriages that are not religious at all. The couple's free and open choice to *say the words*, and thus to conjure for us all of the imagery of a life, not months or years but a *life* spent together, forces us to assume that those who take the vow actually mean it. They do not have mental reservations. (If they did, integrity would demand that they state them.) They do not mean to keep some parts of the vow and not others. (If they did, integrity would demand that they tell us.) At that moment, as they exchange their vows, they mean, or we are entitled to assume that they mean, to stay together unto death.

Very well, the vow, when taken, is seriously meant. In time, however, the vower changes his or her mind: I thought I would want to be with you for my entire life, but I was wrong. What do I do now?

Plainly, to require (as a moral obligation—I am not here speaking of law) the one who wants to break the vow instead to keep it, imposes a considerable cost, certainly psychologically and perhaps in other ways. Smedes anticipates this with his reference to "promises he intends to keep even when keeping them exacts a price."[18] We have already seen that integrity is not integrity unless it entails some risk—unless there is the possibility that holding on to it will be costly. And when a married individual falls out of love—or falls in love with somebody else—the cost is ready to be counted. Smedes suggests that the marriage vow already anticipated this possibility, and the person now seeking to break the vow knew all along that keeping it could have a price. That knowledge is, in Lynne McFall's terms, what makes integrity integrity.

Here Smedes may be onto something, but if he is, what he is onto is a little scary. Let us concede what is surely true, that our nation takes marriage vows too lightly, that our divorce rate is a national embarrassment. Let us agree that we should do something about this. Is Smedes suggesting that marriage means that there is *no* turning back, not for *any* reason? That once one is married, one is indeed stuck, and therefore must stick— no matter what?

Certainly, many Christian theologians defend this position. For example, Philip Edgcumbe Hughes argues that even when "peace has given way to hostility," nothing justifies ending a marriage; his plain implication is that even in the case of spousal battering, separation, not civil divorce, is the proper remedy.[19] Although not many of us might agree with Hughes in the most extreme cases, his views appear to be strongly grounded in Scripture—at least in the New Testament, where Christ states unequivocally that "any one who divorces his wife, except on the ground of unchastity, causes her to commit adultery; and whoever marries a divorced woman commits adultery" (Matt. 5:32). Similar passages in Mark (10:2–12) and Luke (16:18) do not even include the exception for unchastity.

Quite famously, the Roman Catholic Church does not allow remarriage following a civil divorce. But there is reason to think that even the Roman Catholic position has been less absolutist than commonly supposed—at least in the United States. The Church courts now annul an estimated 50,000 Catholic marriages a year, compared with 450 in 1968.[20] (Pope John Paul II has tried to address one possible cause for this rapid increase: acceptance by the Church courts of psychological evaluations from psychiatrists who do not share the Church's doctrine on the nature of marriage.)

But the argument that Smedes is making, even though it rests on an analogy to God's promise to do what is promised, is not strictly a religious argument. It might be better cast, for our present purposes, as an argument about what a spouse legitimately may demand of another spouse. In that sense, it might be cast as an *interpretation* of the vow—the promise—and it becomes an argument about the integrity of that vow. Says Smedes: "Nobody knows what she is getting into when she gets married. . . . A man or woman can become several different persons before a marriage is finished." But, he asks, so what? "[I]n one most important sense, we can stay the same person we were when we first got married: the person who makes and keeps the promise is always 'the one who will be there' with the other."[21]

For Smedes, then, the keeping of the vow is a matter of will; it is not happenstance but determination that keeps a marriage from failure. That determination requires a mature form of commitment to begin with: the marriage partners must recognize from the start that they will both change, and that they will have moments when they have other desires or when they seriously doubt that they have done the right thing. But the purpose of the vow, Smedes argues, is to liberate us from the possibility of yielding to those desires and doubts. By limiting our freedom to answer the call to love other people, we free ourselves to be better and truer people for our spouses. That is the sense in which a married person need not change.

Note Smedes's use of the word *can*: we *can* stay the same people we were when we got married, meaning that it is a choice, not an obligation. It is a choice in the sense that deciding whether to keep a promise is always a choice; he plainly does not mean that all choices are equally moral. Nor, I suspect, would he say that the fact that one has a *reason* to choose to abandon a marriage means that one has a *justification* for it. So many of our most common reasons—tiring of the hard work of marriage, falling in love with someone else, desiring someone younger, or older, or just *different*—surely pale in comparison to the risk that one accepts upon taking the vow. Of the desire for another this seems particularly true. Aristotle, who would have had no patience with the notion that one should leave a marriage because one's longing for somebody else makes staying married painful, put the point nicely: "it shows weakness of character to run away from hardships."[22]

Nevertheless, although I have strong respect for the Catholic position and for the traditional Christian position generally, one cannot resolve the question of the integrity of the secular marriage vow with reference to the religious position. And it must be said, as a secular matter, that circumstances may arise in which nearly everyone without a prior religious position on the matter would agree that an end to the marriage is appropriate. The most obvious of these is the one that Hughes discusses: the spouse who is somehow damaged by the other's hostility. The battered spouse plainly falls into this category, and should be made free of any remaining marital commitment. Another is the spouse who has been betrayed by the other's infidelity (which is, as we have seen, the only explicit New Testament exception). Can we establish a useful standard for sorting the cases representing some sort of moral imperative from those in which one spouse simply wishes to pursue his or her self-interest?

ENDING THE COMMITMENT

In America, we like to talk of rights, and when we do we do not look beyond the decision that the individual makes. (See chapter 13.) That is why to talk of the end of a marriage as a right, although legally correct, could lead to monstrous consequences. In morality, the *reason* for an act matters: thus, even though we might concede that the integral marriage, entered with sincerity and good faith, must at times come to an end, we cannot be indifferent to the reason why the couple cannot stay together.

Let us begin with a reason that is both depressingly common and of questionable moral force: "I must leave you because I am in love with somebody else." To understand why this justification is a weak and even craven one, we might usefully sort those possibilities that were necessarily in the contemplation of the parties who took the vows and those that were not. Because the vow is one of fidelity, it plainly contemplates infidelity, and is a promise not to engage in any. Loving another in a romantic way is a breach of the vow, but cannot be offered as a justification for a larger breach because a breach cannot excuse itself.

Loving a husband or a wife and promising to do it forever is no protection against the unexpected love for another. But marital commitment, however understood, is at least partly aimed at cabining the natural impulses that would otherwise lead both men and women astray—although the word *astray* is, of course, heavily loaded. Nearly all of us surely feel at some points in our marriages the tug of attraction to others. The vow plainly does not eliminate those feelings, but it does reduce our freedom to indulge them—not only our freedom to run off and have affairs but even, as the theologian Margaret Farley has pointed out, our freedom to spend danger-ous amounts of time contemplating such action.[23] Recall what we have already observed: the marriage vow is an undertaking to alter the future, to realize one's humanity by liberating oneself from a variety of possible even-tualities. So if we lose a degree of freedom, we lose it by free choice but also for love and in an exercise of power: there are aspects of the future that we *can* control.

As I noted earlier, the addition of romantic love to the ideal of marriage has had the pernicious effect of encouraging married people to believe that falling out of love is a reason sufficient in morality to end a marriage. But we do not really believe that, which is probably why we heap opprobrium on a person we believe has "deserted" his or her spouse. The excuse might serve to end weaker relationships, such as that of boyfriend and girlfriend. But recall Smedes's point, that the marital vow is not limited to a promise of fidelity "as long as you provide me with all the satisfaction I have com-ing." Indeed, only our severe misunderstanding of the nature of romantic love—our sense that it must be delirious, happens only spontaneously, and can never be willed or created—makes us think that such a reason is even creditable. Not only is "I don't love you any more" thus morally insufficient to justify ending a marriage; it is insufficient as a justification to cease act-ing with love and honor toward one's spouse. Again, the obligation to act with love and honor flows from the commitment that one has made, not from the emotions one happens to feel at a particular time. To say other-wise would be much like saying that the biblical commandment to love our neighbors carries an implicit exception for those neighbors we happen to despise. The same is true of marriage. To make "I don't love you any more" into a sufficient moral reason to end a marriage is to turn the com-mitment stated explicitly in the vow into an irrelevancy. After all, any two people can stay together as long as they both shall love each other. A mar-riage supposes that two people will stay together as long as they live.

That is the point of a commitment that is both limiting and liberating: it reduces our freedom to treat people badly, and it relies on nothing but its own force. If we keep our deepest commitments only when we happen to feel like it, they are not commitments at all; they are mere whims.

Let us consider a simple example:

Example 8-1. After ten years of faithful marriage, a husband falls in love with another woman. He tries to remain faithful to his vow, but finds the ache for the other woman too great to ignore; his yearning is making him a lesser person. Thus it is no longer possible for him to keep the commitment he made. Not only integrity but emotional stability is at stake. He further believes that his wife will be better off free of him and able to start anew. And so he leaves his wife, ending their marriage, in order to fulfill the need that will not go away.

Observation 8-1(a). The integrity of one's desire to be with somebody else is not, by itself, adequate justification for violating the marriage vow, which is what happens when a spouse leaves. Again, there is no true integrity without cost, and pain over the desire for someone else is quite often the cost of marital integrity. Indeed, as I have argued, that precise risk—the possibility of that very pain—is anticipated in the marriage vow.

Observation 8-1(b). The fact that one's desire to be with another person is not a sufficient condition for the ending of a marriage does not mean that the desire is irrelevant. When that desire has so altered a spouse that he or she fears that the original basis of the marriage itself has substantially disintegrated, we are closer to a justification for breaking the commitment—but we are not yet there. We are not yet there for the reason that Smedes proposes: even changes in oneself are anticipated in the vows. The question is whether those changes are sufficiently great that the husband who sees the need to leave is truly incapable of keeping his commitment, or whether he could indeed keep it, even if at significant personal cost.

Observation 8-1(c). If the husband who desires to leave could keep the commitment, but at significant personal cost, one might say that integrity demands that he do so. At the same time, the wife whom he desires to leave must not be treated in our moral calculus as a cipher. It may be that she desires the marriage to continue, that she can see no other way that she wants to live. But it is also possible that she would, for the sake of her own integrity, no longer wish to live with a husband who wants to leave; or, indeed, that she might put aside both her desires and her commitments and, out of her love for him or out of a larger generosity of spirit, simply yield her claim and allow him to go.

This last point bears emphasis. Fidelity to one's partner for life is only one side of the obligation of marriage. Even if, as Margaret Farley argues in her fine book *Personal Commitments*, one spouse always retains a claim on the other, the claim need not always be exercised. To follow the example, the fact that the husband who wants to depart may have a moral obligation to stay if his wife wants him to does not mean that his wife necessarily should want him to. Quite apart from her own needs and desires, which may lead her, like her husband, to prefer someone different, the very love that she holds for her husband might provide reason enough for her to decline to exercise her claim. After all, the point of the claim is not to give her a privilege to punish her husband; it is to enable the two of them, as a unit, to continue and perhaps to complete the task on which they embarked when they decided to marry. Note, however, that the claim is voidable only at the option of the spouse who has been wronged; it would mock the original commitment (and provide some peculiar incentives) to say that the husband, for example, having fallen in love with another woman and betrayed his wife, can now use his own behavior as an adequate excuse to declare that the marriage bond has been sundered!

Very well, if love for another is not enough,* what reasons will suffice to excuse the decision of one spouse (or both) to put an end to the marital commitment? Margaret Farley attempts an answer, offering three situations in which a "just love," as she calls it, may sunder a commitment originally made in love. These are (1) impossibility; (2) loss of meaning; and (3) the existence of an "alternate superseding obligation."[24]

By *impossibility*, Farley means the actual inability, whether for physical or emotional reasons, to do what we have promised. She cautions against what she calls "cheap grace"—the temptation to *say* that something is impossible because we do not want to do it any more, and reminds us that what she calls the "way of fidelity" demands of us that we anticipate and work to avoid the conditions that might make fulfillment of our promises impossible. *Loss of meaning*, for Farley, refers to a commitment that "seems to have lost its point." She supplies the example of a man and woman who married only because they wanted to have children together, and then found that it was impossible to do as they had planned. But she warns that loss of meaning does not excuse the failure to love and, indeed, that the commitment to love may be one from which we are never released. Finally, the *alternate superseding obligation* that Farley has in mind is the existence of a moral principle, perhaps a competing promise, that conflicts with the promise in question. The most difficult competing obligations to resolve, she points out, are the obligations we have to ourselves; what happens, for example, when the obligation to self asks one thing and the promise we have made to another asks for self-sacrifice?

---

*I do not propose that those who reach different outcomes are immoral. Obviously, in some cases the discerning individual will determine that love for another *is* reason enough to end a marriage. How that decision, once made, should be implemented I will come to shortly.

Farley, whose analysis is hardly limited to marriage, does not actually answer these questions. She does not tell us what really is impossible or when meaning is irretrievably lost. To do so would defeat her purpose, which is to encourage moral reflection: so she promulgates general standards and offers a series of examples but sensibly, if frustratingly, leaves the discerning individual to work out the concrete application. Yet, at the core, surely Farley is right, and the Catholic position is finally too idealistic—or perhaps the better word is *romantic.** Some marriages must end. It does not matter whether one believes that God ever wills divorce. (I certainly do not believe it.) Sometimes, in the task of marriage as in the others that God sets forth, human beings fail. They fail to nurture the bond that God has established and so let it fall into disrepair—and sometimes, no matter what the couple might desire, the bond cannot be rebuilt. Sometimes, the easier case, one spouse is clearly at fault in the breaking of the bond: a batterer or an adulterer, for example. But sometimes, bad things just happen. Sometimes, despite the best will in the world, a marriage that began in love and optimism *does* become a prison. Sometimes one spouse suffers horribly, even if through no fault of the other. Sometimes both do. Sometimes the marriage becomes, in Farley's word, "toxic" for one partner or both. And those, I think, are the circumstances in which keeping the vow might become "impossible."

I emphasize the word *might* because the occurrence of none of these events forecloses altogether the existence of the obligation to *try*. The conflict is classically Kantian. Kant viewed the human mind as locked in a struggle between inclination, which one could not help feeling, and duty, which was done by choice. Thus, to Kant, the statement "I cannot remain married to you" would always be a triumph of inclination over will, a triumph he condemned. Yet here, as so often, Kant in his idealism demands too much of mortal humans. Instead, I would here agree with Farley that discernment is of first importance. Recall the careful definition in chapter 2 of what one must discern: not *What are my most basic needs and desires?* but *What is the right thing to do?* And recall, further, our specification, following Lynne McFall, that doing what is right will often be painful; indeed, that the test of integrity comes only when doing the right entails a significant cost. But after the discernment is done, the spouse who desires to leave might still say, in effect, "I am sorry, but I know that what I am doing is right." And it is a decision that nobody else can make.

---

*Perhaps this is an appropriate place to specify that Farley is a *Roman Catholic* theologian.

Of course, the distinctions Farley tries to draw may turn out to be useless to those who are actually involved in a marriage that seems destined for collapse: for the betrayed, all betrayals are the same. To rank them according to motive—this reason is acceptable, that reason is not—is to violate the fundamental rule of marital integrity, that a commitment is quite different from a promise. Again, to return to Smedes's central argument, a promise is an indication of a determination to try, including an acknowledgment of the possibility of failure, whereas a commitment before God is a liberation from the possibility of other futures. A commitment is a choice about how to spend a life. It admits no second thoughts. There are reasons that we usually hold our weddings in our sacred places.

But, as I have said all along, a commitment may fail; for all the best intentions, it does not always work. This is where the impossibility criterion that Farley proposes is crucial. It is not, however, quite sufficient, even though I agree with her that the core is found in genuine discernment. In the case of undoing the marital commitment, as in the case of civil disobedience (undoing the presumptive duty to obey the law, which I discuss in chapter 11), the integral spouse must also consider the criterion of proportionality. Farley recognizes this, for she warns that in discerning what is right, the spouse who wants to break the promise must bear in mind that the original commitment gives the other spouse a claim, a claim that is properly conceived as an independent moral fact.

Thus the question is not alone *What is the right thing to do?* The further question, especially given the claim that one's spouse and one's children are entitled to make, is this: *Is it worth the price?* Here again, only the spouse who is contemplating departure can finally make the decision about whether to depart; although others may be pained, there is no moral caliper against which the outcome may confidently be measured. But the ingredient of proportionality suggests that there will be times when what seems at first to be obviously right turns out not to be worth the cost. Even in the worst of times, that question—whether the choice is worth it—must remain a factor in the decision, lest what began, one hopes, as a marriage driven by integrity, by the deeply willed desire to keep the commitment, ends as a divorce driven by self-indulgence.

(nine)

To Have and to Hold

So far, we have viewed the marriage commitment through the lens of an integrity that rests on the form of the vow and the faith that the vow was reflectively taken and seriously meant. Yet there are some couples for whom this simply will not be so: they will not have thought matters through before marrying and so, as we have seen, will more easily convince themselves that the time has come for the marriage to end. In this chapter, we will examine both the dilemma of those couples and the possibility that there is lurking behind all this a vision of what we might call an *integral marriage*.

INTEGRAL DIVORCE?

First, let me summarize where we are. The decision to live a committed life is not a favor that one spouse does for another, but a promise, usually made in the name of God. This means that a spouse who is no longer inclined to be married has no power to release the other from the commitment. Just as the undertaking of the marriage must be voluntary, so must its cessation.

The marital commitment, moreover, is sufficiently serious that we should provide incentives for those who are contemplating marriage to do the hard work of discernment to determine whether it is right. As we have seen, if divorce is too easy, the incentive to discern is less. But once we go down this path, we may reach an interesting inequality. When one spouse leaves the other, announcing that the marriage is at an end, the spouse who is left behind has an option: "My marriage is at an end," he or she may say, or, if so inclined, "My marital commitment survives this betrayal."

The Roman Catholic tradition requires the second, except in rare circumstances. Most Protestant traditions nowadays exist without any serious theology of divorce, although they certainly recognize that it happens. Because they have no strictures on remarriage following civil divorce, they pretend that there is no need to face the situation that occurs when the civil society declares that a marriage is at an end; but the religious spouse who is left behind sees matters otherwise. One would suppose that a church, where marriage is revered as a sacrament, would honor the marital commitment of the left-behind spouse and refuse to allow the putative divorced spouse to remarry without the consent of the deserted husband or wife; or, in the alternative, that a church would, as a few denominations have, evolve a formal ceremony in which the religious bonds that formerly bound the married couple might be sundered. Margaret Farley has suggested that, at a bare minimum, the ceremony for a remarriage after divorce should not be the same as the ceremony for the initial marriage. In any event, what is truly bizarre is that a church in which marriages are sealed in the name of God would give decisive effect to a civil divorce.

But one need not consider marriage a sacrament—or make ending a marriage difficult—in order to understand that a divorce can cause great harm and should therefore be discouraged. In traditional Judaism, for example, the formal *halakkah* (law) allows relatively easy divorces, but "such a step is considered morally reprehensible."[1] And Christian churches that allow a civil divorce to undo a religious marriage do not, presumably, think divorce itself a positive good.

Yet when decisive effect is *not* given to a civil divorce, much mischief can result. The Roman Catholic Church in theory gives *no* effect to a civil divorce; more precisely, it does not allow remarriage in the Church following a divorce. An annulment is easier to obtain when both parties consent; one spouse can in effect hold that consent for ransom. The same phenomenon has been reported in some Orthodox Jewish communities, where, in accordance with biblical law, a wife, even after obtaining a civil divorce, may not remarry unless her husband grants her a religious divorce, or a *get*. Following claims that some unscrupulous husbands were obtaining civil divorces but demanding payment from wives seeking religious divorces—or just refusing to grant them—the New York legislature enacted a law that requires a husband seeking a civil divorce to remove all "impediments" within his power to the wife's remarriage. (Some civil libertarians were aghast at this legislative recognition of religious concerns, but it is hard to see what option was available, unless the Orthodox Jewish wives whose husbands held their divorces for ransom were simply to sit and suffer.)[2]

Of course, even in faith traditions that do not honor civil divorces, such cases of ransom are the exception. What is true, and very painful, across all religious and social categories, is that divorce is a process that tends toward enormous bitterness, so that what began, one hopes, with integrity and love ends not just in self-interest (as we saw in chapter 8) but in that special pain that comes from knowing that one you have loved is now *trying* to hurt you—or the sometimes even more profound pain of knowing that you are now trying to hurt one you have loved.

It is no easy matter to give a useful account of an *integral divorce*, because the pain and sorrow almost inevitably get in the way. Aristotle described the difficulty of being virtuous when in the grip of strong passions, drawing an analogy to drunkenness, and in the case of divorce, his analogy surely fits. Too often, the spouses who once loved *do* become drunk, as it were, on their own anger and pain and despair, which means that what advice the student of integrity might offer about discernment and right action—or what advice any counselor might offer about spouses treating each other with respect as a kind of memorial to what they tried to do together—may wind up smashed to bits.

And yet one must obviously try, inspired, perhaps, by the knowledge that many couples *do* manage to divorce in ways that show mutual respect and even abiding affection. That, too, is a kind of integrity: for if the divorcing spouses are incapable of keeping the whole of their vows, at least they can keep the part (if their faith includes it) about honoring one another. Indeed, they may even be able to keep the part about love: not out of the romantic love in which the marriage began, but, as Margaret Farley notes, out of the moral (and religious) obligation to love all others that is at the heart of human generosity and therefore, perhaps, at the heart of integrity as well.

FOR THE SAKE OF THE CHILDREN

I have not previously said much of children, but here I must, for both the necessary discernment and the existing set of claims on the spouse who seeks to dissolve the commitment become far more complex when children are present. We talk about the deleterious effect of divorce on children, but in a society that has come to value the individual's freedom above the individual's commitments, we too often lack the integrity to transform our talk into action. So let us be very clear: the responsibility of parents to do what is best for their children is a moral absolute. Those who are not willing to carry out this duty should never bring children into the world. But once the children exist, the duty is not weakened because the parents failed to think it out in advance. Too often, parents who want to part do not adequately consider the effect on their children. The effects seem to be significantly worse in upper-income families than in lower-income families. Some psychologists even hint that a dead father is likely to be a better parent than a divorced father—meaning that children seem to cope better with parental death than parental separation.[3]

From the point of view of the child, this seemingly counterintuitive view makes sense. After all, although the parent who dies is obviously missed and although children whose parents die go through crisis, the crisis may not be the same as the child who feels actively betrayed by the parent who, *by choice*, did not do what he or she gave the child reason to think was an absolute promise. For even when the parents manage to pull it off without trying to tear each other apart, divorce is always confusing and frightening for children, for it represents, as Margaret Farley has pointed out, the sundering of the very union that brought the children themselves into existence. In this sense, one might say that the child perceives, with that terrible and unforgiving moral precision of the young, that his or her parents have acted in a way that appears to be inconsistent with the demands of integrity.

Many couples stay together for the sake of their children, and although it has become quite fashionable to mock the choice, it can also be a mark of integrity, and those who make the choice plainly stand on psychologically safe ground. Divorce alone can be hard enough for children. Add to that the unfortunate fact that for all the good intentions that divorcing parents may have about how they plan to "co-parent" and the great respect with which they plan to treat each other, despite all the fine promises never to try to manipulate the children into taking sides, none of us is quite as mature as we like to think. There is plenty of good evidence that children of divorce are usually unhappy, which is one reason that it was a relief to hear family-values guru William Bennett tell the annual convention of the Christian Coalition in 1994 that divorce, not homosexuality, is today's great threat to the survival of the family.[4]

Of course, divorce is sometimes unavoidable, and when it is, the responsibility of the parents is to see to it that their children fall into the exceptional and rare category of those whose damage is slight. How to do this nobody is quite sure, although there are plenty of people willing to offer advice. In practice, for all divorced children to wind up in the exceptional category may seem a bit pie-in-the-sky, even mathematically impossible, like the proposal said to have been put forth by a leading member of the clergy back in the seventies that America's goal should be to ensure that every family has an income above the median. But here Albert Camus, of all people, comes to our rescue: "The struggle alone toward the heights is enough to fill man's soul."

This suggests that divorced parents can never find the soul fulfillment they seek unless they struggle to make sure that their children find it too—which begins with making sure that their children always know that they, not their parents, are the most important people in their parents' world. Sometimes this can be accomplished in a divorced family; more often, this can be accomplished only by a decision by the parents to swallow their own pains and needs. The trendy contemporary philosophy that we can make others happy only when we are happy ourselves is too often a smokescreen for the pursuit of self-interest. The choice to live the committed life—to remain, for the children's sake, a *family*—will usually be the better choice to make. And if the children sense a degree of parental unhappiness, they will still often be better off than if the parents part.

To be sure, a couple that remains together with its tensions unresolved, fighting and feuding, cannot reasonably be said to be helping the children. So it may be that one of the costs of the integrity of marital commitment is that the husband and wife, having made the decision not to end the marriage, must put aside as many of their differences as they are able. This notion could create costs of considerable significance, for it proposes that some needs will go unmet, some tensions unresolved. It is surely the inability to surrender those needs or tensions that in the end often makes the stay-together strategy seem unworkable. And so a part of discernment here returns to Farley's point from the previous chapter: the proper inquiry is not only *What is right?* but *Can I do what is right?* And sometimes, despite the best of intentions, the answer that a moral person will give is *no*.

Here I part company with the traditional teaching of Catholicism. The end of a marriage represents human failure, but it is not human defiance of God. In Matthew's Gospel, Christ explains that divorce was allowed in the Mosaic law because of the hard-heartedness of the people, which would evidently make divorce necessary. But Christ could not possibly have meant that after his ministry, nobody would be hard-hearted any longer. In other words, although the God of the New Testament surely calls upon married couples to stay that way, God also recognizes that we, here today, are hard-hearted, meaning that our love for one another is imperfect. So God necessarily recognizes that we will sometimes fail.

Conservative evangelicals, often caricatured as an odd mixture of cruel misogynists and hopeless romantics, certainly understand this. Thus any number of evangelical congregations have taken steps to present themselves as what might be considered, for want of a better term, divorce-friendly. Moreover, as the sociologist Judith Stacey points out, James C. Dobson, founder of Focus on the Family, has urged women to leave abusive husbands, notwithstanding his full acceptance of the Pauline vision of the wife as living a life of submission to her husband; and the shelves of Christian bookstores are nowadays full of literature aimed at helping women to cope with divorce.[5]

STICKING WITH WHAT WE ARE STUCK WITH

But what happens when all has been weighed up and thought out, when the husband who no longer loves his wife or the wife who no longer loves her husband decides that integrity demands staying the course, for a while longer or forever? I have discussed what the couple should do about its children, but what should they do about each other?

The first point that must be stressed is that the marriage will never be the same, and the beginning of integrity is the recognition of that fact. There may be aspects that will be better, especially if the spouses decide, as they should, to make it that way, but there is a good chance that some aspects will be worse. For example, the husband may inform the wife that he no longer feels sexual desire for her, or the wife may inform the husband that she is no longer capable of sharing a bedroom with him. This list, left unbounded, could go on for some time as the couple renegotiates the marriage. But it is a mistake, and an offense against the original commitment, to press it too far.

Here, once more, discernment is of first importance, that is, the spouses must consider long and hard what they are not *capable* of doing, and sort it from what they are not *desirous* of doing; for having decided, in Hauer-was's term, to stick with what they are stuck with, they surely must, out of the force of their original obligation to one another, make of it the best they can. This is the point of understanding the marital commitment as *willed,* the idea that parts of the obligation may supersede one's desires.[6] Thus a more sensible emotional focus is not on listing the things they can no longer do together, but on listing the things they can; rather than avoiding what is no longer comfortable, they should be emphasizing what is. To do less defeats the purpose of the discerned and willed decision not to end the marriage.

The second point is that when a marriage is carried along on the power of the original commitment rather than on the power of the couple's continuing delirious romantic love, the third rule of integrity—to say openly why one is doing what one is doing—must be applied with some care. As we saw in chapter 4, the rule cannot possibly be interpreted to mean always telling everything to everybody. For example, if the couple is staying together because of the claim their children have upon them, it would be sheer madness to say this to the children, for the purpose would therein be defeated. That does not mean that the couple struggling to do the right must devise elaborate lies—"We love each other more than ever, kids, really!"—but only that this is an instance, like the military decisions in time of war discussed in chapter 4, in which the benefits of integral behavior can be obtained only at the cost of some candor. The question of how much candor is proper can be resolved, once more, only through the hard process of discernment.

Let us here consider an example:

Example 9-1. After many years of marriage, a husband tells his wife that he no longer loves her. Perhaps he is even in love with somebody else. Eventually, he decides to remain in the marriage for the sake of the children. However, he informs his wife that he will not be affectionate with her in either public or private, neither touching her nor kissing her, because, he says, to do so would make a false statement: he would be proclaiming a level of romantic devotion that he does not feel. Consequently, he concludes, integrity will not allow him to behave as though he loves her.

Observation 9-1(a). Many married people evidently go through precisely this analysis, remaining married but unaffectionate. But the argument fails, for two reasons. First, the message that is transmitted by the husband's public affection toward his wife is not necessarily, as he supposes, that he loves her madly. It may be instead that he is committed to her; that is, that he is displaying his integrity by living the commitment he has made. By treating his wife with open affection, even an affection he does not fully feel in any romantic sense, the husband is saying to the world that his respect for his commitment enables him to do what he would not do, for example, were he and his wife merely boyfriend and girlfriend. There is nothing false about his actions or the message, once the basic decision, to keep the commitment, has been taken.

Observation 9-1(b). The husband has fallen into the trap I discuss in chapter 4—the trap of selfish integrity—the trap that says that integrity is bounded not by obligations one has undertaken or duties imposed by external norms, but only by one's own immediate desires, interests, or needs. There are often good reasons to follow one's own immediate desires or interests, and much of public choice theory, for example, rests on the assumption that one will do so; but discerning and following those desires and interests bear no necessary relation to the discernment of right and wrong that is crucial for the integral life as I have defined it.

Thus the fact that the husband does not desire to be affectionate toward his wife does not conclude the discussion of what integrity demands of him; indeed, it may not even be relevant to a course of conduct that is in itself a fresh violation of the vow. Indeed, to make married life so painful and scary for one's spouse is a betrayal of a special kind. A marriage, like the family itself, should be a place of refuge, a place of emotional and spiritual (and physical) safety in a frustrating and unfriendly or even hostile world. To make the family even an emotionally unsafe place for one's spouse will almost never be an act of integrity; it will almost always be an act of selfishness.

But the role of the spouse who desires to leave is by no means the end of the story. I mentioned earlier that the other spouse's claim must not be viewed as a license to punish the spouse who is viewed as the betrayer. The point bears emphasis. Integrity both allows for anger and encourages its expression, but it does not allow for vengeance, at least not in a marriage. So it is wrong for one spouse to make the other pay—in money or in anything else—as the price of reconciliation.[7] Deals of this kind may be cathartic and may even make the couple feel that matters have in some way been evened out. But the feeling is false. Betrayals of the marital commitment can be forgiven—must be forgiven if the marriage is to continue— but they cannot be balanced. So if the spouse who feels wronged agrees that the marriage should continue, it must not be on terms intended as penal.

Something similar must be said of the spouse who, having expressed the desire to leave, has decided, for the sake of the children or the original commitment, to stay. Holding the whip hand, there is a temptation—a natural one—to dictate: "We shall live on these terms and none other. Take it or leave it." But to treat a spouse this way is to behave like the Christian husband who says to his wife, citing the language of St. Paul's letter to the Ephesians (to be discussed shortly), that he is the "head of the wife," and that the wife must therefore live on such terms as he decrees. This temptation to power, if we might thus paraphrase Nietzsche, is one that the spouse, in both cases, has an obligation to integrity to resist; for to do otherwise is to transform the marital commitment from Smedes's vision of "the one who will be with you" to a far less moral vision of "the one who will tell you what to do."

A BRIEF NOTE ON THE INTEGRAL MARRIED LIFE

The psychotherapist M. Scott Peck, in his phenomenally successful book *The Road Less Traveled,* warns us that the marital relationship, especially when surrounded by traditional religious understandings, can interfere with the ability of individuals to make emotional and spiritual progress and even to relate properly to God. Evidently, it is to the married individuals, not to the married couple as a unit, that God relates. This in turn is part of the larger contemporary project of trying to get people to relate in a healthy way to themselves, apart from the larger network of obligations in which they are embedded.

Although, as a student of integrity, I have obvious sympathy with the idea that people need to understand themselves better, as a Christian, I am just as obviously skeptical of Peck's view, because Christ blessed the institution of marriage explicitly by performing his first miracle at a wedding in Cana of Galilee. But even from a purely secular point of view, Peck's vision has an important weakness: it risks treating the marriage relationship itself, with its mutual promises of love and fidelity, as well as its reciprocal claims and duties, as simply one more crude societal impediment to self-actualization rather than an institution with its own rules and expectations.

I emphasize this point not only because, as I have explained, I agree with Lewis Smedes that it is dangerous to think of marriage as a contract, but also because Peck's view, which could in practice lead to breakup at the first sign of trouble, makes it difficult to pierce the marriage veil and to examine and, if necessary, criticize the dynamic of the marriage itself. Yet to do so is of first importance, because the integrity of a marriage is measured not simply by whether the couple stays together or whether each spouse keeps the vows; it is measured as well by how the marriage is conducted day to day.

The first point to emphasize, although it may seem obvious to many readers, is that the marriage cannot survive at all in the absence of both an abiding mutual respect and an abiding mutual commitment to work at it. What may be less obvious is that, in this society at least, integrity requires both these steps. After all, the love that the couple proclaims when the vows are exchanged necessarily implies a mutual respect: that, at minimum, is what the modern possibilities of free choice and companionate marriage imply. As to the need to work, that, I fear, is what too many couples forget. Precisely because marriages so often begin in the giddiness I have described, many people do not know what they are getting into; and if, as Rubin and Heller suggest, newlyweds believe that their initial delirium will continue forever, the fact that it eventually vanishes, if unprepared for, can lead to bickering, depression, and doubt. That is when the real work of marriage begins and when the couple has its first opportunity to build a mature relationship; but that opportunity will best be seized if the couple has realized from the beginning that matters will not always be easy.

When my wife and I were married, a friend gave us a beautiful sampler that hangs still on the wall of our bedroom. The sampler is in the form of an acrostic (fans of language maven Willard Espy will recognize it at once) and looks like this:

$$\text{fault} \quad \frac{B}{\text{husband quarrels wife}} \quad \text{fault}$$

Translated, it reads: "Be above quarrels between husband and wife. There are faults on both sides." I do not think she could have offered us better advice. What Aristotle wrote about the end of friendship may often apply to the end of marriage: "Quarrels occur when the outcome of a friendship is different from what the parties desire, because a failure to obtain what one wants is almost as bad as getting nothing at all."[8] Understanding this weakness in ourselves and in our partners is another part, and at times the crucial one, of working at a marriage.

Working, always working: that, surely, is how one keeps this most vital commitment. How hard must one work? This is not, obviously, the place for a primer on successful marriage, even if I knew what to write, which I do not. Some 31 percent of married women say that they work harder at the marriage than their husbands do. In the same survey, 40 percent of married women say that they and their husbands rarely or never argue.[9] I wonder how much overlap there is, whether there are fewer arguments if husbands work as hard as their wives to make the marriage a good one. I am certain that if both parties work as hard as they can to keep their promises to each other, such arguments as there are will be neither as painful nor as lingering as they might otherwise be.

There is a further point concerning integral marriage that, although it cannot be resolved here, must at least be mentioned. No two marriages are the same. One of the sharp dividing lines is over the role of women. Modern feminists since Betty Friedan have powerfully exposed the ways in which the so-called traditional marriage can be stultifying for women. But here the data may be surprising. Although more than half of women tell pollsters that they prefer what is called, perhaps with some loss of accuracy, a "shared" marriage, about four in ten continue to prefer "traditional" marriage, in which the husband is the head of the houschold—and some studies suggest that the number in the second category is actually growing.[10] Nine out of ten women take their husband's name when they marry.[11] (Some five percent choose to hyphenate their surnames.) I mention all of this not to express a preference for either form of marriage—which choice a particular woman or man should make is a matter for careful discernment—but rather because, given that millions of people each year choose to enter traditional marriage, a note on day-to-day life is incomplete without a mention of it.

In the traditional Western vision, a family was like a little sovereign state with the husband/father at its head. It was not that wives and children had no rights, but that the very concept of "rights" was foreign to the understanding of the family. This was the awful genius of the choice to treat the marital relationship as status rather than contract: in *Balfour v. Balfour*, a famous nineteenth-century contracts case that I teach to my appalled first-year students, a husband leaves his wife and promises to give her money. When he reneges, the court declines to order the money paid, because, in the judges' understanding of the *status* of marriage, the wife could not reasonably have believed that he meant the promise to be legally enforceable. In fact, at common law, it used to be said (with some degree of hyperbole) that the king's writ did not run into the home, meaning that the husband/father was free to run it as any other ruler would run a fiefdom.

The notion that the husband is head of the household, in the sense of being absolutely in charge, is common to nearly every culture on earth. And the risk is always the same: without the existence of restraints, the power will tend to corrupt. In many cultures, and in fairly recent history in the United States, the right to beat one's wife for her defiance has been considered a part of the power of the husband as head. But this corruption should not surprise us: We have already seen that living with integrity is all but impossible when one is able to act without risk.

We should not blame traditional marriage or traditional cultures for this nonintegrity. But we should also recognize the corrupting tendencies of power that is exercised without restraint. What restraints are possible? Changes in law have accomplished some: nowadays, the king's writ *does* run into the home. But even within traditional marriage, no restraint will be more important than an effort by both spouses to move toward significantly greater equality within that home that the husband traditionally heads.

As a believing Christian, and thus a member of a faith that has too often restricted the ability of women to use their God-given gifts in the world, I must be particularly sensitive to the risk of nonintegrity. Consider the image of the traditional marriage presented by St. Paul, most notably in his letter to the Ephesians: "For the husband is the head of the wife as Christ is head of the church" (Eph. 5:23). As a Christian who believes in a divinely inspired Bible, I am constrained to take this language seriously rather than to pretend, as some critics would prefer, that it doesn't exist. But I am also constrained to add that men have sacrificed whatever authority the vision once granted, and have done so through their own sin. St. John Chrysostom, in his commentary on Ephesians, warned the husband to "bring in love as a counterpoise to obedience."[12] Too many men did not. Instead, they read the Pauline text as being simply about Christ as the giver-of-laws rather than about Christ as the one-who-loves, and so eventually became corrupted by power. Perhaps this was inevitable. After all, as we have seen, integrity suffers when there is little risk in its exercise. The office of head of household thus had to lose its integrity in the unfair world that we have all built. The greater the power that one possesses, the less the likelihood that one will do the hard work of discernment on which all integrity, religious or secular, ultimately rests. Thus even taking Paul at his word and taking his words literally—the husband is head of the wife and thus boss of the wife—the privilege is one that was bound to be forfeit if granted to fallen man. Inevitably, holding such power, men would grow corrupt, would cease to act with integrity, and, no longer acting with integrity, would have no fair claim on the exercise of that power.

Another way of looking at the matter is this: God, for reasons no human will know, inspired Paul to appoint the husband as the head of the wife. But in our mortal fallibility, humans, mainly men, constructed a world in which the exercise of that office is often unjust. For that we should blame men, not God—not women, and certainly not feminism, which has been but the bearer of the tidings and has, in that way, played a role in the fulfillment of God's mysterious purpose. Religious conservatives who rail against feminism would do well to consider the centuries of male nonintegrity that gave feminism birth; and, given the large numbers of people who continue to enter into traditional marriages every year, men and women alike must resolve to do better.

One may sum up the relationship of integrity to marriage this way: marriage is not a game, and nobody promised that it would be easy. Marriage is a serious and lifelong undertaking that is often entered into too lightly and, nowadays, too often ended when troubles begin to mount. Sometimes, to be sure, marriages must end; sometimes, we can make no other choice. But when another choice can be made, we should make it. Because keeping our promises matters. Because our husbands or wives matter. And, of course, the children matter.

Marriages, we can surely agree, will be richer and stronger if those who contemplate them take their vows with sufficient seriousness to engage in the hard work of discernment before ever taking them—and then engage in the hard work of making them real once they have been spoken. But even if the husband and wife have thought long and hard about the risks, matters still may not work out—and they certainly will not work out if the couple treats the wedding vow as a single act of commitment rather than an act that must be repeatedly renewed over time. Success in marriage, in other words, demands not one vow on the wedding day, but a whole series of vows, repeated, even if silently, perhaps as often as every day.

I do not want the reader to mistake my point. Marriage is not easy, but it can and should be rewarding. Marriage of any kind, whether shared or traditional, whether companionate or arranged, will be rewarding—will be worthwhile—only if the spouses work to make it so. But this, surely, is their minimum obligation to each other and to the commitment they have made. Sometimes the work will be hard; sometimes the mountain ahead will seem too high, but the summit is usually worth the climb and we owe it to ourselves and our spouses to try to get there.

I have said so much of Lewis Smedes that perhaps we should grant him the last word. "We are our promises," he says, "and we lose hold of ourselves when we take no pains to keep them."[13]

(ten)

The Integrity of
Fun and Games

Having taken the time to delve into our deepest commitments, we can now consider what we do for leisure—our sports and games—and how the ways in which we organize them, too, can provide lessons in how we value or do not value integrity.

Games quite literally have rules; games, unlike most other areas of life, are in fact *defined* by their rules. So from the way we play our games, we learn about the way we think of rules; and from understanding how we think of rules—and, in particular, how we think about breaking them—we learn about our respect, if any, for the virtue of integrity. In particular, we teach a good deal about our integrity when we choose to follow too literally the late Vince Lombardi's well-known, perhaps notorious advice: "Winning isn't everything—it's the only thing." Lombardi's epigram might be defended as the mark of a tough but fair competitor. (Lombardi is also credited with the gentle admonishment: "Gentlemen, we did not lose. Time simply expired before we had an opportunity to take the lead.") Charlie Brown once put his own depressing gloss on Lombardi: "Winning isn't everything, but losing

isn't anything." It is this last attitude—not that winning is good but that losing is disastrous—that is perhaps the epitome of poor sportsmanship. And
therein hangs a tale.

SPORTSMANSHIP

When I was a law student back in the late 1970s, I spent one summer
working for a large and prestigious New York law firm as what was called,
then as now, a summer associate. (I hated the summer, but that was the
fault of my personality, not of the firm.) Like every firm, mine freed the
summer associates for a single day from the drudgery of sitting in the middle of the library in our ill-fitting suits, pretending we knew what we were
doing. On that one day—known as the summer outing—the firm treated
us to a fabulous afternoon and evening at a rather posh country club hidden in some distant green-hilled suburb. The afternoon was sports: tennis,
volleyball, swimming. The evening was a fancy dinner. All in the interest
of keeping the troops happy.

I spent most of the afternoon on the volleyball court with perhaps a
dozen other summer associates. We were, I should make plain, a leisurely
bunch, enjoying the sunshine and the game, hitting some shots, missing
others, trading anecdotes and clever barbs, laughing a great deal, and keeping only the vaguest sort of score. In other words, we were having fun.

That is, we were having fun until one of the firm's partners, a well-known
lawyer still, joined the game. And then it all changed. It is not simply that
having one of our bosses in the game altered our attitudes, although that is
surely true; we laughed less and probably stopped telling anecdotes, at least
the ones about people in the firm. That was bad enough. What was worse,
however, was *his* attitude. Suddenly score had to be kept with great rigor:
the partner said so. Suddenly the teams were not fairly chosen: he wanted
to move this player here, that one there, and wanted, in particular, to even
out the number of "girls" on the two teams. Suddenly there was criticism:
this fellow wasn't hustling, that woman should have dived for the ball.
Worst of all, suddenly there were these vicious arguments: this shot was out
of bounds, that player reached over the net, the other one spiked the ball
illegally. He began enforcing rules most of us had never heard of.

The summer associates with the greatest degree of self-possession, the
future leaders of America, drifted away to spend their afternoon in more
relaxing pursuits. The rest of us—the wimps, I suppose you might say—
stayed in the game, pretending to enjoy this new and manic pace, trying

to ignite in ourselves the blazing competitive fires that he was demanding of us. And so we kept score and we fixed the teams and we dived for the balls and we argued. We followed all the rules to the letter and, I would venture to say, nobody had any fun.

Now, given what I have already said about the importance of following rules, I should pause and explain myself. Although we had not been following the rules—or not very hard—before the partner joined us, we were not breaking them for any personal advantage or convenience. It was simply that the game itself was being played in a leisurely fashion, and so we were letting offenses slip by that in a more competitive, more serious game might have seemed to be of first importance. In a sense, we were not really playing a game at all: we were simply using the volleyball court and hitting the ball back and forth. You might say, in the language of chapter 1, that the rules about the rules were, for a while, that we would use just enough of them to enable us to enjoy what we were doing but, by common consent, would not enforce them in ways that would make the game seem to matter. The essential change when the partner joined us was that the game suddenly mattered; more to the point, having been a *game* of volleyball, what we were engaged in now became a game of *volleyball*, the emphasis switching from the fact that our activity was a game—implying fun and a none-too-serious attitude—to naming our activity and therefore squeezing us into a mold we had previously been avoiding with some pleasure.

What happened in the end was instructive. The team the partner had joined ended up losing a very close set of games. If memory serves, I was on the other side. If my recollection is right and we indeed snatched victory, I suspect it was because we were able to turn our anger into power and because his team was too cowed, to say nothing of stunned, to play very well. But the ending was predictable: he was enraged about losing, kicking sand around and moaning about the team with which he had been saddled. He was, as they say, not a good sport.

The idea that there are good sports and bad sports—and that it is better to be the first than the second—reflects something valuable about our society: we very much want to be people for whom winning is *not* everything. We want to take pride and even pleasure in a game well played, even when the result is not what we might have wished. When we criticize Bobby Knight, the petty and short-tempered genius who coaches basketball at the University of Indiana, for his childish behavior when things do not go his way—throwing a chair or kicking a player (his son, as it happened) or cursing at officials (the university was fined $30,000 for that one)—we are not suggesting that the man doesn't know his basketball, but only that he doesn't know his sportsmanship.

One of the forces that has been most destructive to the ideals of sportsmanship is television. Thirty years ago, Roger Angell of *The New Yorker* described vividly the distortions in our view of sports perpetrated by "the young men in blazers who run sports TV." Wrote an obviously bemused Angell, "their dream is fifty weekends of world championships—in football, in baseball, in surfing, in Senior Women's Marbles, in anything—that are *not to be missed* by the weekend watcher."[1] The point is that television, by virtue of both its immediacy and its need to profit from its telecasts, has an incentive to market each telecast as independently important. And that importance turns out to be measured in terms of winning and losing.

It is only the advent of broad television coverage that has led to this remarkable spectacle of players dancing in celebration after touchdowns, home runs, and other big plays. Not that dancing is bad in itself. Enthusiasm can be a part of sportsmanship, and exuberance is a marvelous thing; not all players need mimic the supposed stoicism of the golden age (whenever that was). The trouble is that the joyous celebrations can cross the line between pride and poor sportsmanship. Players on teams that are in the lead often point mocking fingers and mutter insults at opposing players. By disrespecting their opponents, they fall into the trap of supposing that all that matters is who has more points.

Although I think taunting is poor sportsmanship and thus runs against the grain of integrity, I am not at all sure that we should try to legislate integral behavior (see chapter 12). Nevertheless, the professional sports leagues have tried. The National Football League has cracked down on celebrations in the end zone.* The National Basketball Association has outlawed taunting. But none of this would be necessary were our young people better taught about how to win, and, in particular, if they learned to respect their opponents rather than despise them. They might, for example, heed the advice of Joe Paterno, longtime coach of successful football teams at Penn State, who told his players why he doesn't approve of post-touchdown celebrations: "When you get into the end zone," he is supposed to have said, "I want you to behave like you expected to be there." And, he might have added, with respect for your opponents.

Years ago, I watched the traditional interviews in the losing team's dress-

---

*Of course, this is the same National Football League that once considered forbidding players to pray together on the field after games, evidently on the ground that doing so showed a lack of competitive spirit!

ing room after the final game of the World Series. I remember the television reporter saying to one of the game's great stars something like this: "Well, even though you lost, you had a spectacular season, and I know it must feel good just to be here." To which the great star replied, towel around his shoulders, head hanging: "It doesn't mean a bleeping thing if you don't win."

And he was partly right: on television, it doesn't mean a thing if you don't win. Announcers don't care about the brilliant defeat, about playing by the rules, or about much of anything except who is ahead, how much time is left, and whether the other team can catch up. But the bad sportsmanship that television so often magnifies is only a corner of the world of sports; there is also real life.

It may be, of course, that bad sportsmanship is an inevitable concomitant of competition and human nature. Some feminist critics—but not feminists alone—have argued that we give far too much prominence to sports that involve competition rather than cooperation, thereby teaching our children that success lies in being opposed to someone else, in working *against* rather than working *with*.[2] And although there is something to this criticism, it can be taken too far. Our most popular national sports are all team sports, and the youngsters who enjoy them do indeed learn the value of cooperation, except that we call it teamwork. Those who refuse to be team players are criticized and, one hopes, corrected.

Competition *can* get out of hand. Plato urged the training of the bodies of his elite guardians along with their minds: and not Plato alone. Everyone who has tried to build a superstate has taken pride in athletics. The very evil—Stalin, Hitler—have seen athletic achievement as crucial to the nation's pride, as though victory on the athletic field would show the world which system was best. "Catch up and surpass" was Stalin's famous dictum, and the Soviet Union was frequently accused of breaking the rules in order to achieve it. As for Hitler, the entire world could cheer the humiliation of his self-styled Aryan supermen by the black American sprinter Jesse Owens at the 1936 Olympics in Berlin. But note what the world was cheering: a victory in open competition.

It is an error to make success in athletic competition the basis for measuring one political system against another, but a degree of competition is surely healthy, in sports as in other areas of life—as long as the competitive urge is not transformed into mercilessness. Indeed, in some areas of life we may actually *need* competition. Despite volumes of social and economic critique, we have not yet discovered a better means than competition in a free market for creating wealth and economic growth. Elections are necessarily competitions, and so are the great ideological struggles. Two people may compete for the affections of a third, and although the struggle can be quite painful, no form of cooperation is likely to resolve *that.*

What turns competitiveness into sportsmanship is a respect for one's opponent and one's teammates and the rules by which the game is played. Sportsmanship implies a desire to win but a willingness to lose, to accept defeat as also a part of the game. In this sense, a youngster who is taught about sportsmanship learns much that is valuable about life: how to play the game by the rules, how to win without bragging, but also how to lose without kicking sand or throwing chairs. In losing, as in winning, we may be measured by the degree of our integrity, our wholeness in seeing the game as more than a contest over outcome.

And, as the story of the volleyball game at the summer outing reminds, not every game and not every sport must be played in a way that turns it into ruthless competition. Sometimes we can play for fun. Joey Jay, the first Little League baseball star to become a major league baseball star, complained about what he saw as a loss of the ethic of fun as Little League became more organized and more competitive and began turning some kids away on the ground that they were not good enough: "I can't think of anything worse than turning a recreation program into an elite society."[3]

PROFESSIONAL "SPORTS"

The elite society to which Jay refers is the world of the sports professional. Apart from what we have already said about winning and losing and following the rules, what is the role of integrity as a concept in professional sports?

The answer is less clear than one would hope. Certainly to the proprietors—some would say the perpetrators—of big-time sports, integrity matters. Consider major league baseball, which created the powerful position of Commissioner of Baseball after the 1919 Black Sox scandal, in which several White Sox players were accused of throwing the World Series for money. Acquitted at trial, the players nevertheless found themselves banned for life from the sport, one of the first acts by the first baseball commissioner, Kenesaw Mountain Landis, a sitting federal judge who took over the post in 1921. Happy Chandler, for many years the commissioner of major league baseball, once explained why the team owners created the position: "[T]he American people needed a symbol of complete authority and absolute integrity."[4] So from the very first, the baseball commissioner was given broad powers to act in the "best interests" of baseball; he was authorized, in so many words, to protect the "integrity" of the sport.

In recent decades, that broad power has been used to suspend an owner, George Steinbrenner, who committed a crime (illegal campaign contributions) and was banned from participating in the affairs of his team, and to force out of baseball altogether Pete Rose, the player who got more hits in his career than any other, because Rose bet on baseball games in which the Reds, which he managed, were playing. Rose's defenders argued that he bet only on his own team, but integrity demands something loftier than the sort of technical justification that a lawyer might offer; one would only wish that if players who are connected with gamblers are suspect, team owners who have interests in racetracks and casinos would fall under a similar pall—for not the least of the aspects of integrity is consistency.

Rose was the fifteenth player or coach barred for life, nearly all of them for gambling or because of efforts to "throw" ball games. (A sixteenth player's lifetime suspension was overturned by an arbitrator.) A. Bartlett Giamatti, the former Yale president who, as baseball commissioner, imposed the punishment on Rose, said that he had no choice in the matter because of his responsibility "for protecting the integrity of the game of baseball."[5]

But if the American people needed the symbol, the owners have always been determined to keep the commissioner's job symbolic, which is why they axed Commissioner Fay Vincent in 1993: they would rather not have somebody else tell them what integrity demands. So, shortly after firing Vincent, the owners changed the commissioner's job description to exclude certain matters from his broad powers. But no matter, according to the owners: they only reduced his authority over subjects not related to integrity.[6] (Of course, the owners are still the ones who get to define what involves integrity and what doesn't.) At this writing, in the summer of 1995, the owners have not yet hired another commissioner, and they seem quite happy to leave things that way. After all, integrity is one thing; running their business the way they want is something else altogether.

Even though the Supreme Court once decreed that baseball is a sport and not a business[7]—thus exempting it from the antitrust laws—nobody can doubt that a business is what the owners of the teams are running. Nowhere was this clearer than in the agonizing major league baseball strike that began in August 1994 and stretched on to the beginning of the 1995 season. In this case, application of the principle of integrity allows us to get a better sense of the issues actually at stake—rather than the non-issues that are said to be at stake.

One nonissue is that the players are overpaid because their average salary is $1.2 million. (The median is $400,000.) In the first place, the skill that professional baseball players possess is quite rare and, if one judges by the sport's popularity, quite valuable. Moreover, the owners themselves are the ones who have bid the salaries up through open competition in a market. But there is an entirely separate point. Professional athletes are simply entertainers, and many successful entertainers make far more money than baseball players do. For example, top recording artists may make $20 million or more in a good year. The heavyweight boxing champion of the world might make as much or more for a single bout. Network news anchors—probably the most dour of entertainers—routinely accept salaries of $5 million or more. A best-selling novelist like John Grisham or Stephen King may earn in excess of $10 million in a good year. They write books that are purchased by a million or so people and are made into films that are viewed by a few million more. But many times that number attend major league baseball games in an average season, and many millions more watch on television.

But even these are the pikers. According to the *Forbes* magazine list of the highest-paid entertainers, the film director Steven Spielberg earned something over $300 million during 1993 and 1994 combined. Is he overpaid? By what standard? He makes films that people pay lots of money to see. The public obviously believes it is getting its money's worth, because it keeps going back; the studios obviously believe they are getting their money's worth, because they continue to bankroll his films.

Team owners demand a salary cap. But if all the major studios or all the leading publishers agreed among themselves to limit to a specific dollar figure their total payments to directors or writers in a given year, they would be violating the antitrust laws. The antitrust laws effectively prevent them from colluding, forcing them to bid for the services of the directors or writers most in demand.

One still sees much written about the "greed" that is said to drive the whole dispute; sportswriters fall all over one another to insist that the players and owners show no respect for the fans. But this is sophistry: nobody is under an obligation to give his or her services away. What major league baseball lacks (the same is true, in lesser degree, of other sports) is not altruism but market discipline. It lacks market discipline in part because of the franchise system, but mostly because of its exemption from the antitrust laws.

Consider: Why are the salaries of the players so high? The simple answer is that the services the players provide are priced at the market level. However, the market itself is a peculiar one. Ordinarily, if Firm A is overpaying for its labor, Firm B will open in direct competition and with lower labor costs. Firm A will then reduce its labor costs in order to compete with Firm B or go out of business. In baseball, however, as with any other major league sport, the franchise system makes it impossible for Firm B to open up in competition with Firm A: only one franchise is allowed in a city, except for a very few large cities, and even then only one franchise is allowed per league. Consequently, if Team A overpays for its labor (its players), there are fewer market forces to make it control its costs.

But imposing a salary cap produces the reverse problem. In most markets, if Firm A is providing a product superior to that of Firm B, Firm B can, through additional investment, improve the quality of its offerings. Under a salary cap, however, Firm B is prohibited from making the investment it needs, if the investment happens to be in labor. Consider an analogy. Firm A builds a better personal computer than Firm B because Firm A employs better engineers. Firm B wants to spend more money to hire more engineers so that it can build computers as good as those made by Firm A. But Firm B is not allowed to do so because of an industrywide agreement limiting the amount of money that can be spent on personnel!

During the negotiations over the most recent professional football collective-bargaining agreement, one owner was quoted as saying that he did not need an industrywide agreement to tell him how much money to budget for personnel. Here was a rare but clear example of integrity in professional sports. The owner in question understood quite well what he was doing—running a business—and was willing to say so. But, more than that, he was willing to say that the responsibility for making his business profitable was his alone. Which makes perfect sense. If he wanted to cut back his costs, he would decide; if he wanted to spend more, he would decide. And if his business lost money, he would have only himself to blame. That is the way markets are supposed to work.

Major league baseball, armed with its silly exemption from the antitrust laws, possesses a degree of freedom to adjust the markets to its liking. No other industry would be allowed to impose an industrywide salary cap— that is, to engage in collusion in a decision on how much to budget for labor costs—and all the self-righteous moaning about how some clubs lose money is no substitute for the market discipline that would, in any other industry, drive those firms out of business or at least cause them to be sold to new owners who believed they could turn a profit.

It is something of a commonplace among disgusted baseball fans to assert that the players are overpaid and that their reluctance to allow their salaries to be limited is greed. And many baseball players *are* greedy, their charging fees for autographs for children being only one of many depressing examples. But it must be noted that relatively few of us would be in a hurry to enter an industry that, by policy, held all firms to a preset salary budget. The major league baseball players naturally share that hesitation, and, as successful entertainers, they happen to possess a rare and valuable skill that they would like to be able to sell in a free and open market. And one thing integrity forces us to say of a salary cap is that it represents a view that markets should not be free.

Still, do not misunderstand the point. Merely because there seems more of right on the side of the players than on the side of the owners in the baseball dispute does not mean that the players are entirely admirable. The 1994 strike dealt professional baseball a blow from which it will be many years recovering—if it recovers at all. When all has been written about baseball as a business and the players as union workers, the end result is that the "sport" loses its charm; it is not easy for a child to grow excited about seeing a player who was out on strike for a year keep his salary in the millions of dollars. It does not matter if this is what happened; this is a sufficiently widespread perception that fans have grown tired of the whole thing. Attendance was down dramatically in 1995, and ABC and NBC, which had been sharing television broadcast rights, announced that they were no longer interested. A bewildering variety of special promotions are altogether failing to bring the fans back into the stadiums. And integrity requires us to concede one of the forces that is bringing the sport to ruin: it just isn't fun any more.

FOR GOD, FOR COUNTRY, AND FOR . . .

What about collegiate sports, which once were played for fun and honor? Nowadays, college sports, too, are big business, with basketball and football in particular generating hundreds of millions of dollars in revenues every year. (In 1994, CBS agreed to pay one and three-quarters *billion* dollars for the right to broadcast the college basketball championship tournament through 2002.) Successful coaches at major colleges can earn hundreds of thousands of dollars from endorsements, radio programs, and speaking tours. In the spring of 1995, the state of Alabama adopted a new ethical code, requiring many state employees to report their outside income—but exempting coaches of college teams, whose outside income is almost certainly the greatest.

The players, of course, see none of this money, except in the form of scholarships. Although they earn huge amounts of cash for their schools, they are not paid a penny. The reason is that they are said to be amateurs, competing, no doubt, out of sheer love of the game. The colleges and universities, through the National Collegiate Athletic Association, the governing body of major college athletics, have adopted a bewildering set of rules to enforce this pretense. For example, students who receive athletic scholarships are sharply limited in the amount of outside income they are allowed to earn. Greg Anthony, a star on the 1990 championship basketball team at the University of Nevada at Las Vegas, founded his own very profitable company while in college, which might seem the sort of entrepreneurship that ought to be encouraged. But the NCAA said he could not keep his scholarship if he kept his company. Anthony, fortunately, was making enough money from his company that he could afford to give up his scholarship, which he did. (No NCAA rule prohibits well-to-do parents from giving their children who play collegiate sports as much money as they want; what is important is that the students not earn it. You figure it out.)

Every year, some variety of this saga is played out: A poor kid from the inner city becomes a big star at a college far from his home. For all his college years, his parents do not see him play except perhaps on television, because they cannot afford to travel. Finally, when the youngster plays for the championship, a sympathetic alumnus of the college slips the parents plane tickets to the big game. Bingo! The rules have been broken, the school risks probation (an NCAA punishment that restricts tournament play and sometimes television appearances), and the impoverished parents usually wind up promising to pay the money back.

To be sure, the NCAA rules are aimed at combating genuine abuses: the specter of alumni slipping money to athletes behind the field house, or schools competing for top recruits with lavish but secret promises of cars or cushy jobs, and so on. But all of this is at issue principally because of the NCAA's vigorous refusal to allow the athletes to be paid even a small amount of money for their highly profitable labors. Even Walter Byers, a former executive director of the NCAA, has expressed the view that the group should rethink its opposition to paying the athletes.[8] After all, every other student on campus is allowed to work, and if a rich alumnus guarantees a summer job to the best sophomore in the chemistry department, nobody cries foul. On the contrary, schools knock themselves out to create programs of that kind.

The principal difference in athletics is surely a fear that with money comes cheating—that the kids' heads will be turned by the dollars at stake, that gamblers may get a toehold, and so on. But the money is already there, and the players can see that their coaches are awash in it. (One major public university recently investigated allegations that its highly successful basketball team was switching uniform makers because of the coach's new endorsement contract. The coach backed down and nothing came of it.) But if the NCAA really is worried about the influence of money in sports, perhaps it should stop negotiating multimillion-dollar television deals for itself based on the labor of unpaid students who are wise enough to know hypocrisy when they see it.

THE BLACK COACHES WERE RIGHT

Of course, the pay-for-play issue is not nearly as hot a controversy in college sports as is the eligibility issue—that is, the burning question of who will be allowed to play. And like so much that is divisive in America, this issue arrives with a racial spin. In the early 1990s, the NCAA adopted Proposition 48, a set of rules that, in its original form, required high school students to attain certain minimum grades and standardized test scores before they could receive scholarship assistance or compete as freshmen in intercollegiate sports. The rules, which were softened a bit in January 1995 to allow nonqualifying students to receive scholarships even though they would not be allowed to play, were aimed at a fairly obvious and well-understood problem: the recruiting of players not capable of doing college-level work who would be admitted solely on the basis of their ability to put a ball through a basket or run a hundred meters in ten seconds.

Proposition 48 and its successors have been staunchly opposed by the Black Coaches Association, which has argued vehemently that the standards are unfair to black students. The coaches argue that the standardized tests incorporate a racial bias. The literature on this point is inconclusive, and, in such debates, both sides tend to take their positions as matters of faith. It must be said that the coaches are on shaky political ground here, not on the merits of their position but because the minimum scores required on the tests, whether biased or not, are actually fairly low.* The original Proposition 48 required scores of 700 (out of 1600) on the SAT and a 2.0 grade point average (GPA) in eleven college preparatory courses. (Students may alternatively take the ACT, where the qualifying score is also fairly low.) The great majority of American high school students could easily reach these levels, and do. In 1995, the required number of college preparatory courses increased to thirteen. And under new rules set to go into effect in 1996, the qualifying levels are replaced by a sliding scale, so that students achieving 700 on the SAT will need a 2.5 GPA and students achieving only a 2.0 GPA will need to score 900 on the SAT.

A stronger argument for the coaches is that the NCAA should not be dictating to individual schools which students they should admit and what standards they should apply. If one school happens to make a specialty of educating students deemed marginal elsewhere—the present-day mission of a number of traditionally black colleges—it is hardly the province of the NCAA to say that in the case of students who happen to be athletes, that mission may not be fulfilled. Indeed, the low-scoring students at the black colleges often have higher graduation rates than better-scoring students at more prestigious colleges. One might try to argue in response that the academic program is more rigorous at the more prestigious colleges, but this assertion, even if true, is well outside the purview of the NCAA. If a college feels itself disadvantaged in sports because of the high expectations it places upon its students, perhaps it should be content to keep its academic rank and field losing teams, rather than using the NCAA regulatory process as a crutch to keep the teams winning and the alumni happy.

Of course the NCAA argues that it is not trying to prevent anybody from getting an education, that it is simply concerned about exploitation. But the devotee of integrity is constrained to note that there seems to be a plain absurdity in the NCAA's ruthless determination to monitor the standardized test scores of freshmen when it seems unconcerned about their character. In 1995, Richard Parker, one of the nation's most skilled and thus most sought-after high school basketball players, pled guilty to sexually assault-

---

*It should be noted in passing that there is reason to think that some black students who take the tests are the victims not of racial bias but of poor teaching. For example, at a few schools in Washington, D.C., the median scores on the SAT consistently fall *below the predictions of random chance.*[9] When an identifiable group of students really does worse on a test than they would through guesswork, they are almost certainly making common errors and the common errors may be the result of poor teaching.

ing a fellow student. This was no misunderstanding. According to the prosecutors, Parker and a classmate enticed a fifteen-year-old girl into a stairwell in the school building, where they attacked her. This was an act of some brutality, although the trial judge was mysteriously content to suspend Parker's sentence. Did the assault make a difference in his eligibility to play college basketball? Not, evidently, to the NCAA, which cares only about test scores; and of the schools that were recruiting him, only a few withdrew their scholarship offers before the glare of publicity focused public attention on the case.*

But the biggest lie of all is that the reason for the tougher standards is the concern that without them, the schools will exploit their young basketballers and footballers. The concern is a legitimate one. But there is an easy answer to that concern, an answer that the black coaches proposed and that the NCAA voted down contemptuously at the January 1995 meeting: Do not allow freshmen to play varsity sports. Make them wait a year. Give them time to grow accustomed to the change from high school to college, time to mature, time to learn to work hard and make progress in their courses.

Until the early 1970s, freshmen were not allowed to play varsity sports at the college level, and the black coaches are not the first to challenge the NCAA's policy shift. Educators have long questioned it. So have some white coaches. The aforementioned Joe Paterno has put the point succinctly: "When a kid plays football games before he attends a class, something is wrong."[10] And in the arena of college football, where the season often starts in August, this can literally occur: a young man can win an athletic scholarship, play in early September, break a leg, never play again, and never attend a class—but the school would have broken no rules!

Eliminating freshman eligibility, as it is called, would have several advantages over the iniquitous Proposition 48 and its successors. First, instead of relying on predictions about how well students will do in college, we would be able to learn directly whether or not they are capable. Second, we would not only weed out those students lacking the essential smarts to

---

*My point is emphatically not that Parker, having committed a serious crime, is undeserving of a college education. My concern is that the NCAA has no stomach for enforcing moral requirements on entering students with the same fervor with which it presses its academic rules. If you do not like the idea that an organization of colleges should be able to tell its members what moral rules they must enforce, query why the organization should be able to tell its members what academic rules they must enforce.

do college work, but we would also discover which of these young potential athletes are able to maintain the classroom discipline needed to do the
work. Third, we would avoid the nettlesome spectacle of the NCAA telling
colleges which students they may admit and which they may not.

But the NCAA was not impressed by these arguments. Nor should anybody be surprised. The NCAA voted the no-freshmen-eligibility proposal
down for a simple reason: the NCAA does not actually believe what it says
about student athletes. If it did, it would monitor and regulate the rates at
which student athletes are graduated rather than their admission requirements, for the proper question is whether student athletes are actually
being educated, not whether some test predicts that they will be. But the
big schools would never go along with such a notion, because so many of
them do not care about whether their students are educated or not, as witness the substantial rates of failure to finish, most notably among basketball and football players.

Title IX, the sometimes controversial federal guarantee of rough equality for women's and men's college sports, seems to have opened an era
when women's and men's teams feel equally free to play fast and loose
with the rules. In the spring of 1995, the University of California at Los
Angeles won the collegiate softball championship with the help of a
player named Tanya Harding (that really is her name), who was both the
hitting and pitching star of the playoff tournament. This should not have
been a surprise, however, because Harding was already an established
star of the Australian national softball team. Harding arrived in Los Angeles just in time to play softball, played brilliantly, won the Most Valuable
Player award, and then left to return to Australia, all this without complet-
ing a single class. When the school was criticized, the reaction of her college coach was almost contemptuously ho-hum: "It's frustrating because all
of a sudden Tanya Harding is a terrible person for quitting school to fulfill
an Olympic commitment."[11] But the coach had matters backward. Nobody
thought Harding was a terrible person. Critics thought that UCLA did a terrible thing.

"Matching men's cheating," wrote one disgusted columnist of the Harding incident, "is one place where gender equity isn't needed."[12] But UCLA
broke no rules, as its athletic department at once pointed out, supported
by the NCAA, which muttered that there was no "problem with her eligibility."[13] Which seems to be all the group could find to worry about. Harding tested well enough to meet the NCAA's silly criteria for student athletes.
She just didn't get an education. But then, that isn't really why she was
there.

SPORTSMANSHIP REVISITED

When we teach our children to play games, we teach them—I hope—what it means to be a good sport. Being a good sport means not only playing fair, following the rules, but also giving one's victorious opponent full credit. There is an old saying in chess circles that no healthy player has ever lost a game. The reference is to the common chess-player's habit of insisting, after every loss, "I wasn't feeling well" or "I had a touch of the flu" or "I didn't get a wink of sleep last night." The chess player and poet Alfred Kreymbourg tells the marvelous story of the man who, after losing a game at a New York chess club, offered as his excuse that he was worn out from doing nothing all day.[14]

Professional sports fans are past masters of this skill of fixing blame. The weather was the problem, or the injury to a key player, or a foolish decision by a coach. Quite often the blame falls on the referees: had they called the game fairly, our side would have won, but instead they botched the big call. On hearing all of this blather from fans, and sometimes players (who ought to know better), one longs for the wisdom of Casey Stengel, longtime manager of the New York Yankees, who is supposed to have upbraided one of his infielders with this *bon mot*: "Don't make excuses on the bad hops. Anybody can catch the good ones."

Of course, sports is hard work. Playing at the professional level is hardest of all. And at the highest levels, determination can often count for as much as talent. So one can understand the burning desire to win that afflicts all professionals: without it, they would have remained amateurs. Still, one wonders whether this determination has to lead to simple bad sportsmanship—not merely the cheating that I discussed in chapter 1 but the refusal to give credit to opponents or, indeed, to give them a fair shot.

The literary agent Morton Janklow told me the following story. Back in the days when Forest Hills hosted the United States Amateur tennis championship instead of the United States Open, the great amateur Ted Schroeder was contesting a difficult match against the sensational Pancho Gonzalez—a match Schroeder would ultimately lose. At a critical point, Gonzalez served what appeared to be an ace: that is, his opponent was unable to return the serve. The line judge, whose job it is to make these calls, said that the serve was out, meaning that the point would go to Schroeder. The crowd could not believe the call. Neither could Gonzalez. Even Schroeder himself protested, signaling that the ball was clearly in bounds. But the line judge refused to change his call, and the umpire refused to overrule him. Play resumed. When Gonzalez made his next serve, Schroeder let the ball go by, making no effort to return it, and Gonzalez won the point he should have had on the previous serve. In the end, Gonzalez also won set and match—by two points. But Schroeder preserved his integrity. Indeed, he followed all three rules for integral living: he decided what was right, did it at cost to himself, and was quite open about what he was doing.

The sports journalist John Feinstein tells a similar story about a professional golfer who penalized himself a single stroke at a tournament because he thought he might have broken a rule (by moving a ball marker) and could not remember whether he had or not. Nobody else saw the alleged violation; the golfer himself made the decision. Because of that penalty, he missed the cut by a single stroke. (In a professional golf tournament, after two rounds, the players with the lowest scores continue and everybody else is out.) But even in losing, he could tell himself that he did the right thing.

An unfortunate comparison is the University of Colorado's football team, which won the national college football championship for 1990, but only because of a victory that was tainted by a bad call by the officials—a call so bad that, had it been right, Colorado would definitely have lost the game and, ultimately, the chance for the championship.

In October of that year, trailing the University of Missouri by four points with time running out, Colorado had a first down near the Missouri goal line. (For readers who are not football fans, a first down means that Colorado had four chances to move the ball.) Four times Colorado tried to score a winning touchdown, and four times the team failed. Because all four downs had now been used up, possession of the ball should have switched to Missouri, which could then run out the clock—that is, hold the ball until time expired—because only two seconds were left in the game. However, the referees inexplicably lost track of the number of plays that had been run and gave Colorado an illegal *fifth* down, which it used to score the winning touchdown. Asked about the error, Colorado coach Bill McCartney shrugged and said it wasn't his responsibility: "I feel strongly about the fact Colorado earned the victory, and do not apologize for the victory," he said.[15]

McCartney, a devout Christian who preaches the importance of solid values in everyday life, got this one exactly wrong: his team did *not* earn the victory. His team won the game, 33–31, but by accident. However, neither he nor his school made any effort to give the game back, as some urged, which would have cost Colorado the national championship. (Giving the victory back is not unheard of: "In 1940, Cornell relinquished a tarnished 7–3 victory over Dartmouth, and to this day the game stands in the record book as a 3–0 win for Dartmouth," *Sports Illustrated* reported after the Colorado fiasco.)[16]

And then there is the case of Gary Kasparov, who is, at this writing, the chess champion of the world. At the prestigious Linares tournament in 1994, playing against one of the handful of female grandmasters in the world, Judit Polgar, Kasparov allegedly moved his knight to one square, then realized that the move was a mistake that would cost him the game, and so took the move back and put the knight on a different square. Under the Laws of Chess, as they are called, once a player has released a piece from his grasp, the move is complete and cannot be changed. Kasparov initially denied letting go of the knight at all, but his opponent, a seventeen-year-old wunderkind, as well as other witnesses and a tape of the game made by a Spanish television station, apparently told a different story.[17] Kasparov eventually conceded that the knight might have left his fingers for about "a fifth of a second,"[18] but the rules draw no distinction as to time. If he let go, his move was at an end.

Kasparov's incredible talent and his will to win are both admirable, but his handling of this incident is not. Given that his integrity was being called into question, perhaps Kasparov should have conceded from the first that he might after all have let go of the knight—like Feinstein's golfer, whether he could remember it or not—and then moved it and waited to see whether Polgar could find the riposte that would make her the first woman ever to defeat a reigning men's world chess champion. Instead, he managed to look small-minded and to leave open questions about the very integrity that he sought, through his feverish denials, to safeguard.

Integrity, as I have explained since chapter 1, usually means following the rules, even when following the rules costs victory. Sometimes integrity means breaking the rules, but only with a good and clear and openly articulated reason that appeals to a superior moral virtue. "Otherwise I would lose" is not one. Part of the work of raising children to live in society is teaching them which situations are which. Playing and watching sports are among the ways that children learn about the world. If we teach them here, in the arena of fun and games, that winning is the highest value, they will carry that lesson on to other, more serious areas of life, where we can expect them to act corruptly. If, on the other hand, we teach them here, in the arena of fun, that rules are made to be followed, we prepare them for lives of integrity in which something far more important than winning must be at stake before they are allowed to break the rules.

(eleven)

Coda: The Integrity of Civil Disobedience

Bur if the desire to win is not a sufficient reason to break the law, what is? The integral life, remember, is a discerning life, one in which we spend time in moral reflection. What do we do when our discernment leads us to conclude that the laws of the society are unjust? On the one hand, as we have seen since chapter 1, integrity demands a healthy respect for the rules laid down. On the other hand, as we have seen since chapter 2, many of the most honored figures in the pantheon of integral Americans are people we admire precisely because of their willingness to break laws they considered unjust.

We face this dilemma often in our lives, although at a less exalted level than the great civil disobedients of our history. We imagine ourselves to be a nation of laws, and our political rhetoric is full of old saws and wise sayings to reinforce our imagination, but the uneasy truth is that we are a vigorously lawless nation. Whether our problem is too many laws, or a national flaw in character, or something else, we disobey our laws in ways and at a pace that should make us the envy of lawbreakers everywhere. We cheat on our taxes, we exceed the speed limit, we cross against the light, we litter—and we do none of these things out of a sense of integrity.

When seemingly minor breaches of law in the name of convenience become our habit, we begin to lose regard for others. That we understand this is evident every time a parent asks a child to think about what would happen if *everybody* did it—the *it* being anything from littering to running into the street. But sometimes only one person must act in an antisocial way in order to mess things up for lots of others. We saw an extreme example of this in the late spring of 1995, when a passenger who apparently was late for his flight dashed past the security gates at the Houston airport without waiting to be screened. The unarmed guard could do nothing but call for help. When authorities were unable to locate the man, the entire concourse was shut down and every single passenger—several thousand in all—had to pass through the security gates anew.

Perhaps it is precisely because so many of us so often break the law out of naked self-interest that we seem to admire so deeply the integrity of lawbreakers who stand up against unjust laws, the civilly disobedient who face punishment unflinchingly. Many of the heroic figures of our history would bear that description, none more so, perhaps, than the Reverend Martin Luther King, Jr., whose shining example and shining rhetoric constitute a virtual textbook on the principles of nonviolent civil disobedience. Given our admiration for the integrity of many disobedients, it is useful for the student of integrity to pause and consider just what it is about them that we admire—and whether there are lessons even for those of us who may lack both the certainty and the fortitude that give disobedience its great power over the imagination.

DISOBEDIENCE AND INTEGRITY

I begin with the proposition that every person of integrity must be, by definition, a morally reflective individual. Thus every person of integrity will judge the actions of others or of the state (or of herself) against some moral code, will at times decide that the state is acting immorally, and will occasionally perceive the necessity of creating an identity between her private moral judgment and her public action. Integrity will demand it. I am not concerned here with whether in some other moral scheme, different from hers, the imposition of her morality as public law is justified. I insist only that the time will come when she sees the need to challenge the practices of the state because they do not accord with her moral judgment.

Sometimes the citizen who is unhappy with the laws will seek to change them through the processes that already exist in the state for that purpose.

In the United States, such action might include petitioning the legislature, supporting a new slate of candidates, or challenging in the courts the law that individuals perceive as unjust.

More interesting to the student of integrity is how to treat individuals who break the laws to which they object. Sometimes they break the laws openly, presenting a public appeal to some morality that is said to be higher than law. The appeal may be religious. In any case, such an appeal requires a public and open disobedience of the law. The classic American examples of this appeal are the sit-ins and other nonviolent disobedient activities associated with the civil rights movement of the 1950s and 1960s. A more recent example (and I intend no analogy) is Operation Rescue, in which pro-life activists have blocked the entrances of facilities in which abortions are performed.*

Sometimes individuals break the objectionable law covertly. An example is the Sanctuary movement that flourished in the eighties, the church-based drive to save Central American refugees from deportation by shielding them from the Immigration and Naturalization Service. So is the practice (I am assured by my friends that it exists) of shuffling figures on one's federal income-tax return in order to avoid providing money for a cause that one dislikes. This category might also include noncooperation, such as the protesters of Operation Rescue who, at times, have chosen a strategy in which they allow themselves to be arrested but refuse to give the authorities such basic information as their names or addresses.

Every coherent moral and political philosophy allows for the possibility that citizens will break the law for moral reasons. We generally subsume all those actions under the category of civil disobedience. And philosophers are largely agreed (but not unanimous) that civil disobedience must not be violent and must somehow be proportional to the moral harm to

---

*My subject here is only nonviolent acts of civil disobedience. I do not deal here with the question of violence versus nonviolence, which is covered in my book *The Dissent of the Governed* (Harvard University Press, 1996). I will note that the rhetoric used to justify acts of political violence is often identical to the rhetoric used to justify acts of nonviolent resistance. In the minds of those who commit violence, nonviolent action will sometimes appear to be less effective than violent action; indeed, as the philosopher David Lyons among others has pointed out, nonviolent action at times entails greater social costs than violent action. Suffice for the moment to say that the circumstances in which violent resistance are justified, at least in the United States of America, are so rare as not to need any special discussion, and those who believe otherwise quite properly bear an enormous burden of persuasion.

be avoided or undone. It is difficult to disagree with these precepts. For the student of integrity, the more interesting question is one over which philosophers have battled for centuries: Do civilly disobedient citizens have a general obligation either to act publicly in their disobedience or to stand punishment for what they have done? Must all of us follow the famous example of Socrates in the *Crito*, who willingly drinks poison to show his respect for his city, even though the law under which he has been sentenced to die is manifestly unjust?

A growing number of contemporary theorists reject the idea that individuals have even a presumptive obligation either to obey the law or to stand punishment for their disobedience.[1] Such notions are often looked on as quaint relics of a more primitive era in the development of political philosophy. The arguments of Gandhi and King, the twentieth century's twin icons of nonviolent resistance, are derided by contemporary philosophers through omission; they are treated as mere political polemics, not even worth a serious scholar's mention, to say nothing of a refutation.

The model of integrity I have been defending suggests, by contrast, that the answer to the question is yes: the morally reflective citizen, after due deliberation and discernment, may act to disobey the law, but must then be willing to say openly what he or she has done and why. Indeed, the rules fit civil disobedience perfectly. Having discerned what is right and what is wrong, the individual must now act—here, break the law—and, having acted, must also be forthright about what he or she has done.

But are matters so simple? Consider what is sometimes known as the "Nazi exception." For example, the legal scholar Michael Perry, in his book *Morality, Politics, and Law*, writes:

> the position that disobedience must be open or public to be legitimate is ... untenable. In the United States during the era of slavery, did those who operated the underground railroad act illegitimately because they acted covertly? ... [P]urposes other than the open protest normally associated with civil disobedience may underlie a valid claim that disobedience is morally justified. Sometimes a law is so wicked that the actor rightly acts to circumvent it. The person who contrary to the law assisted Jews to escape Nazi Germany acted morally.[2]

Not only that, but for similar reasons there is no obligation to stand punishment either: "If someone was illegally engaged in helping Jews escape from Nazi Germany, to have given himself up would have made it impossible for him to continue in that aid. It would have been perfectly moral for him to try to avoid punishment." Moreover, if someone helping Jews escape from Nazi Germany had been detected, he would have been no more obligated to refrain from attempting to escape Nazi Germany than were the Jews he had been helping.[3]

Obviously, no one will disagree with the force of these views. But they draw their force significantly from the moral consensus on the status of particular regimes. One is a state based on the enslavement of other human beings, the other a state with a fundamental policy of genocide.

Consequently, there is a reason that the examples resonate powerfully with the modern reader: Both are drawn from regimes that are essentially unjust. It seems quite unlikely that the disobedient citizens who sheltered Jews in Nazi Germany were saying to themselves, "The government isn't so bad if it would just stop killing the Jews"; such a position about the Nazi regime would have been morally monstrous. More likely, the disobedient Germans would not be engaged in law reform at all. The judgment to help Jews escape would be partly moral, but also pragmatic, logical, even the result of instrumental rationality. Given my goal, the citizen has asked herself, how best can I attain it? The answer in Nazi Germany was evidently that change—in the sense of saving Jews—could be brought about only by evading punishment. But note that changing the law was not the objective of the disobedient citizen who was hiding Jews. This is not to deny that she would have celebrated had the law been changed, but she was not hiding Jews in order to convince the state of the futility of its persecution of them. She was hiding them to save their lives.

But of course there is a reason that she was not hiding them in order to change the law. She undoubtedly disbelieved in the possibility of changing the law. If a society possesses a sufficiently unjust law that will not be changed (except, perhaps, by force), the society itself may be described as an unjust one. If the society is unjust, then the presumptive duty to obey its law is nonexistent. Consequently, the citizen of Nazi Germany who hid Jews was not engaging in civil disobedience at all. She was engaging in rebellion, for she denied the authority of the state in which she lived. In other words, the Nazi example involves disobedience by those who challenged the justice not of one law but of the state itself. In my view, the same is true of the example drawn from the period when slavery was legal in the United States.

So examples of this kind actually teach us very little about the proper moral consequences of disobedience in the United States. No doubt there are disobedient citizens of the United States who also deny the authority of the state, and who also consider the government fundamentally unjust and therefore consider themselves freed from any presumptive duty to obey its laws. We have seen this recently not only in the attention paid to the so-called militia movement but in the rhetoric of the self-described Constitutionalists, who deny the authority of all constitutional amendments adopted subsequent to the Bill of Rights. For such citizens, the decision that moral action requires sheltering oneself from prosecution will often be an easy one. But the rest of us are under no obligation to *agree* with the moral judgment of the dissenter.

Most Americans probably consider their government—their society—essentially just, and my empirical hunch is that most Americans consider the laws promulgated by their own government presumptively entitled to respect. And for people who would concede that the United States as a society is radically different from Nazi Germany (some members of the left and right fringes, I know, would not), for people, in short, who find this society, with all its flaws, essentially just, the disobedience of its laws will surely carry an obligation that is different from the one that might have attached to disobedience of Nazi law by German citizens who considered their society an unjust one.[4]

For the student of integrity, disobedience to law, even in a just society, is ultimately a matter for discernment by individual conscience. That does not mean that the state cannot or should not punish its disobedients; it means only that the moral assessment must necessarily be made first by the citizen, in reflection. But in the course of that reflection, a member of a civic community must give weight to the contrary opinions of the majority: we are not, in civil society, laws unto ourselves. Perhaps, on somber moral reflection, a citizen will come to the opinion that the majority is wrong. But for an individual who believes that the society in which he or she lives is essentially a just one, there is no fitter signal of personal integrity, of wholeness of being, and of membership in the society than to be public in one's disobedience, to make the act itself a communication. So it would seem that people of integrity who live in societies they consider essentially just have a strong and perhaps irrefutable reason for standing punishment when they disobey the law.

JUST AND UNJUST SOCIETIES

Since the era of classical antiquity, human beings have debated the source of the obligation to obey the laws of the societies in which they find themselves. Because virtue requires it, said the Greeks. Because God wills it, insisted the Christian tradition. No, said the Enlightenment thinkers, the reason is that there is a social contract among us all.

The debate continues today with remarkable fervor, a sign that in the West, anyway, we are never entirely happy with the thought that others may be able to tell us what to do. Of course, there have been some changes. Hardly anybody believes in the social contract anymore because none of us ever actually agreed to be bound, and the case for tacit consent (Locke's notion that you have to accept the society's burdens once you accept its benefits) has, on somber reflection, proven to be shoddy. Lots of theorists have tried to fill the void with a variety of creative arguments for a presumptive obligation to obey the law in all, most, or some circumstances. Others deny that individuals have even one strong reason for obeying the law simply because it is the law.[5]

I would like to sidestep that debate just a bit, for it runs outside our general subject, and consider the possibility that whatever may be the moral obligations of citizens *qua* citizens, not all citizens are similarly situated. There are always some—in America, I suspect it is most—who believe that the law is presumptively entitled to obedience just because it is the law. They do not engage in deep philosophical analysis on the point; it is simply what they believe. Respect for law is, one might say, part of the American ideology, the American Core I mentioned earlier. For the citizens who already think the law entitled to obedience, there is a compelling reason to be open and public in disobedience, and to stand punishment if the society chooses to administer it.[6]

I would suggest that the individual's own assessment of the justice or injustice of her society must carry moral force in her decision on whether the society's laws are presumptively entitled to obedience. Out across America (albeit relatively far from the academy) are millions of individuals with a deep and abiding faith in the essential justice of their nation's institutions, a faith that leads them to presume, in their own minds, that the commands of law are entitled to obedience. One of the reasons for the love-it-or-leave-it rhetoric of the 1960s was surely an unwillingness on the part of many Americans to believe that there could be fellow citizens who did not share their faith.*

True, we do not know the source of this faith. For some, the faith is a

---

*Faith of this kind is not consent in the contractarian sense. The faith would, however, play a large role—perhaps the major role—in the decisions by those individuals who shared it on whether disobedience of law was right or wrong. Thus, for the purpose of determining obligation, the faith might plausibly be described as the functional equivalent of consent.

form of patriotism. For others, it has religious roots, as in the "two-kingdom" tradition of Luther. And whatever its source, we must be cautious about suggesting that the faith alone is what makes the laws legitimate. When we condemn politicians who take bribes or kids who sell drugs, we are not saying to ourselves, "The reason we Americans should obey the law is that we think so," which would have an unsettlingly recursive character. We are supposing, I think, that there is a *reason* somewhere out there for our ready assumption that the American Core generally requires obedience to the law—we just are not quite able to articulate what that reason is.

But that is all right. The philosopher Joseph Raz has this answer: "[I]ll-articulated as many people's thoughts sometimes are in substance, they often amount to an assumption of semi-voluntary performative submission to an authority, because it is a morally worthwhile attitude to have."[7] In the American context, this would mean that most of us find it "morally worthwhile" to treat the law as presumptively entitled to respect. We could not hold this view if we did not also share the faith that I have described in the basic justice of our society and its governmental arrangements. Perhaps this faith is best captured in the often misused word *patriotism*—for the real patriots are those who believe that paying taxes to the United States of America is a privilege, not those who steal the word, then arm themselves and dress in camouflage uniforms and denounce the federal government as an illegitimate occupying force. In our experience, the true disobedient is committed to the reform, not the destruction, of the state; the disobedient usually seeks to persuade her fellow citizens of the justice of her cause. As Ronald Dworkin has put the point: "Civil disobedience, in all its various forms and strategies, has a stormy and complex relationship with majority rule. It does not reject the principle entirely, as a radical revolutionary might; civil disobedients remain democrats at heart."[8]

Of course, one must be careful here. Dworkin's generalization does not describe all civil disobedients, but it is true of many, and in America probably most. Once this affection for majority-rule democracy exists, its source scarcely matters. The point is not, however, that we have a special obligation to obey laws that are generated through the democratic process. Even a democratic society can produce very bad laws. To strain the example that opened the chapter, the moral case for disobedience in Nazi Germany would not have been weakened had Hitler been elected democratically or had a majority of Germans approved genocide at the polls. But the case for a presumptive obligation to obey the laws of a just society does not turn on whether that society styles itself as democratic. (We would then have to define democracy. Try!) It turns instead on the individual's faith that the law must, in most cases, be obeyed. Our inability to track that faith to its source does not make the faith less real.

Consider an example:

Example 11-1. A resident of the American South during the era of chattel slavery objects on religious grounds to slavery and therefore agrees to make his house available as a stop on the Underground Railroad. When confronted by the authorities who are searching for escaped slaves—and for the people who are helping them escape—he denies any involvement.

Observation 11-1(a). One could conclude that he is not showing integrity because he is being covert. Perry would excuse him on the ground that openness in his disobedience would make it impossible for him to achieve his ends. I would answer that this instrumental notion is beside the point. He need not be open about his disobedience, but only if he rejects not the law alone but the justice of his society, in this case the slave South. If he sees his society and its people as essentially just, he has a presumptive obligation to obey the laws and thus to stand punishment if he breaks them.

Observation 11-1(b). The fact that we, as twentieth-century Americans, would likely regard as absurd the suggestion that the people along the Underground Railroad had an obligation to go public and face punishment is evidence that we do not view the society in which they lived and struggled as a just one.

Observation 11-1(c). Even if he elects not to be public in his disobedience, he is still taking a risk in his actions—he could still be caught and punished—and for that he indeed gets points for integrity.

The main point is that the individual reflection that integrity demands may be addressed to a larger target than any particular law; judgment can be passed on the society as a whole. Surely the respect that underlies the obligation to obey can be shattered in a radically discontinuous manner by a radically unjust result of democratic processes. As in the Nazi example, a law may be so bad that it sunders not merely the presumptive obligation to obey that particular law, but also the self-conscious link of the individual to the community. Indeed, the force of the Nazi example as one in which the ties of obligation are sundered helps explain why it has become so ubiquitous. In the sixties and early seventies, it was commonly used by rhetoricians of the left, marking as Nazis and Fascists and storm troopers the

police, the National Guard, the Federal Bureau of Investigation, and anybody else who could be described as the satraps of oppression. Nowadays,
the rhetoric is used on the far right, with the National Rifle Association's reference to federal agents as "jack-booted thugs" (a statement for which the
group later apologized) only the most prominent example. Whether used
by the left or the right, the point is the same: if you can convince your fol-
lowers that the other side is like the Nazis, you can hope to dissolve even
the presumptive obligation to obey the law that most of us grow up with.

One of the reasons, then, that discernment is particularly important in
the case of the civil disobedient is that the citizen who contemplates defying the law must also take time to reflect on whether it is the particular law
or the larger society that is the symbol of injustice. There will always be a
temptation to say that it is the second if so saying excuses us from any
obligation to stand punishment, and that is why it is important to reflect
long enough and hard enough to be sure.

THE DISOBEDIENCE OF DR. KING

Martin Luther King, Jr., the principal exponent of nonviolent resistance to
unjust law during the American civil rights movement, held that the individual whose integrity moved her to disobey the law had a moral obligation to stand punishment. His reasons are instructive and, for people who
consider the state essentially just, they are to my mind unrefuted as well.

King laid out his thesis squarely in an address that he gave in 1961: "I
submit that the individual who disobeys the law, whose conscience tells
him it is unjust and who is willing to accept the penalty by staying in jail
until that law is altered, is expressing at the moment the very highest
respect for law."[9] The thesis over the years has been the subject of much
criticism and debate and, as I mentioned, is not popular among contemporary philosophers. But its ringing, aspirational justification squares better than the alternatives with the faith that most of us share in the essential justice of our society, a faith that, among people of integrity, may
generate a presumptive obligation to obey the society's laws.

It is no accident that King was a man of the cloth, for the religions are
natural centers of dissent. A religion fully lived denies the authority of the
rest of the world over the aspects of life that are, to the religionist, of central importance. "Above all," as the theologian David Tracy has pointed
out, "the religions are exercises in resistance."[10] And so they have been in
American history, witnessing openly for change. Sometimes these resisting

religious voices are right, sometimes they are wrong. Sometimes they win, sometimes they lose. But we are always a stronger and better nation for their presence.

For King, disobedience had one purpose: change. And for a citizen who believes her society essentially just, change is necessarily the reason for action, because her faith in society's justice carries with it an optimism about the society's capacity to undo its acts of injustice. This is why King's disobedience was relentlessly optimistic, why he premised his justification for disobedience on the supposition that the hearts of others could be moved by the spectacle of the state's oppression. In this sense, he believed in the essential justice of the state, which is why he was able to say, in accepting the Nobel Peace Prize in 1964: "I refuse to accept the view that mankind is so tragically bound to the starless midnight of racism and war that the bright daybreak of peace and brotherhood can never become a reality."[11] King believed in a state comprising essentially decent people who would finally be willing to change its laws. Consequently, his vision of the state and its people was much like the vision that animates contemporary liberal political theory: a nation of reflective, deliberative individuals who are willing to engage in dialogue about policy and to change their minds if convinced that they are wrong.

King's optimism, his sense that dialogue, once joined, can lead to change, is illustrated by his most famous writing on the topic of disobedience, the *Letter from Birmingham City Jail*, in which he wrote: "Nonviolent direct action seeks to create . . . a crisis and establish such creative tension that a community that has constantly refused to negotiate is forced to confront the issue. It seeks so to dramatize the issue that it can no longer be ignored."[12] The idea was to change the system by changing the minds and hearts of the people who ran it. This faith in dialogue was intimately linked to his justification for the claim that the disobedient citizen should stand punishment. Thus, in the same essay, he penned this well-known passage:

> In no sense do I advocate evading or defying the law as the rabid segregationist would do. This would lead to anarchy. One who breaks an unjust law must do it *openly, lovingly* (not hatefully as the white mothers did in New Orleans when they were seen on television screaming, "nigger, nigger, nigger"), and with a willingness to accept the penalty. I submit that an individual who breaks a law that conscience tells him is unjust, and willingly accepts the penalty by staying in jail to arouse the conscience of the community over its injustice, is in reality expressing the very highest respect for law.[13]

Clearly, this argument makes sense only if one first accepts the essential justness of the state. One who believes the state unjust can have little hope that an open and loving act of disobedience will accomplish very much (although, in the right circumstances, it might accomplish a little). But one who believes that the state is essentially just necessarily believes that unjust laws can be changed. She shares the personal moral judgment of most of her fellow citizens, a judgment that counsels a respect for law and a presumptive obligation to obey. She can show no greater love for the ideal of just law and no greater faith in the capacity of just societies to change than by submitting herself to punishment under the law that is unjust.

King's argument is entirely persuasive for those individuals whose goal in disobedience is change. But even in a just society, there may be other goals that prompt disobedience. The principal "other goal" is circumvention—not so much changing the law as avoiding its effect. To the circumventer, avoiding punishment is the point of the strategy. I recognize that the judgment on whether morality counsels disobedience must ultimately be left to each individual. But as a student of integrity, I must confess to a skepticism on circumvention: if one truly believes that the society is essentially just, then, following King's argument, one should be trying to change it for the better. If one feels free to disregard the presumptive obligation, expressed in the American Core, to obey the law—if, perhaps, one does not believe that it exists—then perhaps one does not after all consider the society just.

Having said that, I must concede that in American society, circumvention is surely the most common form of disobedience. In the literature of disobedience, the frequent examples involve such actions as exceeding the speed limit or making a U-turn in the wee hours of the morning or trespassing on private land far from anyone's sight.[14] These are not examples of disobedience after discernment, however, except in a very crude sense, and the moral justification for avoiding punishment is not particularly strong. They are examples, rather, of personal convenience, of putting self-interest ahead of community judgment on legal norms. In this sense, the individuals in the examples are not civil disobedients at all, at least not in the traditional sense, and they are displaying no integrity—they are simple, humdrum lawbreakers. They are not, in Ronald Dworkin's phrase, engaged in activity that is "very different from ordinary criminal activity motivated by selfishness or anger or cruelty or madness."[15] They are simply trying to get away with something, and figuring, no doubt correctly, that it is not worth anyone's trouble to prosecute them. But they are making no moral claim. Were it worthwhile to prosecute—were the town to announce a sudden crackdown on early-morning speeders (indeed, were a police car to appear in the rearview mirror)—the speeder would no doubt slow down. Were the rancher suddenly to appear with a shotgun, the trespasser would surely scurry for safer territory. In neither case is it likely that the disobedient would purport to have a *moral* claim to support her disobedience.

Do not mistake my point here. In classing those who speed at four o'clock in the morning as lawbreakers, I do not mean to say that they are necessarily immoral. I am no paragon of lawfulness: I do the same thing. The point that each of us must finally confess, however, is that there is no integrity in our wee-hour disobedience, and the evidence of that is the unlikelihood that we could, with straight face, present a justification for our behavior that sounded like morality rather than convenience.

It seems entirely plausible, moreover, that when we make our U-turns at two in the morning, we conceive of ourselves not as protesting the law, not even as violating it, but rather as interpreting it. Perhaps we are thinking, "The rule against U-turns could not have been intended to cover this situation. I will interpret it in accordance with its purpose—as a safety rule—in order to make sense of its terms in the real world in which they must be applied." Perhaps the law enforcement authorities might even connive in this interpretation. Cognitive dissonance problems aside, if this is what we believe, then we may not be disobedient at all; we may be *obeying* the law as we understand it. And certainly we are not disobedient in the strong sense of an individual whose integrity compels disobedience because the hard work of discernment has determined that the law is unjust.

Michael Perry offers the further example of a black person who uses a whites-only bathroom, asking: "In what way does a black person's violation of the law contravene the norm of fairness?"[16] The answer is that if the black person does it for convenience alone, without regard to moral judgment about the law itself, then that person is arguably in the same position as the early-morning speeder: both are humdrum lawbreakers making no moral claim. If, on the other hand, the black person is engaged in a strategy of circumvention, then the goal is to change the law. If (as might be the case) the black person considers the state itself essentially unjust, then there is little to be gained by standing punishment. If, however, the black person considers the state essentially just, then we are back once more to the civil rights movement, and the protester must confront King's argument that when integrity counsels disobedience of the laws of an essentially just society, she shows the highest respect for the ideal of just law when she stands punishment. If she seeks to avoid punishment, she is challenging the justness not simply of the law but—at least implicitly—of the society that has enacted it. As an African American in the age of segregation, the disobedient in Perry's example would have every right to do so; and it is part of the power of King's example that he was able to face a society that insisted on such massive injustice and state nevertheless that the nation and its people were essentially good.

But, again, the goal of King's disobedience was to provoke dialogue; the goal of the dialogue was change. In his vision, a just society was one that could be inspired by the open and loving defiance of others to change the objectionable laws. Conversely, a society that could not be moved by nonviolent protest was not really a just one. If the black person who uses the bathroom reserved for whites is trying to change the law but also considers the society essentially just, then she has a strong reason for standing punishment for her disobedience. Consequently, she has good reason to reject the strategy of circumvention.

It is possible, however, to envision situations in which an individual might consider her society a just one, and therefore concede a strong presumption in favor of standing punishment for disobedience, but nevertheless reject the presumption in favor of circumvention. I have in mind the situation of something like the Sanctuary movement, which stands on a different footing because of its different goal.

This movement, which flourished in the eighties and is still around in diminished form, was made up of Americans whose personal moral judgments insisted that returning Salvadoran refugees, or passively allowing their arrest and deportation by the government, was wrong. According to King's argument, if they considered the law unjust and the state just, the members of the movement should have stood punishment. If they accepted the state as essentially just, their presumptive obligation was to make their case by legal means or, if they chose to break the law, to let the punishment itself serve as their argument.

But the obligation is only presumptive. Although it gives the individuals in question a very strong reason to obey the law or stand punishment, the presumption can be rebutted. The members of the Sanctuary movement, by choosing the strategy of circumvention, in effect proclaimed their rebuttal of the presumption in their particular case. Although in most ways the Sanctuary movement was just like any other disobedient group, it differed in one crucial respect: its goal was not simply to change the law but also to save the refugees. Had its disobedience been open, had the members of the movement stood punishment, then saving the refugees might have been impossible. For the movement's adherents, this difference was plainly sufficient to place their circumvention in a different moral light.

Similarly, the pro-life activists of Operation Rescue have at times adopted a strategy of noncooperation, under which they are arrested and charged (it is difficult to envision a covert blocking of the entrance to a clinic), but refuse to give authorities such basic booking information as their names and addresses. The logic of this strategy is that if the protesters refuse to cooperate, the machinery that seeks to prosecute them will slow down and perhaps grind to a halt. This is an extension of the notion that one form of protest is to overwhelm the system of criminal justice rather than use it as a forum for moral debate—a notion that was common in the antiwar movement of the sixties. If the strategy works, then even though the protest is public, the noncooperation must be classed as circumvention—for the protesters are trying not to stand trial for their offenses.

I have already mentioned my skepticism on circumvention as a strategy in a just society. If one must circumvent, however, the decision should at least be preceded by genuine discernment. And I think it important to the ideal of dialogue that even those who decide to keep their disobedience secret find some other means for joining debate in the larger society. All of us, no matter how morally reflective, no matter how morally certain, must be ever aware of the possibility of learning from the often quite different moral sentiments of others.

However, the conclusion that particular acts of disobedience should be concealed is fraught with both practical and analytical risks. One of these I have mentioned before: there is always the risk that the disobedients have "discerned" no obligation to stand punishment simply because they do not want to. Two more bear brief discussion.

First, it is quite conceivable that any disobedient individual could recast her moral conclusion to say that her purpose is not simply to protest the law: morality, she might say, requires her to avoid its effects. Indeed, the protester will often be tempted to do so. As the philosopher Carl Cohen has observed, however, "Such claims are often mistaken and are sometimes outrageous."[17] So, for example, the tax protester might say that it is not only the immorality of the tax that is her concern, but also the immorality of the jail sentence that follows upon conviction. No one could say that this seamless argument is exactly wrong, but it does not seem a particularly appealing case when weighed against King's lofty rhetoric on open

and loving defiance. The principal point, then, is that an individual convinced of the justice of her society and the injustice of one of its laws ought
to search her soul to be very sure that circumvention really is the only
effective strategy.

Second, the claim that the Sanctuary movement, or any other protest movement, stands on a different footing because of the necessity of secrecy
reduces moral judgment to a question of instrumental rationality—the issue
is not the end but the means. The goal of the disobedience is no longer
changing the law by changing the hearts of the lawgivers, nor is it to engage
in a dialogue with one's fellow citizens; instead, the goal is freedom to act
as though the objectionable law did not exist. In a sense, the goal is a laudable one, for it is difficult to criticize people of integrity for acting out the
dictates of the reflectively formed conscience. Yet it is difficult to see how
circumvention as a strategy advances the public dialogue that ought to char-
acterize our societal reflection on tough moral issues. Writes the philosopher
John Rawls:

> [C]ivil disobedience is a public act. Not only is it addressed to public prin-
> ciples, it is done in public. It is engaged in openly with fair notice; it is
> not covert or secretive. One may compare it to public speech, and being
> a form of address, an expression of profound and conscientious political
> conviction, it takes place in the public forum.[18]

In short, the proposition that even in an essentially just society, one's
integrity can demand a quiet and hidden circumvention of the law, without legal consequences for the protesters, should sit uneasily upon the
consciences of integral individuals who believe in dialogue and who consider the law of their society presumptively worthy of respect because the
society itself is essentially just.

DISOBEDIENCE AND DIALOGUE

Another consideration that weighs in favor of openness of disobedience in
a state that is essentially just is the commitment that such a society ought to
have public moral dialogue as the preferred means for resolving difficult
questions of policy. For those who view the liberal state as a place in which
citizens undertake rational deliberations about morality and policy, the principle of dialogue has an obvious appeal. The Enlightenment emphasized
the ability of humans to come to moral conclusions through exercising their

faculty of reason, and the Neo-Enlightenment liberals of the current era make the exercise of reason the rule—that is, conclusions that are reached through less rational decision processes (as liberalism itself defines rationality) are excluded from the universe of discourse. The rationality requirement is in theory a mediating force. It permits communities with different moral and epistemological premises to argue with one another over policy, so long as they are willing to put aside their respective preferred means of understanding the world in order to engage in the form of dialogue that is available to everyone.

In general, I find this model attractive, although, as I have noted elsewhere, I confess to some dissatisfaction with the use of a rationality requirement as the tool that mediates the dialogue. My particular concern is the use of the requirement to exclude religious views from our public dialogues.[19] My own strong preference is to envision the liberal state as one in which citizens may enter the dialogue in ways and at times of their own choosing, but in which they are encouraged to be morally reflective both prior to and subsequent to entrance. The advantage of dialogue so understood is that it includes individuals whose concepts of how fundamental morality is discovered might be at war with the liberal notion of rationality. This is a difference that matters, because a dialogue that excludes dissenters by defining their views as irrelevant is not a truly liberal one. All should be welcome, provided only that they seek to be morally reflective and to listen generously to the counsels of their opponents.

In a world of reflective, self-aware individuals who treat fellow citizens with respect, it is difficult to understand why any particular form of dialogue must be excluded *ex ante*. To try to envision a reflective and self-aware individual who separates her basic moral convictions (including her religious convictions) from the rest of her world view is to imagine a poorly integrated personality, for the effort would destroy anyone else as a person. On the other hand, once the religiously devout citizen, or any other citizen, chooses to participate in public dialogue, she commits herself to listen as well as to speak, and to think and act in a reflective and generous spirit.

There are risks to any strategy of change that values public dialogue, among them the obvious risk that the bad guys might win; but that risk occurs in every form of government and, for that matter, in every form of anarchy. Of more immediate concern in a nation such as ours, where too many citizens lack the energy or the patience for direct participation in the dialogue of governance, is the risk, not an insubstantial one, that one side or another will win not because it has the better argument but simply because it wears the other down. There is no satisfactory response to this challenge, except to note that, in a curious fashion, this possibility of change through sheer perseverance also reflects an ultimately positive judgment about human character—a judgment that formed a vital part of the optimism of Martin Luther King, Jr. According to King, people did not necessarily change because they wanted to. People sometimes changed because they had to, wound up saying yes because they tired of saying no. In an essay not published until after his death, King wrote:

America has not yet changed because so many think it need not change, but this is the illusion of the damned. America must change because twenty-three million black citizens will no longer live supinely in a wretched past. They have left the valley of despair; they have found strength in struggle; and whether they live or die, they shall never crawl nor retreat again. Joined by white allies, they will shake the prison walls until they fall. America must change.[20]

I do not know where or how to draw the line between a retreat in the face of superior force and a genuine change of heart that has been enriched through the process of public moral dialogue. I have a faith, however, that one is wrong and the other is right. I do know how to draw the line between an individual who believes her society and its law to be essentially just and one who does not; the line is drawn when she decides whether she has a presumptive obligation to obey the law just because it is the law—a decision that will in turn influence her determination whether to accept punishment for disobedience. One either believes in the efficacy of dialogue in a just society or one does not—but the one who does not cannot truly believe that the society is just. The greatest love that one can have for a society and its people, the greatest respect that one can show for the differing moral visions that create the objectionable law, is to sacrifice one's self-interest in order to change them.

The connection of this understanding to civil disobedience is clear. King's emphasis on religious faith and love for others in disobedience obviously reflects such a spirit. For individuals who accept the respect for law that is part of the American Core, who have come to believe in the obligation to obey, it is possible to act with similar faith and similar love simply by taking disobedience public. In openly resisting the law in order to change it, we invite dialogue; indeed, we insist on it. In King's terms, we "provoke" it. And in the process we demonstrate our respect for our fellow citizens and for their quite different conceptions of justice by submitting to their will. We may lose out in the dialogue—we may deserve to lose out in some cases—but we will not lose the morally worthy satisfaction of having acted correctly. And that is the principal, often the only, satisfaction that integrity offers.

(iii)

Ruminations

Let me be weighed in a just balance, and let God know my integrity

—Job 36:1

(twelve)

Can Integrity Be Legislated?

W E live in a regulated world; when something goes wrong, the contemporary solution is to regulate it. Legally. So if integrity is such a good thing—and if we truly have less of it than we ought—then why not mandate it? Why not pass a law that says this person or that one *must* behave with integrity? In fact, we have tried to do just that, sometimes with a fair degree of success, as when we have regulated the securities markets, and many other times to our considerable embarrassment. We have tended to do it well when we have regulated something else under the name of integrity: prohibiting false advertising, for example, or forcing full disclosure in a prospectus. These are regulations, really, of honesty and fair dealing.

But we have done worse when we have tried to force people to act as though they are people of integrity. Our embarrassment has been particularly acute when we have tried to regulate the linked and diabolically volatile arenas of politics and speech. In this chapter, I offer three brief examples—not of our successes but of our failures. In examining them, we can perhaps learn what *not* to do; but in a political era that demands more searching and reflective justifications for government programs, that is surely important too.

NOT-SO-SPECIAL PROSECUTORS

In our regulatory age, we feel the need to prevent damage to our politics the same way we prevent damage to our environment: find the right rules, set up the right agency, and it's done. We have different instincts about how to do it, of course. Liberals tend to think that we need special prosecutors, and conservatives seem to think that we need term limits, or they used to; the elections in 1992 and 1994 seem to have messed things up a bit, so that congressional Republicans, at least, seem less sure about term limits, and Democrats who have seen the appointment of a record number of independent counsels during the Clinton administration are not so sure the statute was a good idea after all. Indeed, no President's administration in the admittedly brief history of the Ethics in Government Act has been investigated by as many independent counsels—what we call, colloquially, special prosecutors—as Bill Clinton's. Does this mean that the Clinton administration is unusually unethical? Of course not. It means that the Act itself, a well-intentioned but poorly reasoned piece of legislation, has gotten out of hand. And therein lies a lesson, for that is what often happens with regulations of integrity and other virtues. They get out of hand because they are trying fundamentally to regulate something that is (as we have seen) difficult even to define, much less to spot. The result, as we shall see, is to trade in ethics in favor of law, always America's habit and often America's nightmare.

A *New York Times* editorial, responding to complaints from the Clinton administration that the independent counsel appointments were becoming ridiculous, engaged in a bit of unintentional misdirection: "Proliferation of independent counsels is not a reason to revoke a law of proven value to clean government."[1] The trouble is that the law's value to clean government has not after all been proven, and the editorial simply asserted it; it cited no evidence, presumably because there isn't any.

For example, the Iran-Contra prosecutor Lawrence Walsh spent $36 million of public funds in his investigation and wound up putting *one* individual in jail. Now, one might say that we should not judge the success or failure of a prosecutor based on how many miscreants he locks up, and one would be right. (Although if the prosecutor in question were elected, the reelection campaign would not be much fun, except for the other party.) But it is reasonable to ask whether the discovery that nobody else can be put away is worth $36 million. Real-life prosecutors have to work out budget priorities, just like other government officials; special prosecutors evidently do not.

One might also suggest that Walsh might have been able to pack a few more people off to the federal penitentiary but for the fact that President Bush pardoned the lot before the prosecutor got his chance. This is a fair point. But it is a measure of how far the prestige of the independent counsel has fallen that Bush was *able* to issue the pardons. Richard Nixon, to take the simplest example, would not have dared—not after the public revulsion at his firing of Watergate special prosecutor Archibald Cox that led within ten months to his fall from office. But there are now so many independent counsels looking into so many relatively minor offenses that the public (and the media) cannot possibly keep track. In short, special prosecutors have become mundane, and the interminable Iran-Contra investigation did its part to make them that way.

But the larger problem with the independent counsel provisions of Title VI of the Ethics in Government Act is that they draw the wrong lesson from Watergate, and thus are based on a mistaken premise about the relationship between integrity and lawbreaking.

The Ethics in Government Act, which in one of its many earlier incarnations was called the Public Officials Integrity Act, was adopted in 1978, designed, in Hubert Humphrey's words, as "a major step toward a stronger, more accountable Government which can better command and justify public trust and confidence."[2] The Act set forth standards for disclosure of income and assets for certain public officials, created offices and agencies to look into alleged ethical violations—and provided in Title VI for the courts to appoint special prosecutors to investigate wrongdoing in the executive branch. (Amendments to allow courts to appoint special prosecutors to investigate members of Congress were defeated at the time and have been defeated as often as they have been raised.)

It is plain that the drafters did not imagine that Title VI of the Act would become what it has; they did not contemplate that there could possibly be so many investigations of so many relatively minor offenses; they were moved by a larger force. In the words of Senator Charles Percy, one of the bill's main sponsors, "Our common goal is that we want no more Watergates."[3] Again and again, supporters invoked it like a talisman, the magical name, Watergate (which has lost much of its magical presence because of the proliferation of silly neologisms for lesser offenses: Irangate, Iraqgate, Whitewatergate—and remember, during the Carter administration, Billygate?—today's schoolchildren must think my generation mad to make such a fetish of the word). They spoke of "the experience of Watergate"[4] and "the lessons of Watergate"[5] and even "the horrors known as Watergate."[6] Indeed, the statute itself began as a bill entitled the Watergate Reorganization and Reform Act.

This history matters. We sometimes forget how profound a set of wrongs Watergate entailed. It involved political espionage, we like to say, but that only begins to tell the tale. The evil of Watergate was, put most simply, a concerted effort to subvert the democratic processes, followed by a craven and panicky effort to cover up what had been done by commandeering the investigative processes of the Justice Department. It didn't work, of course; when the public saw the President of the United States fire the top officials of his own Justice Department in October 1973 because they would not dismiss the first special prosecutor, Archibald Cox, it was really all over. When the President's men fell, they fell very far and very hard— as did the President himself.

Archibald Cox was not, of course, an *independent* counsel; that is why he could be fired. One of the justifications for the Ethics in Government Act's provisions for *judicial* appointment of the prosecutor was so that the prosecutor might avoid Cox's fate. But a key part of the story is missing: firing Cox did no good. His lack of independence did not protect him personally, but Richard Nixon's lack of respect for legal process turned the public's collective stomach.

The dismissal of the Justice Department's leaders, the firing of Archibald Cox, and the sealing of his offices, guarded by agents of the Federal Bureau of Investigation, in what came to be known as the Saturday Night Massacre, led some commentators at the time to suggest that Richard Nixon had all but set up a Central American–style junta in Washington, D.C. (I believe I might have said a word or two on that theme myself, from my lofty nineteen years of experience on the face of the earth.) But the Republic was stronger than that. Instead, matters began at once to unravel, and they unraveled fast. Ten months later, Gerald Ford was President.

I emphasize these details for two reasons. One is to explain why it is not obvious that independence of the prosecutor is really necessary, as Gerard Lynch, a law professor who was himself once an independent counsel, has pointed out.[7] (I must confess that I am among those who believe that this deficiency makes the Ethics in Government Act unconstitutional,[8] but I must also confess that the Supreme Court rejected that argument years ago.)[9] Over the years, plenty of executive-branch wrongdoers have been indicted, tried, and convicted by ordinary prosecutors simply doing their jobs; and, again, Richard Nixon's efforts to subvert this process met ultimately with failure.

The second reason for the details is to remind all of us how vastly the offenses of the Nixon administration differed from what tends to be charged now. Allegedly using cocaine in a nightclub (what Hamilton Jordan was investigated for) or even losing money on a high-flying Arkansas land speculation (all, so far, that anybody with any evidence has accused Bill Clinton of doing) simply do not compare with trying to steal the Republic. When we refuse, as the Act refuses, to draw distinctions among possible criminal offenses, we begin to lose perspective. As Amitai Etzioni has written: "In order not to trivialize its moral voice, a community must focus on serious, recent, and especially repeat infractions—which are all too common—rather than taint everyone in sight with a broad brush."[10]

Assuming that Title VI of the Ethics in Government Act survives a GOP-controlled Congress that talks wistfully of repealing it, these suggestions might make useful amendments—that offenses must be serious and recent, perhaps even committed while in office, rather than the present statutory standard requiring the attorney general to seek an independent counsel whenever she believes further investigation of a covered official is needed. But they would not solve what may be the largest problem of all: the Ethics in Government Act, by focusing our attention so relentlessly on criminal conduct, actually dilutes the standards of public virtue that it was designed to uphold.

By establishing and exalting a special process for investigating possible criminal behavior by presidential functionaries, the statute raises the stakes too high (and lowers the standard far too much) in policing wrongdoing. Tocqueville observed a century and a half ago that Americans "think that oppression and tyranny should be treated like theft, by making prosecution easier and the penalty lighter."[11] Perhaps he was right. Perhaps it is still true today. We Americans really do not like to think of misbehaving officials as tyrants, and feel more comfortable if they can instead be labeled criminals.

It is difficult, however, to make all executive misbehaviors into crimes. In particular, it is difficult to criminalize a political lack of integrity—although several of the supporters of the Ethics in Government Act implied that they hoped to do just that. Yet because Title VI provides for independent investigation, indictment, and prosecution of miscreants among the President's minions, the focus in considering whether someone has misbehaved is on the narrow question of whether a crime has been committed. Members of the Congress (who would not dream of applying such a standard to themselves) constantly demand special prosecutors to look into one mess or another, as though the principal goal is not to ensure that the executive branch performs its work with integrity but rather to embarrass the President and, with luck, to throw a few of his cronies into jail.

Against this background, it is small wonder that those who are investigated by independent counsels generally refuse to resign, and that those who are investigated but not indicted—former attorney general Edwin Meese is a prominent example—proclaim themselves vindicated. Critics may complain that mere absence of criminal wrongdoing is too low a threshold for judging the integrity of executive behavior, and they are surely right, but it is the Congress itself, not the executive branch, that has effectively established the threshold. If Title VI did not exist, the Congress and the executive branch would be thrown back on the old rules, under which public officials were expected to resign when their improprieties became too great an embarrassment to the President—not to stay in office because the congressionally mandated criminal investigation might yet prove them to have met a significantly lower ethical standard.

Yet it is scarcely surprising that the Congress would make the category mistake that has led to the bizarre spectacle of executive employees, including a lengthening string of Presidents, acting as though the only standard of sound ethical behavior is the absence of criminal indictment. Ever since Watergate, and to some extent before, the Congress has pressed for deeper involvement in the micromanagement of the executive branch. That is what has created such ill-conceived (although possibly constitutional) innovations as the War Powers Resolution of 1973. Yet a Congress that would rather participate in decisions to commit troops (which is what the resolution allows it to do) than enact a statutory charter that defines the mission of the armed forces of the United States ought not to profess surprise when the President and his advisers define the mission in its stead.

Similarly, it seems that the Congress would rather have an independent counsel trying desperately to pin criminal charges on government officials whose ethics are shady than to create a clear and enforceable set of ethical guidelines that lead to a fall from office if transgressed. But in that case, the Congress (and the rest of us) ought not to profess astonishment when the miscreants hang stubbornly on, hoping for the vindication of non-indictment. For that, finally, is what Title VI of the Ethics in Government Act has wrought: no matter what I might do in office, as long as I am not indicted, I retain my integrity.

TRUE LIES?

In our fiction, which is also our truth, politicians lie, and they do it a lot. Not only do they lie in order to achieve public office, but they lie once they get there. Probably there is no conceivable—or at least sensible—legislative remedy for a politician's lies in the course of his or her work, which is why it is well that we hold periodic elections. But what about the problem of lying to get elected?

Remarkable though it may seem, the states have occasionally tried to regulate this—to make it a civil offense, and sometimes a crime, to lie in order to get elected.[12] In 1982, the Supreme Court decided the rather remarkable case of *Brown v. Hartlage*,[13] in which the state of Kentucky tried to strip a successful candidate of his seat on the county commission on the ground that he had violated state law by "mak[ing] an offer to the voter of pecuniary gain"—in other words, offering a bribe. And what was the bribe that Commissioner Brown had offered? He had promised that he would, if elected, reduce his own salary. This undertaking, frowned the Kentucky court, "is so vicious in its tendency as to constitute a violation of the Corrupt Practices Act." Why was it vicious? Because the salary is paid with tax dollars. So if the salary is reduced, taxes are reduced, and there is more money in the pocket of the voter, and . . . well, you get the idea.

Really. That's what happened.

The Supreme Court (unanimous for once, which happened in those halcyon days) held that the First Amendment prohibited applying the law that way. Why? Because of the "chilling effect"—one of those great if overused phrases of our constitutional jurisprudence—and also because, even if the Kentucky court correctly analyzed the effect of the promise, it was no different than a promise to lower taxes or to increase efficiency in government. Indeed, when *Brown* was decided, the nation had just two years earlier elected by a landslide a President who promised to do both those things. Following the Kentucky court's analysis, that was like offering a bribe. (Why didn't the Democrats think of that argument?)

But understand the possible ethical sensibility underlying the Kentucky court's perhaps overly wroth opinion. The court might have been concerned that promises that have the effect of putting money in the voters' pockets appeal to our baser natures; that we are called to think of ourselves as atomistic individuals rather than members of a community. In that way (the court might have reasoned) our political integrity is indeed subverted, because the voters dwell not on the larger questions of right and wrong that should, in theory, occasion hard reflection before a ballot is cast, but on the more mundane and self-interested problem of fulfilling their own appetites. (A very similar dilemma confronted voters in Oregon in 1995, as supporters of expansive casino gambling promised every voter about one hundred dollars a year should the gambling initiative pass.) Again, one thinks of Martin Luther's stricture to suffer all things when only our own needs are involved, but to do all things to fulfill somebody else's. Perhaps Kentucky was simply trying to use the statute as a lever to get candidates to talk this way so that voters might vote this way.

And even if that possibility seems too far-fetched, consider the next logical point. Take the U.S. Supreme Court's opinion this time as our text. Suppose now that the candidate *does* promise to cut taxes or to make government more efficient. Suppose further that the candidate is then elected. And suppose that the candidate then breaks those promises. Does the First Amendment mean that his or her behavior cannot be punished?

Any number of states have tried to restrict deceptive campaign advertising, with decidedly mixed results in the courts.[14] But I have in mind a different problem: a lawsuit, for example, by a voter who feels that he or she was duped, a suit, say, for breach of contract.* I suppose that the courts would probably dismiss it—citing once more, the dreaded "chilling effect"—although the people most likely to be chilled are voters, who have come to assume that politicians will *not* keep their promises, leading to an eerie contest in which the voters sometimes seem to be voting for the candidate with the best promises, not the one most likely to keep them.

This leads us to the larger problem with the integrity of our elections, a problem that no regulation can resolve. It is our conceit that free speech, particularly in political campaigns, leads to a better-informed electorate. Unfortunately, there is reason to think that more and more voters may be opting to cast their ballots while steeped in what political scientists call "rational ignorance": a state of ignorance that one makes a rational decision to maintain. To put the matter simply, a voter chooses rational ignorance when he or she knows that there is more information to be had about a candidate but chooses not to get it because the cost of obtaining it is greater than the value of having it. In an era when fewer and fewer voters seem to think that they (or their votes) matter, it is not hard to see why so many would make this choice.[15]

Indeed, as a moment's thought will reveal, there is no logical reason to vote at all—not if the rationale for the vote is that it will influence the election. The larger the number of voters, the less effect one vote is likely to

---

*During the debate over the Republican Party's Contract with America in 1995, I published a brief magazine article speculating on the possibilities of winning a breach-of-contract suit should some parts of the contract not be kept. From the correspondence I subsequently received, it is plain that I did not manage to convey the point that the article was tongue-in-cheek. So I offer my apologies to puzzled readers.

have. So there is a sense in which we do not, quite, vote in order to affect the outcome. We vote for the symbolic value of showing that we belong to the political community or out of anger or joy or simple civic duty (there's integrity for you), because we also know that if everybody decided not to vote because their votes didn't matter, then nobody would vote.

So perhaps the integrity of the electoral process is supplied, if at all, not from the candidates' side but from the voters' side; and that, in a democracy, might not be such a bad thing. That is, it might not be a bad thing as long as we, the voters, can do what the Kentucky court might have wanted us to: vote to express the higher rather than the lower aspects of our human nature.

INTEGRITY OF SPEECH

The journalist Nat Hentoff, with forgivable hyperbole, has called the desire to censor "the strongest drive in human nature, with sex a weak second."[16] For it has been true throughout human history that whatever we have not wanted to hear, we have done our best to silence. As we think about legislating integrity, however, we might try to put a benign spin on the urge to censor: what the censor seeks to do, we might say, is to force individuals *to speak as though they have engaged in moral reflection.*

How can this be? Take the example of the Sedition Acts in the late eighteenth century, which made it a felony to publish false and derogatory statements about the federal government. The drafters might have supposed that no morally reflective person, no one who had thought things out, would really write the sort of nasty stuff that could weaken the newly established and not yet fully accepted central government. Or consider the campus rules against "hate speech" that were so popular in the 1980s and now seem to be dying out under the pressure of judicial decision and national controversy. Surely—so the drafters might reason—the individual who gives vent to a racial epithet or endorses a negative sexual stereotype would not have said the words had he or she only taken the time, like Socrates, to stop and think. The idea, then, is that we can build a better community if we force people to behave as though they are acting with integrity, whether they are or not.

The same reasoning could apply to a variety of other forms of regulation of what people say: prohibition of violent pornography, punishment of dissent from policies the government deems benign, even the law of libel and slander. Indeed, the law of libel and slander is of particular interest to the student of integrity because it is the least controversial of all these regulations, and yet it is, in form, very much like them. What is the law of defamation, after all, but a way of making sure that a person who recklessly harms another must pay? That the harm comes from one person's speaking or writing has little legal relevance; it is still genuine harm and it can still be compensated. The only important exception that the Supreme Court has drawn established rules that make it all but impossible for a "public figure" to win a libel judgment.[17] (The justices originally limited their special exception to a "public official" rather than a "public figure." Had they stuck with that wise distinction, a substantial chunk of tabloid America might not exist.)

By punishing defamation, the law provides an incentive for the defendant to think harder next time before speaking or writing, as well as for some other writer, never sued, to think first; in short, the law encourages integrity. For the student of integrity, this approach might seem a very good idea. The question is whether it is such a good idea that it should be extended to the many other contexts to which it might obviously (or not so obviously) apply.

Perhaps the most obvious of those other contexts is hate speech, the speech in which we give vent to one of the truly horrific aspects of our humanity: the ability to despise others for being different. Hate speech rules, surely, are an effort to encourage people to behave as though they have discerned right and wrong; for if they engaged in moral reflection, they surely would not express themselves through words dripping with, for example, racism. What morally reflective person could *be* a racist, or, at least, could be willing to speak like one?

The trouble with the hate speech rules, however, is the same as with any other regulation of speech: not so much the famous "chilling effect" that we were just discussing, but the risk that in trying to get everyone else to behave with integrity, the lawgivers may lose sight of what integrity demands of *them*. The accident of the government winding up on the right side in its regulation of hate speech is just that—an accident—and there is nothing in our history to suggest that such power over speech, once granted, will be used solely or even mostly for the good.

However, given what Hentoff correctly points to—our very human national taste for censorship—it seems unlikely that the unpopularity of hate speech rules is based on a more general public distaste for regulation of speech. Some defenders of the rules put opposition down to racism and let it go at that. And although I have no doubt that racism is *one* reason that people oppose the rules—some people, again, have a very human taste for hatred of others—I do not think it is the only reason worth mentioning.

Another reason, I suspect, is that many people have detected in the rules a bias with which they feel uncomfortable. Hate speech rules have struck many people as cramped, treating some groups as though somehow they *deserve* to be offended. Some legal scholars have argued, for example, that campus rules against racial epithets should be limited to epithets directed at those who have traditionally been subjected to discrimination.[18] The trouble is that others may be wounded too. I remember from my days in law school an evening in the gym, when the Black Law Students Union basketball team trounced a team of white students, and I stood on the sideline (I was never much good at the game, but I loved my team) and harangued the other team for playing, as I put it, "suburban basketball." Later that night, one of the white players told me how much he had been upset by what seemed to him a racial attack; not long ago, another one of the players wrote me a letter to tell me how it bothered him.

I think I owe an apology, and this is it. I am sorry, truly, for engaging in what I can only call racial harassment. I certainly understand how, at a given moment, such language can affect a white person as painfully as a black one. When otherwise thoughtful scholars argue the contrary, they blink at a simple and very personal reality. I quite understand that the case for the hate speech rules rests on the genuine suffering that words can cause and have caused, particularly to those the nation has oppressed. But it is important not to be so enthusiastic about telling the story of one set of experiences that we ignore another; if we lose caution here, we wind up proposing, whether we put it this way or not, that the members of one group—here, the white kids—are somehow *deserving* of what they get.

The reluctance to acknowledge the pain that particular groups may suffer is also apparent in the simple fact that nobody (as far as I know) has proposed, as part of the hate speech rules, to ban the taking the name of the Lord in vain—that is, cursing. But for a devout Christian, hearing God's name repeatedly abused in day-to-day conversation can be crushing, alienating, infuriating. Nor can one escape by arguing that Christians have never been oppressed in America, for that argument simply betrays an ignorance of history. Of course they (we) have been. Roman Catholics have been lynched for saying the wrong prayers, Mormons have been shot and burned for using the wrong holy book, Baptists have been driven from one community to the next to find religious freedom. That, and much more, is also the nation's oppressive history, even if we choose not to dwell on it.

When I suggest that hate speech rules might be too narrow, I am not proposing reform: add in this group and that one, and then everything will be fine. I am proposing instead, as the philosopher Richard Rorty has pointed out, that our many different perspectives on these stories are often just different—not better, not worse, just different. Integrity does not demand of us that we suspend judgment on our different interpretations of morality or, indeed, of history. Integrity simply demands that we take the time for genuine reflection to be certain that the one we are pressing is right.

I stress these points not because I necessarily expect the reader to agree, but because the politics of regulation of this kind is complicated. I am not even saying, really, that the regulations are a bad idea: Who really wants to listen to some of the racist nonsense that gets spouted in the name of free speech? We make a mockery of our precious freedoms when we use them for purposes so pernicious. No, I am saying that when we set out to make people behave as though they were people of integrity, we have to prepare ourselves for the possibility that their visions of what it means to live with integrity may be quite different from ours; a possibility, if we are but willing to acknowledge it, that can actually enhance the state of political dialogue. Sometimes, as in the case of the racist, we truly have nothing to learn from opening ourselves to the possibility that the other side is right. But that is the rare case. The madness of what somebody once called our "politicized politics" is that more and more of us, on more and more issues, seem to take the view that we have nothing to learn from the other side. To see the error, indeed the tragedy, of that position is the first step toward building an integral politics. What other steps might be necessary is the subject of the next chapter.

(thirteen)

Toward an Integral Politics

EVERY time an American community holds an election for any office something remarkable happens: when the votes have been counted, the losers leave office peacefully. No tanks are needed for a rival political party to lever open the doors of the White House; people need not risk their lives against riot police to force the ouster of the defeated governor; the mayor who fails to win reelection does not have his opponents murdered. We simply assume that the winner will take office, and, time after time, our assumption comes true. This happens at every level, whether we are electing a President or a dog catcher, and it is the signal feature of our politics.

Even today, as we move into what appears to be an increasingly bitter and even mean political era, nobody seriously doubts that if the bad guys are voted out (and it doesn't matter who you happen to think the bad guys are), they will step aside and let the good guys take office. So a political party that is out of power plots the overthrow of its opponents by figuring out how to get the right voters to the polls—not by figuring out how many troops to march into the streets.

I mention this because smooth transitions to power remain rare and wonderful things in our troubled world, and because I think it is important to begin any discussion of American politics with the simple optimism that all of us, whatever our partisan preferences, should draw from the plain fact that in the United States of America, democracy works. We may not always like the answers that our democracy provides; we may not always like the leaders whom our democracy elects; but the glory of our nation is that the system works.*

That glorious system, however, is under threat. The threat comes not so much, as today's media hoopla would have it, from America's many frightening fringe groups, although the groups are real and deserve the condemnation they receive. The threat comes, rather, from the increasing alienation of people from their government, a trend that, if not halted, may yet spell the end of genuine democracy in America. Indeed, a part of democracy is already collapsing, for more and more people see government as a distant, indifferent, and even hostile enterprise, over whose decisions ordinary citizens have little sway.

A few days after the November 1994 elections, I gave a lecture on the role of religion in American society at a small Christian college in western Pennsylvania. Later on, I talked politics with members of the audience. One was a middle-aged white woman who had voted Republican and supported, so she said, the Contract with America. Rather than bog us down in ideology, I decided to talk specifics. I asked her how she felt about federal funding for school lunch programs. She said she supported it in principle—in fact, she thought federal funding was a very good idea. She added, however, that she simply did not trust the federal government to do it. Washington—that was her name, and not hers alone, for the bureaucracy and the Congress together—Washington, she said, would mess it up. Washington would hire too many bureaucrats, would write too many regulations, would somehow ruin things. Of that she was absolutely certain.

And not only that: she felt, keenly, a sense that Washington did not trust local people. People like her. Washington thought that if she, and people like her, made the decisions, the decisions would be wrong. And she resented it.

I am not attempting to elevate an anecdote into a national trend. But nobody doubts that this sense exists or that it is widespread. Conservatives say it is the fault of liberals, whose big-government philosophy has frozen out local people who disagree with particular policies. Liberals say it is the

---

*This may be why the American tradition rejects the category of political criminal, the person who commits a crime not out of passion or a desire for personal gain but out of devotion to an ideology. Who would believe in the notion of a "political prisoner" in a nation that shares a faith (rightly or wrongly) that all can be fixed through the ballot box?

fault of conservatives, whose relentless attacks on "the government" have turned it into the enemy. As so often, there is a little bit of truth in both accusations. But placing blame is less important than recognizing that the survival of American democracy into the twenty-first century will require finding ways to overcome the alienation that is driving citizens away from the political mainstream.

When conservative politicians succeed with the rhetoric of "devolution" and "term limits," liberals often respond that the clever words are only gimmicks that mask terribly oppressive cuts in funds for desperately needed programs. But this ubiquitous answer, although sometimes fair, is inadequate. Most Americans are generous, not mean-spirited, and if they are attracted to what seem to liberals to be gimmicks, it is worth examining the gimmicks to see what they offer. And what they offer is quite simple: democracy.

The trouble is that America is too big—not the government, although that may be too big too, but the country. It is too big to work as the easily governed agrarian republic that the Framers of the Constitution envisioned.[1] In the world as the Framers imagined it, Tip O'Neill was precisely right: all politics *was* local. The federal government had little to do. The aspects of governance that affected people most were carried on at levels they could influence: the state house, the parish, and the town meeting. The cumbersome machinery for electing a national legislature every two years was designed to slow the national legislative process to a crawl: unable to anticipate modern transportation and communications, the Framers assumed that the rascals could do relatively little damage in two short years.

Of course, the Framers also limited the franchise in ways that we can now see as inexcusable: women could not vote, nor of course could slaves, nor, in many places, could men who did not happen to own property. This made the nation as a whole less democratic, but it may have made the nation *more* democratic within the narrow sphere of those permitted a voice. After all, the limits on the vote meant limits on the number of voters one had to persuade in order to carry the election. The classic First Amendment image was, for the late eighteenth century, precisely right: one *could* stand on a street corner and orate and, if skillful, gain an immediate audience.

Over the two centuries since the Constitution was written and ratified, America has progressively expanded the franchise, so that men without property, then the freed slaves, then women have been granted the vote. This is all to the nation's credit, although more credit would be due had America awakened sooner to its own moral obtuseness. Still, the nation is, on parchment, far more democratic now than it was two hundred years ago.

At the same time, democracy has grown distant from the lives of the American people. Of national democracy, this is particularly true. Fewer and fewer Americans believe, the polls tell us, that the government cares about people like them.[2] This frustration, more than any other, creates the danger that many a demagogue tries to exploit and that our politics must find a way to assuage.

The reader might reasonably ask what any of this has to do with integrity, but the point, as will become clear, is a simple one: a politics of integrity is what is needed to draw people back to their faith in our democracy. In this chapter, I hope to offer at least a preliminary sketch of what characteristics an integral politics might possess.

MOVEMENTS AND INTEGRITY

American politics is under siege—by causes. Just about all of us have a few. By a *cause* I mean a desire to put into place an institutional structure that will guarantee that our particular political desires remain triumphant (at least until the next cause comes along and sweeps away the structures we foolishly think will stand forever). The institutional structure matters, because the idea is to find a way to protect the triumph against some future majority that might have a different idea. So many people who want the government smaller demand a Balanced Budget Amendment to the Constitution. Many people who support universal health coverage envision a federal agency (once established, hard to abolish) to administer it. You get the idea.

When people who believe in many different causes band together, we have a political movement. Movements of this kind might be considered a good and noble thing for democracy—groups of citizens working toward a common goal!—if the movements did not turn out, far too often, to be the modern incarnation of what James Madison had in mind when he warned, in *The Federalist No. 10*, against allowing our politics to be taken over by "factions."

Madison defined a faction as "a number of citizens, whether amounting to a majority or a minority of the whole, who are united and actuated by some common impulse of passion, or of interest, adverse to the rights of other citizens, or to the permanent and aggregate interests of the community."[3] Factions, he believed, are ruinous to democracy, although he also believed that the constitutional design—along with the sheer ungovernable size of the new nation—made them less dangerous here than elsewhere.

Of course, advocates for every cause will insist that although their opponents are probably factions in the Madisonian sense, they themselves are not, for they have at heart the nation's interest, not something narrower and more ephemeral. And I am sure that they always believe it. Sometimes, certainly, it is true. (As usual, the civil rights movement is my case in point.) But the collapse of our politics into vaguely defined group interests—what business is said to want, what women are said to want, and so on—brings Madison's definition much closer to our reality. So does the relentless (one almost wants to say *ruthless*) insistence of too many of today's activists on characterizing their political opponents as outside the mainstream—even when their opponents turn out to comprise a majority of their fellow citizens.

Our commitments are admirable, but they carry the seeds of tragedy. The deeper our commitment to our causes, the weaker may be our commitment to democracy, for it is in the nature of the true believer to have little patience with majoritarian structures that get in the way of progress. Rather than accept the possibility of defeat in democratic politics, we try to enshrine our commitments as beyond the reach of argument, by shoehorning them into the vast and intimidating structure of constitutional rights or by crafting a rhetoric that makes those who stand against us necessarily stand with the forces of evil. *Un-American* used to be a big word in the vocabulary of silencing, as, today, are such terms as *reactionary* (from the left) and *not normal Americans* (from the right).

I must confess that the great political movements of our day frighten me with their reckless certainties and their insistence on treating people as means to be manipulated rather than as the ends for which government exists. Liberalism and conservatism, in their current incarnations, both possess great ideas, worthy of a fair hearing and fair debate . . . and great capacities for hatred. Too many partisans seem to hate their opponents, who are demonized in terms so creative that I weep at the waste of energy, and, as one who struggles to be Christian, I find the hatred painful. What perhaps is worse, the liberal and conservative movements of our day both make common cause with people who hate on grounds that I would have thought history had by now taught us never to tolerate. I am asked, often, whether I consider myself a liberal or a conservative. My answer, always, is "no." Conservatives too often welcome racists; liberals too often welcome people who look down their noses at "traditional values"; and both movements welcome more than their share of religious bigots. (Think of the evangelical leader who stated at a political dinner in 1980 that God does not hear the prayers of Jews; or the feminist leader who stated in 1991 that there are too many Catholics on the Supreme Court.)[4]

I very much doubt that I am alone in my antipathies, which is why I sometimes wonder whether the American people might rush to embrace a political movement that managed to make a forceful case for its causes without having to hate and demonize those who disagree. The next century is arriving soon, whether we are ready or not, and the only way to avoid a twenty-first-century politics that is every bit as nasty (and, if integrity requires us to tell the truth, undemocratic) as the politics of the current era is to craft a set of principles and then to use our only political weapon—the vote—to make sure that our politicians and their movements follow them.

I mean this quite sincerely. I look forward to the day when we as voters will say, "I agree with So-and-so on most of the issues, but I could never vote for somebody who would say this or do that in order to win." We don't do that, of course. We may complain about the nastiness of our politics, and we may wish it would change, but the fact is that just like the fund-raising appeals we examined in chapter 5, nastiness and lies and unintegral behavior work. We reward them with our votes, perhaps because we see no alternative.[5]

Perhaps there *is* no alternative. But I am more of an optimist than that. This chapter, then, is an effort to figure out how to change things, how to begin to bring to our politics a true integrity, which would at last make our democracy as moral as I deeply believe our people are.

EIGHT PRINCIPLES IN SEARCH OF A DEMOCRACY

American politics is a mess. But a careful attention to the demands of integrity may offer us some hope of cleaning it up. What, then, does integrity require of us? The eight principles that I discuss below are a preliminary effort to move toward an answer.

1. The nation exists for its people. Integrity, as we have seen, requires that we try to live our ideals. A politics of integrity, then, believes and lives out its own rhetoric. And what is foremost in the rhetoric of liberal democracy? Why, the importance of the individual—not simply as a possessor of rights but as a full participant in the process of national governance. Thus, the first principle of an integral politics is to remember our Kant: *people are ends, not means.* People, and people alone, are the reason there *is* a United States of America.

One of the reasons for the growing national disgust with politics, I suspect, is precisely that politicians (along with the activists who feed them money and position papers) tend to forget this. To them, people are means, not to be listened to but to be manipulated—persuaded to change their minds if possible, or controlled if not. This vision of the people of the United States as the clay rather than the potters is not unique to left or right in America; it is, rather, an elite mentality, the shared vision of people who have in common their certainty that they know all the answers, if they could but get those pigheaded American voters to come along.

Thus, many of the liberals who have been largely on the defensive since 1980 will pronounce solemnly that their electoral defeats are the fault of the successful manipulation of what must be the simpleminded voters of America, or perhaps the essential racism (or sexism or whatever) of those same American voters. This puts one in mind of a story about the cantankerous old Dixiecrat Lester Maddox, who, while serving as governor of Georgia, was asked about unrest in the prison system. He responded that the problem was not the conditions in the prisons but "the quality of prisoner you get these days." And that is what one hears nowadays from liberals: the problem is not the message but the quality of the voters who keep ignoring it. As long as that is the explanation, liberals will keep on losing.

But conservatives have little reason to celebrate, and if they insist on treating recent elections as ideological transformations, they will have even less. Although they have lately learned the lessons of populism—voters want to vote for people who *listen* to them—they are also falling into the same old traps that power always springs. Instead of listening to the voters who put them in power, Republicans spent too much of 1995 listening to the business groups that paid for their successful campaigns, proposing changes in the securities and environmental laws that businesses had long sought—making it harder to win fraud suits and easier to meet environmental standards—changes that precious few Americans had in mind when they voted the Democrats out and that certainly were nowhere to be found in the Contract with America.*

Indeed, the Republicans, just like the Democrats, seem much more comfortable palling around with their favorite interest groups than actually doing the work that most Americans want done. In *The Revolt of the Elites*, the late Christopher Lasch argued that most Washington politicians, on left

---

*Lobbyists for various business groups were invited to help draft the legislation. Republican protests that the Democrats used to do the same thing with, for example, civil rights groups missed the point: people voted in 1994 for a government that would listen to *them*.

and right alike, actually disdain the common folk of whom they speak so often, preferring the company of one another (even political enemies), as well as lobbyists and journalists, people they consider, in effect, members of their own class.[6] An overstatement? Probably. On the other hand, members of Congress do everything they can to prove Lasch right. A mystifying example is the combination of arrogance and sheer stupidity through which many members of Congress refuse to make their fax numbers available to their own constituents—even those who call and ask. (I suspect that the numbers are well known to the many lobbyists and media stars with whom they associate.)

Republicans who believe that the 1994 elections were principally about ideology rather than about a sense of a government out of touch with its people should ponder the success of Ross Perot's famous line in 1992, that Capitol Hill is the only place he knows where the employees can park and the owners can't. Too many of our representatives, it must be said, spend less time acting like our employees than like the employees of the PACs that fund their campaigns. Perhaps it is too late to do much about that. But integrity would suggest, at a minimum, that Republicans and Democrats alike should let the voters know their fax numbers—or tell the truth about whose views they care about and whose work they're doing.

I do not mean this indictment to be as harsh as it may seem. Most of our elected representatives are people of good will and a strong desire to do the right. And yet the best will in the world is no insulation against the temptation, once one has gained political office, to forget that the people rule.

2. *Some things are more important than others.* A politics of integrity is a politics that sets priorities, that does not tell the self-serving lie that every program preferred by a particular political movement is of equal value. In the political world toward which we are moving, priorities are essential. Ever since the 1970s, voters have been electing Presidents who promise a government that is smaller and, in the public mind (I suspect), more controllable. That is, the American people quite sensibly see government size as related to government accountability. Many elections that seem to be about something else are probably about this: people want a government they feel is reachable.

For this reason, the debate over the proper relative roles of the federal and state sovereignties—a debate that conservatives keep promising and liberals keep resisting—is actually a very useful one to have. As a nation, we have good historical reasons to be leery of the phrase "states' rights," for it has been used both to permit and to mask racial oppressions that should have been deemed intolerable. But that is not the same as saying that it is obvious that anything worth doing well is worth doing only at the federal level. To the citizen, democracy most feels like democracy when the apparatus of government is something that he or she feels capable of affecting. The sense of the federal government as more and more distant from the people (whether the sense is fair or not) is surely a far more important force than ideology in driving the debate over government size.

This is where liberals tend to make a serious mistake. They generally defend a program threatened with reduction or elimination by objecting that the program is a good one: it is cost-effective or it prevents starvation or it fills a need. Often the argument is correct. But it also misses the point of the new politics: it is no longer sufficient in defending a program to demonstrate that it does some good—even a great deal of good. For the government itself is no longer trusted. Consider again the story with which I opened the chapter: the woman in western Pennsylvania who likes school lunch programs but dislikes the feeling that the federal government does not trust people like her to do it right.

Liberalism, and any revised philosophy that favors particular large government initiatives, must have an answer for this woman, and the answer must be more persuasive than "It's a good program," which is no longer sufficient, or the depressingly ubiquitous "The Republicans are starving children," which is hardly rhetoric that will win back lost voters. Lots of programs are good programs, and if the only argument needed to justify a program is that it is a good one, the government will never shrink. And shrinking government is something that the American people very much want, and something that, one way or another, they are going to get.

Any political movement that expects to survive into the next century must make its peace with what a strong majority of voters seem to believe: the federal government (or government generally) cannot do everything that happens to be a good idea. Some things that are very good ideas will have to be scrapped. Some things that work very well will have to be scrapped. Some things that have very powerful constituencies will have to be scrapped. And even some things that are very popular will have to be scrapped.

So our second hesitant step toward an integral politics is to acknowledge that the conversation has changed, that arguments on pragmatics and practicalities will not suffice in an era when the dominant ideology is one of skepticism and mistrust. What is required of both liberalism and conservatism, therefore, is something that for a good two or three decades their proponents have stubbornly refused to do, perhaps because they have not had to: the setting of priorities. Not paper priorities, the sort one puts in a platform, but real priorities, as in concluding that this cherished program is more important than that one. Less than that the voters will no longer abide.

This stark fact—if true—will make life difficult for conservatives, who, having gained a measure of political power, seem to have decided that shrinking government is less important than replacing a plethora of liberal initiatives with a plethora of conservative ones. The same stark fact—once again, if true—substantially wrecks the contemporary program of liberal political philosophy, which has been to find *justifications* for the programs of the liberal agenda. Many of the justifications offered for very controversial liberal programs are quite strong. Affirmative action, for example, no matter what its flaws, responds to a genuine moral claim that we all too rarely articulate. And many of the challenged liberal programs themselves are wonderful. For example, federal funding for alternatives in television and the arts is a glory, not an aberration, of the budget.

But so what? Justifications, no matter how thoughtful, will no longer suffice as substitutes for the setting of priorities. And here, of course, integrity becomes crucial, because it is folly to pretend that all programs are equally important. Liberals (like everybody else) must begin to draw distinctions. So one might say that federal funding for the arts is important and federal funding for school lunches is important, but is federal funding for the arts *as important* as federal funding for school lunches? I don't think so. Others might strike the balance the other way. The point is that in an era that demands the setting of priorities, balances of this kind must be struck.

3. Consistency matters. Third, a politics of integrity requires that the principles for which our parties and institutions stand truly be treated as principles. A principle is not a principle if we will bend it to help our friends.

Consider as an example the current assault on some aspects of the "welfare state."[7] A central theme of the argument against treating government assistance as an entitlement is that reliance on aid supposedly cripples self-reliance. Perhaps it does. But integrity requires that the principles on which the government operates be applied consistently. If welfare programs have bad effects on individuals, they must also have bad effects on corporations, and corporate welfare should receive the same scrutiny—and be subject to the same dismissive rhetoric—as welfare for individuals.

Consider the following examples of corporate welfare, gleaned from 1995 reports by the Cato Institute and the Progressive Policy Institute:[8]

• "Over the past 20 years, the Forest Service has built 340,000 miles of roads—more than eight times the length of the interstate highway system—primarily for the benefit of logging companies." (The cost of this project was $140 million in 1994 alone.)[9]

• "Through the Rural Electrification Administration and the federal Power Marketing Administrations [sic], the federal government provides some $2 billion in subsidies each year to large and profitable electric utility cooperatives."[10]

• "An estimated 40 percent of the $1.4 billion sugar price support program benefits the largest one percent of sugar farms."[11]

Moreover, as the Progressive Policy Institute report points out, the corporate subsidies are deeply regressive, providing benefits to a relatively small group of upper-income Americans, largely with money taxed from those earning far less. In other words, corporate welfare programs are like individual welfare programs, except that they transfer tax dollars from low- and middle-income people to upper-income people, a kind of reverse–Robin Hood effect.

And, as the Cato Institute points out, corporate welfare raises consumer prices, fosters cozy relationships between the government and business, and "converts the American businessman from a capitalist into a lobbyist."[12] In other words, corporate welfare has the same bad effects that individual welfare is supposed to have, only more so, because corporate welfare hits all of us and hits us hard. But the same Congress and administration that are tilting at the windmills of welfare reform for individuals seem content to leave corporate welfare relatively untouched, but for a nip here and a tuck there. (Of course, the recipients of individual assistance do not have political action committees.)

Machiavelli argued that it is more important for a leader to seem to be principled than actually to be principled—indeed, that a truly principled leader, one who tries to live out the deepest moral commitments of a society's public rhetoric, will ultimately be deposed. A politics of integrity must, through its structure and its work, deny the truth of this proposition.

4. *Everybody gets to play.* A politics of integrity does not draw arbitrary boundaries around the public square, screening out some citizens whose political views have been formed in ways of which various elites disapprove. A particular problem of our age has been the astonishing effort to craft a vision of public life in which America's religious traditions play no

important roles, by ruling out of bounds political (and sometimes moral) arguments that rest on explicitly religious bases.[13] Nowadays, one hears quite commonly the argument that it is morally wrong—perhaps even constitutionally wrong, a violation of the Establishment Clause of the First Amendment—for you to try to "impose" on me your religiously based moral understanding. Usually this argument is stressed in the context of the abortion battle. Of course, had this ever been a seriously defended principle of American public life, we would never have had the abolitionist or civil rights movements, to name only the most obvious two.

When I make this point, as I often do, in lecturing about politics and religion, I often get an answer that goes something like this: "But nobody can reason with these religionists. They say that So-and-so is God's will, and what can you say in return?" I am always saddened by this answer, because, as a professor at a university, I run into many closed-minded people, and few of them need divine command as an excuse. But nobody tries to ban them from public debate for their closed-mindedness. Besides, this vision of how religious people reason is a caricature. That there are some who cannot be reached by reason is doubtless true. The notion that most religious people are that way seems to me a quite unfounded insult.

A further argument I hear is of this type: "The difference is that the civil rights laws that were supported by religious people, unlike the abortion restrictions that are supported by religious people, do not infringe on anybody's fundamental rights." So I point out that the distinction is false, that the civil rights laws infringe on the fundamental right of property, by telling people that they may not segregate in restaurants or hotels they happen to own. The fact that it is a good and honorable and just infringement of those rights does not change the fact that it is an infringement of those rights.

Typically, I am next hit with this one: "Yes, but the right to property is less important than the right to privacy." Now, apart from the upper-middle-class bias inherent in that proposition, one can at least say that the right to property is mentioned in the Constitution. The right to privacy is not, and although I count myself as glad that the right exists, I am not so hypocritical as to pretend that something other than a rather uncomfortable judicial alchemy put it there and keeps it there. Besides, it would be crude governance indeed to build a hierarchy of constitutional rights—these are important, those are trivial—and then to say, as a matter of law, that religious opinion can be taken into account in the infringement of some but not others.

I am not suggesting that the pro-life religionists who demand access to the public square deserve to prevail. But I do believe in fair procedures.

There is an air of design about the date of the discovery of a rule against religious politicking: after the civil rights movement (which relied on it heavily) and before the maturity of the pro-life movement (which relies on it heavily). We have spoken of consistency as crucial to a truly reflective integrity, but I have yet to find the pro-choice advocate who will condemn the *Reverend* Martin Luther King, Jr., for daring to ask the state to impose his religiously inspired vision of equality on dissenting segregationists who might prefer to serve only whites at their lunch counters and hotels. In fact, when I raise this point, I am generally told that King's vision was not really religious—that it was grounded in . . . well, natural law or something (his repeated citations to Scripture and theology notwithstanding). Of course, the Roman Catholic Church could argue that its opposition to abortion is not really religious but is grounded in . . . well, natural law or something (repeated citations to Scripture and theology notwithstanding). But nobody on the pro-choice side would say that this fact gets the Church off the Establishment Clause hook.

It does not matter whether one sees the pro-life movement as in any sense the intellectual heir of the civil rights movement. (Indeed, one of the genuine political ironies of our day is that both the pro-choice and pro-life sides can claim a spiritual and intellectual connection to the civil rights movement.) The point, rather, is that a politics of integrity must be consistent in its rules instead of fixing the rules so that one side gets to win. If it is bad to have religious advocacy in the public square, then it was as bad for the Reverend Martin Luther King, Jr., as it is for the Reverend Pat Robertson.

To be sure, the image of religion in our public life is badly tarnished nowadays by the tendency of some Christian conservatives to pour the most virulent anathemas upon those who disagree with their politics.* (Of course, many secular liberals do the same.) Although the religious voice belongs in American politics, it will be an ineffective and scary voice as long as it seems to be a mean-spirited voice. Moreover, advocates of a strong religious presence in American public life must bear in mind that the freedom of religion, our guarantee of religious pluralism, is one of the great glories of our Constitution. Consequently, any suggestion that there is a single best or even official American religion (for example, the "Chris-

---

*I am convinced, both by the people I have met as I travel and lecture on religion and politics and by reviewing survey data, that the often strident voices of the *leaders* of some conservative Christian groups are representative of the convictions of only a relatively small number of the *members*.

tian nation" rhetoric) is not only an offense against religious liberty; it is also, if offered as a basis for government policy, blatantly unconstitutional.

However, the rhetorical excess of some conservatives hardly justifies the antireligious sentiments expressed by some liberals. A strong tradition among liberal intellectuals, at least since John Dewey, has been to treat religious faith as a kind of primitive superstition, if that faith governs (or even strongly influences) one's public moral and political stances. Too many liberal theorists, as I have noted elsewhere, write and speak of religion with a kind of elitist despair, recognizing that it is a force in the world but seeming to wish that it would go away.[14] This tendency puts one in mind of Pliny the Younger, who, early in the second century, wrote a letter to the Roman Emperor Trajan on the treatment of Christianity, which he called "a depraved and extravagant superstition." He tried to get people to see reason, Pliny wrote, even on pain of torture or death, but despite his efforts, he complained, "[t]he contagion of this superstition has spread not only in the cities, but in the villages and rural districts as well."[15] To which one might simply add: Ah, blessed contagion! Would that we had more of it!

More to the point, it does not ultimately matter how many thoughtful scholars and journalists argue that it is wrong to have religious rhetoric in the public square. It is simply there. Hume argued that one cannot derive an *ought* from an *is*; I would answer that you cannot defeat an *is* with an *ought*. Millions of American citizens seem to have decided that the language of their faith is the language with which they feel most comfortable, and so we must, under our first principle of integral politics, take them as they are, rather than commanding them to become something else.

5. We must be willing to talk about right and wrong without mentioning the Constitution. I say this as a longtime teacher of constitutional law and as one who truly loves our foundational document, the greatest and most successful the world has known. A politics of integrity must certainly respect the fundamental (and constitutional) rights of its citizens, and must be vigilant in protecting those rights, even when they are exercised by those we disdain: Nazis, for example, or serial killers. But we must never make the moral mistake of supposing that because I have the right to do something, you lack the right to criticize me for doing it. To pretend that the existence of constitutional protection for an action immunizes the actor against moral criticism is blatantly unintegral: it as much as says to free and equal citizens, "Shut up about your principles!"

Individual rights are a good thing, but to make a cult of individualism can lead to social disaster. It is no accident that the United States has both the highest rate of abortion and the highest rate of private ownership of firearms in the world, for we live in a nation that *has* made a cult of individualism. Our well-known national inability to engage in moral conversation means that once a right exists, nobody seems to feel comfortable urging that it not be exercised. No wonder people who are concerned about the harm that firearms do see no alternative to banning them; no avenue exists for a discussion of the possibility that the "right" to own them should be exercised with greater discretion. And no wonder opponents of abortion believe they must try to make the procedure illegal; not only is there no significant forum for moral suasion against the exercise of the "right" but courts have lately cooperated in destroying such limited forums as do exist, by issuing orders that civil libertarians would countenance in no other context, intended to keep pro-life demonstrators sufficiently far from abortion clinics that their message is likely to be ineffective.[16]

We know that our cult of individualism is out of control when a respected federal judge issues an order—as happened in New Jersey—making it impossible for a town to keep a homeless man with offensive body odor from making the public library an unpleasant place for others. It is as though once an individual has made up his mind to do a thing, no matter how tasteless or repulsive, nobody else has legal recourse.

Newton Minow, who as head of the Federal Communications Commission in the 1960s coined the phrase "vast wasteland" to describe the offerings of network television, has raised similar concerns about the direction the rights revolution has taken. Minow cites the example of a student at a California university who decided to attend classes naked. When challenged on his conduct, the student offered as his defense the First Amendment.[17] Now, I am not convinced that the freedom of speech can plausibly be read to shield public disrobing. Even if it can, however, Minow points out that the existence of First Amendment protection says nothing at all about whether the student was doing something wise or unwise, offensive or inoffensive, right or wrong. So there lies the point: that I have a right to do something does not deprive you of your freedom to criticize me as harshly as you like. In particular, it grants me no protection whatsoever from *moral* critique of what I choose to do.[18]

Even the philosophers of the Enlightenment, justly credited with modernizing our understanding of freedom to include rights against the state, understood this point. John Locke, for example, stated as his first principle that men belong not to themselves but to God—meaning that the exercise of freedom is to be guided by God's commands. Indeed, our modern notion of freedom in the sense of an exercise of free will is largely a Christian invention (see chapter 14). The Greeks had no significant conception of will, which explains Aristotle's maddening insistence on describing virtue as a habit. Christianity needed it, however, to allow human beings a free choice to accept or reject God's offer of grace. And freedom rightly used, of course, meant freedom to follow God.[19]

As a matter of secular ethics, the proper critique of the use of freedom—of rights—is not necessarily that it ignores our particular vision of the will of God (although we also must not rule that critique out of bounds). Whatever the source of the moral critique of how we use our freedom, however, the existence of the Constitution should not be treated as a moral shield. For the Constitution is but a reminder that we possess freedom to choose; it does not tell us which choices are best.

And just as we must be willing to criticize the exercise of constitutional rights when they are used immorally, we must resist the temptation to run to amend the document every time we do not like what is going on. At this writing, American conservatives seem to be lining up to support a great trilogy of amendments: the Balanced Budget Amendment, the Religious Equality Amendment, and the Flag Desecration Amendment. If a cause is just, it seems, the Constitution is the place where we are supposed to enshrine it. Right now, it happens that liberals want to enshrine their programs through the courts and conservatives theirs through the amendment process, but, in reality, both sides are up to the same antidemocratic factional mischief. Conservatives and liberals have grown intoxicated with constitutionalism, staggering together along the same drunken route, propelled by the same bleary logic: the way to make sure that we win is to place our program beyond the reach of politics. But democracy is not about making sure that we win (see my eighth principle). Democracy is about making sure that every voice is heard, that no voice is privileged, and that everybody plays by the rules.

I wonder sometimes what Madison, who worried so much about factiousness, would think if given the chance to ponder our edifice of constitutional rights. Perhaps he would decide that our heavy reliance on the language of rights is simply the crowning jewel in the work that he and the other Founders began. On the other hand, I worry that he would say that by placing so much emphasis on the rights the Constitution protects, we actually promote the rise of factions, because, with all free to do as they like, there is less and less reason for people to work together—as Madison openly hoped they would—in the *national* interest.

Do not mistake my point. Of course there are principles that should be beyond the reach of democratic politics. Of course there are rights with which no majority should be allowed to tamper. But a thriving democracy must insist that the set of untouchable icons be as small as possible. Nowadays, the temptation of power is to do just the opposite, to make the set as large as possible. In fact, the temptation is to place *all* our causes beyond the reach of democratic politics, lest some future majority disturb our work. But if ever we allow that to happen, we certainly cease to be a democracy.

6. *Our politics must call us to our higher selves.* The debasement of political language is particularly embarrassing when the negativity is being spread by our elected representatives. The matter is only made worse when we think that even the polite ones seem too often to be calling us to selfishness. In a politics of integrity, we must try to respond to politicians who call us to our highest rather than lowest selves; in particular, we must respond to politicians who talk of the national interest and our shared obligations, not merely those who promise to enrich us.

The trouble is that, nowadays, every politician tries to enrich us. The devil's definition of an honest politician (and quite an unfair definition at that) is one who stays bought. Nowadays, this notion must seem depressingly cynical. Yet something very close to it captures the unhappy political spirit of our selfish age. Most Americans seem to think an honest politician is one who will buy our votes with promises of wealth and then go on to complete the purchase.

The wealth with which politicians make their electoral purchases comes in a variety of forms, but nearly all of them play to our selfish instincts. Conservatives tend to promise tax cuts, which translate to more money for good, honest, hardworking Americans, and less for the despicable *them*, who may be demonic bureaucrats or demonized welfare cheats, according to one's taste. Liberals promise entitlements and, better yet, constitutional rights, which translate to more freedoms for good, honest, hardworking Americans against the despicable *them*, who nowadays are likely to be wealthy fat-cats or what liberals sadly persist in labeling the "religious right."

Promises of both kinds offer something for the voter, and so appeal to our lower instincts.* (Remember our discussion in the previous chapter of *Brown v. Hartlage.*) Neither kind offers the vision of a better nation, except in the narrow sense that the nation is better when it gives us precisely what

---

*I am well aware of the political science literature arguing that appeals of this kind are precisely what politicians should be doing if government is to aggregate private preferences. I simply disagree.

we desire. In other words, neither kind calls us to duty. One longs for the political candidate who is willing to say, more than three decades after John Kennedy's assassination: "Ask not what your country can do for you. Ask what you can do for your country." At the time, the borrowed phrases sounded a little hokey. Looking back, they sing with an optimism about America that today's cramped and self-regarding politics altogether lack.

One reads from time to time that changes in the economy are to blame; that it is far harder to be generous of spirit or genuinely optimistic in a nation that is undergoing the rapid and unsettling economic evolution with which America currently wrestles. If true, this explanation is a sad one. Holding to our principles of duty and service and regard for others is most important at times of stress; after all, as we have seen, integrity is not integrity if it is never tested.

7. *We must listen to one another.* A politics of integrity is a politics in which all of us are willing to do the hard work of discernment, to test our views to be sure that we are right. As we have already seen, this in turn implies a dialogue, for in the course of our reflections, especially in a democracy, it is vital to listen to the views of our fellow citizens. If our discernment is genuine, then so must our listening be, which is why our seventh principle, simply put, is that all of us must listen with our ears, not with our mouths.

By this I mean that we must strive to avoid an error I confess to committing all the time: the error of allowing others to speak only because we need to hear their views in order to be able to refute them. In true dialogue, as Martin Buber pointed out, we not only seek to persuade the other but we allow ourselves the possibility of being persuaded by the other.[20] An integral politics certainly needs citizens who listen; otherwise, the dialogue itself becomes pointless.

The trouble is that we may lack the capacity for truly open and thoughtful dialogue. I do not say we have lost it; I am not convinced we ever had it. But what we did have and seem to have forgotten is a strong tradition favoring the old saw "I disapprove of what you say but I will fight to the death for your right to say it." Our public dialogue—our very language—has been debased through the move toward increasing negativity and even hostility, so that, in an argument, the first weapon we reach for is often the most extreme: "That's ridiculous!" or "He's such an idiot!" or "She's full of it!" or "I've never heard anything so crazy in my life!" Missing are such stalwarts of civility as "I'm sorry, but I must respectfully disagree" or "Let's talk about this further" or "I might not go as far as that, but I do see your point." Having lost the talent for argument, we call names instead. But dialogue in an integral politics must be civil; if we lose the civility that integrity demands, we trade the possibility of persuasion and compromise for the certainty of provocation and alienation.

In a dry cleaner one day I witnessed a vehement argument between a customer who felt a shirt had not been adequately cleaned and the owner, who was defending his staff. The customer did not want to pay. The owner wanted his money. In their mutual fury, neither one came up with the obvious solution: that the cleaner should try again, free of charge, to get the stain out. Our politics can be that way too: we are so busy being angry at one another that it does not occur to us to try to find ways to work together.

People on the right seem to think that the nastiness of our public discussions is the fault of people on the left; people on the left seem to think that it is the fault of people on the right. But there is plenty of blame for all of us. When we are told, as we often are, that affirmative action is as bad as Jim Crow, we are facing a cruel absurdity; when we are told, as we often are, that only a racist could be troubled by affirmative action, we are facing another. I struggle, hard, with my own habit of concluding that people who disagree with me on the important public issues of the day are obviously deserving of my condemnation. I struggle to understand their points of view, even, as Buber suggested, to search for empathy. I do not claim to do it very well. What is depressing is how solidly that failure places me in the American mainstream.

8. Sometimes the other side wins. This is, perhaps, the most important principle of an integral democratic politics, and yet little need be said about it. The point is simple: in the end, politics comes down to votes. Somebody wins and somebody loses. In practical terms, that means that the people have picked one and rejected the other. Integrity requires us to admit the possibility (indeed, the likelihood) that we lost not because of some shameless manipulation by our villainous opponents, and not because of some failure to get our message across, but because our fellow citizens, a basically rational bunch, considered both our views and those of the other side and decided that they liked the other side's better.

To be sure, now and then the other side cheats, as Richard Nixon tried to do (and maybe succeeded) in 1972, and as some say Joseph Kennedy did on behalf of his son John in 1960 (although evidence is thin). But we cannot deduce cheating from the fact that we lost. And when both sides play by the rules, one would hope that the losers would have the integrity and fortitude to say to the winners, "Congratulations; I'll see you in two years" (or four, or six, or whatever), rather than, "Oh, no, the forces of evil have triumphed, monsters are in the streets, and the Republic is at an end"—which is roughly the tone of far too much postelection commentary from both sides of the political aisle.

"Here, the people rule," pronounced Gerald Ford after Nixon's resignation in August 1974. The fact is one that an integral politics cannot afford to forget.

INTERLUDE: THE ABORTION DISTORTION

Perhaps this is the place to pause and note that in order to get an integral politics back on track, we have to stop allowing so much of politics and principle to be dictated by the nation's moral divisions over abortion rights.

In particular, the press must end its abortion hang-up, its tendency to treat abortion as the most important domestic issue facing America—something almost nobody else believes. When President Clinton announced his 1993 nomination of Ruth Bader Ginsburg to the Supreme Court, I happened to be in my car; the same was true when I heard the news of his 1994 nomination of Stephen Breyer to the same tribunal. In each case, the announcer treated the audience to useless speculation as to each jurist's views on abortion—but mentioned no other issue likely to come before the Court. We heard nothing about the nominee's views on affirmative action or free speech or the separation of powers or the death penalty or, for that matter, interstate banking (which probably affects more people more directly than any of these sexier issues do). Only abortion.

Yet the number of people who consider this the most crucial work of the Supreme Court is probably quite small. Certainly the number of voters (especially on the pro-choice side) who rank the abortion issue as foremost among their electoral concerns borders on the minuscule.[21] I do not mean to suggest that abortion is a trivial matter, either as a matter of constitutionalism or as a matter of ethics. The media, however, should recognize that there are other issues as or more vital to the lives of the American people and stop treating this as the crucial fact that we must know about Supreme Court nominees.

Abortion distorts our political dialogue in other ways as well. So passionately do committed advocates care about the issue that they offer misleading analyses of the data—thus sacrificing integrity in the interest of the cause. Both the pro-life and pro-choice sides tend to offer broad generalizations about the opinions of the American people on the subject, generalizations that are not so much wrong as woefully misleading. Thus the pro-life side will point out that a solid majority of Americans say that killing a fetus is as bad as killing a child—indeed, in some surveys, a majority says that a fetus is human from the moment of conception.[22] This is an accurate reading of the survey data. But the pro-choice side will point out that a solid majority of the American people opposes banning abortion, and this, too, is an accurate reading of the survey data.

These data sets may appear to be contradictory, but, in truth, the American people have resolved them. Indeed, the data have been consistent for more than twenty years—in short, since *Roe v. Wade*[23] was decided in 1973. What the data show is that if you add together all the people who believe abortion should be banned and all the people who believe that abortion should be an unfettered choice, you still have less than half the American people. Strong majorities of Americans support a number of restrictions on abortion: waiting periods, parental permission for minors, and the like.[24] This compromise position, moreover, is more or less where the Supreme Court, which activists on both sides condemn for its often shaky decisions, has positioned the constitutional law of abortion.[25] There is no obvious reason why the Court's decisions have to reflect the views of the American people, and the justices do their most courageous work when they stand in opposition to the polls; nevertheless, activists on both sides, who seem to think public opinion important, would do the nation a favor if they behaved less like the Ravenna forgers we discussed in chapter 7 and more like people of integrity.

Our abortion-centeredness further distorts our politics by making us seem less civil than we are. The abortion debate suffers quite famously from the rhetoric of demonization: the religious zealots who intimidate women and murder doctors against the baby killers who are perpetrating America's own Holocaust. And much of the media's relentless assault on the so-called religious right (what a biased term) seems abortion-centered. When you leave the abortion issue, there are relatively few subjects of our politics on which Christian conservatives seem significantly out of step with the views of the larger society. (There are a number of issues on which I disagree with the Christian conservatives, but I am willing to admit, as I wish more liberal activists were, that I am often disagreeing with a majority of my fellow citizens as well.)

To the media, abortion seems to be the classic example of an arena in which, all too often, the argumentative ratchet turns only one way—and not merely on the editorial pages. A number of newspapers have adopted, as a matter of style, the term "anti-abortion" to refer to members of the pro-life movement, and the term "abortion rights supporters" to refer to members of the pro-choice movement. This decision is troubling because, by using these terms, the newspaper takes sides in the controversy. One side becomes *for* something, the other *against*. It would be as logical to call the pro-life side "fetal rights supporters" and the pro-choice side "anti-fetus," or to call gun-control supporters "anti–gun rights," or, for that matter, to call supporters of historical preservation laws "anti–private property." But nobody, least of all a major newspaper, would countenance such nonsense.

Except in the case of abortion, where the mass media make no pretense to the usual neutrality. Now, I am not an adamant pro-lifer, although I do tend to find much of the pro-choice argument question-begging and, ultimately, resting as solidly as the pro-life argument on undiscussable premises.[26] But the bias of the press on the abortion issue is depressing. In this book, the reader will already have noticed, I use the terms *pro-choice* to refer to people who favor protection of abortion rights over protection of fetal rights and *pro-life* to refer to people who favor protection of fetal rights over protection of abortion rights. My reason is simple: absent a complete collapse of linguistic integrity (that word again), I am willing to call people and groups what they want to be called.

If our politics is to become a politics of integrity, we must not allow one issue to generate so many of the rules and so much of the rhetoric, from either left or right. Particularly the abortion issue. It is shameful that so many otherwise principled liberals and conservatives have made abortion a litmus test of genuine commitment. As Jean Bethke Elshtain has noted: "Dealing with abortion . . . cannot be compared to building a great interstate highway system or desegregating the schools."[27] But the reason is not that our divisions over the issue are insuperable. The reason is that abortion is one of the few moral issues in American history about which it is possible to say, with no sense of irony, that both sides are right.

THE DUTIES OF THE PEOPLE

The greatest error of all in considering how to build an integral politics is to judge the integrity of our politics by the integrity of our politicians. In an electoral democracy, what matters far more is the integrity of voters; in particular, what matters is the willingness of citizens first to envision a national purpose and then to vote consistently in ways that will further it. We, the People of the United States (as the first line of the Constitution reads), when we do less, are already making impossible the politics of integrity that the nation needs.[28]

The point is not that politics would not benefit from a healthy dose of integrity—it would—or that politicians do not deserve criticism when they fail to display it—they do. The point is that the nature of integrity in politics is properly understood as referring to more than an individual's consistency to his or her own internal compass. Politics, more than any other institution of our society except the family, rests on an integrity that focuses outward, toward being true to others, rather than inward, toward being true to one's own self.

Bob Herbert, the *New York Times* columnist, has argued that the obligation of black people who face what he describes as a hostile political atmosphere is to vote—and vote and vote.[29] This would seem to be a sensible prescription for everybody, especially for those who have a complaint about what the government is doing. If you don't like it, go out and do something about it. Get involved. Vote. Cast a ballot, preferably an informed one. That surely is at minimum what integrity demands of the citizen.

But all of this may seem rather pie-in-the-sky. In our busy world, the peculiar secret of our electoral politics may be that despite our partisan furies, the day-to-day lives of most Americans remain relatively unaffected by the outcome of national elections. If this is so, there is no obvious reason to suppose that we will do the hard work that is required to alter our choice for rational ignorance (see chapter 12). Even if the fullest practical information *is* the key to an integral electoral politics, we may lack a ready base of reliable sources to get it. History has taught us that we cannot rely on the candidates themselves to campaign in accordance with the rules for integrity. Instead, we have come to rely on our mass media of communication, sheltered and liberated by the First Amendment's protections, for unbiased and useful information about our politics, which means that if journalists do not do their jobs with integrity (see chapter 7), we, the people, can hardly be expected to do ours.

But this criticism can go too far. If we, the citizens of the United States, are to be people of integrity, then we cannot, past a certain point, blame our politicians for misleading us or our media for misinforming us. If we are too busy or too cynical to go out and do the hard work of democracy—the work of digging up the facts instead of relying on others to spoon-feed them to us—then we can hardly complain when others take advantage of our political laziness or incompetence.

Still, the final truth bears repeating: we cannot expect our politicians to create a politics better than we are. If we the citizens, as we consider governance, think only of our own narrow interests, whether expressed in terms of "our" tax dollars or "our" constitutional rights, we can hardly expect to find a government, at the local, state, or national levels, that operates with a needed vision of national purpose. Instead, we will find a politics as parochial and selfish as we are. In a democracy, it is not only true that people tend to get the *government* they deserve; it is also true that people tend to get the *politics* they deserve.

Edmund Burke warned, famously, that all that is needed for the forces of evil to triumph is for enough good people to do nothing. When we retreat into cynicism or fatalism, we fertilize the ground from which evil springs. I have friends who believe that the forces of evil triumphed in 1994. I have friends who believe that the forces of evil were defeated in 1994. Both groups of friends, I think, are wrong. But there is evil abroad in the land, as there is evil at work in the human soul. If we do not demand of our politics sufficient integrity to keep evil at bay, we will wake one horrible morning and stare the triumphant evil in the face—in the mirror.

(fourteen)

Coda: Integrity, Evil, and the American Core

EVIL, evil, evil—it confounds every moral theory. And the modern mind, as Hannah Arendt pointed out, is not satisfied with Aquinas, who would have us accept that evil is simply a deficiency in good. Evil is palpable, miasmic, as real as anything in the world. We look at Stalin or Hitler or the genocidal slaughter in Bosnia or Rwanda; we look at children here at home, today, shooting other children (one is shot every ninety minutes); we look at bikers displaying the Confederate battle flag; we look at crowds cheering for celebrities who murder or rape; we look at the viciousness—not madness, but viciousness—of the April 1995 bombing of the Oklahoma City federal building; and we can hardly evade the truth that evil indeed exists.

Elaine Pagels, in her book *The Origin of Satan*, argues that the early Christian Church developed the idea of Satan as a way of (literally) demonizing its opponents—as far too many Christians do today. I am neither historian nor theologian enough to say whether she is right, but I think myself on safe ground when I agree with those who say that the devil does a lot of advertising. One does not need a Satan to understand evil; but one does, unfortunately, need evil to understand *us*. Because we mortals do a lot of it.

Evil is probably the greatest challenge for the student of integrity: a challenge because the traditional philosophical understanding of the virtue of integrity has been a life lived in accordance with a consistent set of principles. One can well imagine a set of principles that is utterly immoral—or, let us say, utterly evil—and a life lived consistently in accordance with them. Indeed, we have seen such "principled" evil in history—even in our own century.

So before we close our investigation of integrity, we must take the time to consider two final questions: Can great evil have its own integrity? And, in the face of great evil, what is the responsibility of one who strives to live with integrity?

THE "PROBLEM" OF EVIL

The philosopher Antony Flew once wrote that the Problem of Evil (he used the capital letters) "seems to attract bad arguments as jam-making attracts wasps."[1] Flew had in mind the theologians and philosophers who have tried, without noticeable success, to explain evil away, to suggest that it does not exist or that it is always relative and never absolute, or that we should not use the word, as its only substantive content is supplied by our biases.

As the century draws near its close, our inability to talk about evil weakens moral dialogue. The *New York Times Magazine* ran a cover story in early 1995, asking whether evil has returned; but most Americans, whether able to talk about it or not, surely had no reason to think it had ever left. When I say *evil,* genuine evil is what I mean, rather than the policy choices that pass for "evil" in our fractious political debates: not trimming a few dollars a month from Social Security, but murdering people for their Social Security checks; not muttering a racial epithet, but slaughtering people because of their race; not making violent films in Hollywood, but preaching violence from the pulpit; not demanding the right to own assault weapons, but blowing up buildings to make a point. So although we may have trouble talking about it, we are certainly surrounded by it.

Our modern concept of evil is in some sense a Christian invention. The Greeks did not need it because they did not have a concept of will—not in the modern sense of volition—and thus were not concerned with the problem of *freedom*, the problem of whether human beings might will bad things.[2] Virtue was for the Greeks simply a habit, the habit that virtuous people would necessarily develop as they came to understand how they ought to act. So if people acted in ways that did harm or were otherwise unvirtuous, there was a flaw in their reason, or perhaps they had never been exposed to the good, which is part of the point of Plato's famous allegory of the cave. Then they could be trained to be virtuous, or perhaps even made to be virtuous. But at no point was there a serious issue of will.

Christianity needed the will principally because of the nature of the covenant of Grace, an offer from God that the believer had to accept from his or her own free will. One could not be trained to it; one had to accept or reject God's love. Moreover, to make sense of the concept of sin, one needed the freedom to choose to obey or disobey the will of God. Aquinas put it this way:

> God left man in the hand of his own counsel, not in the sense that he could do whatever he pleases, but that he approach every act, not under the stricture of a natural necessity, in the way non-rational creatures do, but out of free choice issuing from his own counsel.[3]

Of course, the traditional vision of Christian integrity found that virtue in submission to *God's* will, and thus in surrendering the very will that Christianity had in effect invented in its effort to understand Grace. Yet this seeming paradox makes sense. The point is that evil results from the rejection of the divine will and its replacement with the human will. The proper use of the human will, then, is to *will to follow God's will.* In the words of W. S. Tyler: "The truly upright man not only subjects his whole being to the supremacy of conscience, but submits his conscience to the law and will of God as the infallible standard of moral rectitude."[4] The psalmist says "The law of the Lord is perfect" (Ps. 19:7), which means, according to Maimonides, that the believer cannot resort to the excuse that "its burdens are grievous, heavy, and difficult to bear."[5]

The concept of integrity developed in this book updates this understanding by proposing that the standard of moral rectitude is not (necessarily) "the law and will of God" but our reflective and sometimes self-sacrificing judgments on right and wrong. So in the more general analysis we have been attempting here, one can at once see the point. The distinction that the person of integrity must draw in order to avoid evil is between *willing good* and *willing evil.* Willing good occurs when, upon due reflection, we will ourselves to do and speak that which we now know to be the right, even when the burden is heavy. Willing evil occurs—just as in the Christian tradition—when we do *anything else.* This last point is crucial. Evil is not simply the result of a decision to do a bad thing; it is the result of refusing to make a decision to do a good thing. That is the Christian understanding, and it is quite communitarian as well; it rejects important parts of the modern libertarian ethos in favor of a sense of *duty*. The idea is that confident knowledge of the good entails a duty to will it—and therefore to do it—just as confident knowledge of the evil entails a duty not to will it—and therefore to avoid it.

Even if we thus conclude that evil, like good, is a choice (and a choice that any one of us might make), that does not bring us any closer to solving the "Problem" of evil: why a just God would allow it to exist. Fortunately, in our more secular moral analysis, we need not find an answer; we can simply acknowledge that it is so. Perhaps even the devout believer would ultimately agree with what F. C. Copleston wrote in his splendid monograph on Aquinas: "To this question, why God chose this world, foreseeing all the evils which would in fact occur, no answer, I think, can be given."[6] Evil, in other words, for the theologian no less than for the philosopher or the lawyer or the citizen, remains a mystery. But we do know this: God, like politics and like law, sometimes allows it to happen.

THE INTEGRITY OF EVIL

In chapter 4, we briefly examined a question with which philosophers and theologians have struggled for centuries: Can an evil person be described as a person of integrity? The challenge posed by the question goes to the heart of the argument so far. If, as I have argued, a life lived with integrity is a life in which a person discerns what is right and true, strives to live that way, and is open about the rules by which he or she is striving to live, it might seem that Hitler or Pol Pot could say on the Day of Judgment: "I did what I thought was right. I lived with integrity." Indeed, the Bosnian Serbs, who are at this writing conducting what appears to the rest of the world to be a war of aggression, insist that it is a war for the good: that they are trying to right a six-hundred-year-old wrong in which their land was taken.

Is this possible? Augustine, heavily influenced by Plato, thought that the knowledge of good and evil was evident. He called the God-given knowledge of the truth the Idea, our goal in life being to discover the Ideas and then to follow them. Augustine thought that knowledge of the Ideas came only through divine illumination. Thus prayer and contemplation could help us to open our minds to learn from God what was right and what was wrong; evil came from the avoidance of this knowledge or, perhaps, the refusal of this opportunity.

The Hitler who lacks the capacity to discern may fairly be supposed to be insane, but insanity is not the only possible description of an individual who is unable to discern the certain knowledge of right and wrong, the Idea. It may be that the faculty is dulled through nonuse—maybe because it has never been trained, maybe because the mind is so encrusted with prejudice and cant that the faculty has been buried. (We saw this point in the example from Jonathan Lear in chapter 4.) These possibilities in a Hitler help illustrate why all of us, children included, should exercise, and should encourage others to exercise, the discerning faculty as often as possible.

Elsewhere, I have criticized on moral grounds the argument that Hitler was not evil, just insane, because we must not suspend our capacity for judgment.[7] But armed with the Augustinian vision of the nature of good and the Aquinian vision of the nature of evil, we can see that it makes no difference which was true. Aquinas would say that it is impossible for a discerning human being—in our terms, a human being with integrity—to mistake the evil of mass murder and genocide for the good. But how can an adult human being be nondiscerning? There are only two ways, Aquinas would likely say: either the individual lacks the capacity to discern the truth (in Augustinian terms, the Idea) or the individual is being willfully blind, refusing to follow where the divine light leads.

If we do follow the divine light—or, in our more secular analysis, if we do the hard work of discernment—then we are more likely to see the good. Not the good of everything, but the good of, the right answer to, the particular problem to which we turn our reflective attention. Here is where Aristotle was clearly correct: the more time we spend in discernment, the more it will become a habit. The more it becomes a habit, the better we will be able to avoid true evil. Integrity, so understood, leaves little space for evil to take root. According to W. S. Tyler, "[i]ntegrity fortifies against temptation"—and it is yielding to temptation that brings about evil. Integrity, says Tyler, "everywhere fears to sin because God is there"; even when nobody would know of the sin, the person of integrity says "how can I do this great evil, and sin against God!"[8]

To turn once more to our secular analysis, the point of doing good must be something other than seeking a reward. Indeed, as we have seen, identifying, doing, and speaking the good will often carry a significant cost. The cost may be that others will be critical of us. The cost may be forgoing a particular pleasure or desire. Or the cost may be greater. But even if there is no cost to doing right, we must also not yield to the temptation to do wrong simply because that, too, seems to have no cost. Each time we justify going against what our reflective morality tells us is truly right, or each time we refuse to reflect at all, we make it easier to do the same again tomorrow. Tyler puts it this way: "The vices are gregarious. They feed in herds; when you see one, you may be pretty sure there are others in the neighborhood."[9] And again: "Resist the beginnings of evil; once let loose, it will be like the letting out of water."[10]

The vices feed in herds. We forget this not only when we commit small wrongs, thinking we can avoid big ones, but also when we stand by and allow others to do it. When Hannah Arendt wrote in *Eichmann in Jerusalem* about the banality of evil, she was actually writing about what we have called integrity. Arendt pointed out that even huge evils—like the Holocaust—result from many seemingly small decisions by ordinary individuals. One need only look the other way one day, order a particular piece of equipment the next, and one is complicit. There is no need for grandiose conspiracies, or even for massively evil individuals, but only for everyday thoughtlessness. That is the point: our obligation to integrity is to think about all the little decisions we make each day, because those decisions, if made recklessly rather than deliberately, can lead to evils far greater than any one of them alone. Evil, like good, has its synergy, and all of us can play our parts—*will* play our parts—unless we think before we act, rather than later.

I know this sounds preachy, and I do not mean it to be. I am not one who is always or perhaps even often reflective. I am not one who is able always to do what I believe to be right, most notably when there is a cost involved. But I am more convinced than ever that struggling to do those things is what life requires of all of us if we are to avoid falling into evil. Which might be another way of saying that the journey that this book represents has convinced me to try harder.

TOLERATING EVIL

A person of integrity, morally reflective and willing to act, should be able to recognize evil. (How one does it is a question that, for the moment, we shall pass.) When evil—true evil—is found, the person of integrity must choose either to do something about it or to learn to live with it. The choice is not as easy as it may seem: even the person of integrity has limited resources of time and emotional and physical energy. The philosopher Isaiah Berlin, widely regarded as a skeptic on moral truth, surely had this in mind when he wrote that we cannot possibly accomplish all our moral goals.[11] In short, priorities must be set. Some evils must be fought, others, perhaps for the short term and perhaps for the long, can be tolerated.

In chapter 4, we briefly examined the connection between the ideal of toleration and the reality of evil. The word *toleration* has a particular historical origin. It developed as a proposed solution to the religious wars in Europe, especially in England, and its original reference was to allowing all people to worship God as they pleased. In this the concept relied crucially on the belief/action distinction: it dealt with what one thought, not what one did. Indeed, in his justly famous defense of toleration, Locke so strictly limited the application of the term that it did not even include atheism.[12] The state, said Locke, rests on certain religious presuppositions, so that atheism was, in effect, the enemy of order.

Nowadays, the use of the word *toleration* is quite different, for it often refers to people's freedom to do things. When I call upon you to tolerate me, I am asking you to forbear from regulating or even criticizing my choices about how to fulfill my own needs. This is not, of course, integrity; integrity demands consistent attention to what we *should* do rather than what we *desire* to do. Moreover, as the philosopher Charles Taylor points out, "the culture of self-fulfillment has led many people to lose sight of concerns that transcend them."[13] If nothing is larger than we are, we are not so much morally reflective as self-absorbed. But once we discern that something *is* larger than we are, that same something might turn out to be larger than everybody else as well. (At least in our own judgment.)

This, of course, is where toleration and integrity break down, for when we find something larger than other people, we generally have trouble "tolerating" others who prefer to ignore it. To take the most obvious example from our fractured politics, for one who genuinely believes in the personhood, or simply the right to life, of the human fetus, it is difficult to know what to do with the suggestion that one "tolerate" individuals holding the opposite view—at least if toleration means allowing them to have abortions. The same difficulty applies to core issues of religious practice. People who consider it wrong to harm animals have little patience with, say, the Santería religious tradition, in which animals are sometimes sacrificed in order to nourish the personal gods that are believed to govern human fate. And people who believe that racism is a great moral evil are not interested in tolerating educational institutions, private or not, religious or not, that exist in part to further it.

One of the difficulties, then, with any demand that we temper our integrity with tolerance is that hardly anybody is actually interested in doing it. In our politics, we quite famously call for others to tolerate what we want to do, and we quite famously refuse to tolerate what others want to do. Just think for a moment of our debates over gay rights on the one hand and gun ownership on the other. In each case, opponents insist that what they are trying to ban is harmful, and in each case, proponents want to be tolerated in the classic sense in which Brandeis and Warren understood privacy: they want to be left alone.

The trouble with the modern American community is that there is no longer much space (geographical or psychological) in which to be left alone: there is no way, at least no easy way, to go off and do what one pleases in a way that affects nobody else. Clever philosophers since John Stuart Mill have filled volumes with efforts to find the limits to tolerance, but all of them assume, across a broad range of cases, the existence of that space that the modern state makes so terribly hard to find. Perhaps what explains our relentless modern urge to regulate each other's private conduct is a growing sense that there is no longer a significant *empirical* distinction between public and private. Our very homes are becoming so wired to so many others that it is harder and harder to speak of even that most sacrosanct of spaces as *private.*

Although any democrat must count that development a loss, the student of integrity should also see an opportunity. Our growing loss of privacy forces us to confront evils that we otherwise might ignore: it is no longer possible to pretend that few husbands beat their wives behind closed doors or that no politicians tell racist jokes when they think they are alone. We might argue over what, among all that goes on in our increasingly tiny world, is evil—a point we shall presently examine—but we cannot close our eyes. We must, obviously, condemn what discernment has taught us to be wrong. But we must also (following Tyler's point) offer to the potential evildoer an alternative vision of the right. The vision need not be religious. To the extent that the vision has some official recognition, it *must not* be religious. The way to do it in America is to make the case that there exists a set of values in which America believes.

PREVENTING EVIL: TOWARD AN AMERICAN CORE

Václav Havel, the dissenting writer who rose to become the President of the Czech Republic, has warned that our efforts to craft institutional arrangements that meet the necessities of our complicated age are "doomed to failure if they do not grow out of something deeper, out of generally held values."[14] The point applies not just to change but to stability. What distinguishes democracy—especially *this* democracy—is not the fact that we can vote. Many nations on earth vote, and not all of those nations would be considered democracies. What makes democracy different—what makes *America* different—is surely our attachment to a set of prodemocratic values, values that might be termed the American Core.

When I refer to "our" attachment to a set of values, I do not mean to imply unanimity. I do believe that our institutions of government presume some baseline set of propositions that will not be challenged. Over the years, the content of this American Core has evolved along with our national understanding of the lessons of history. But the Core, I believe, exists. If it doesn't, we are in a great deal of trouble.

Why are we in trouble? We are in trouble because nobody grows up to be good by accident. If we are to accept the lessons of this search for integrity, and thus to press toward a morally discerning society, all of our institutions must begin to reflect not only this process but its results. One reason for the popularity of the character education movement is surely that parents understand the needs of their children for clear, firm moral instruction. It is not enough to say that it is the responsibility of the parents to teach their children right from wrong. If we are to look on our society as a community, the responsibility is a shared one: and so the lessons in right and wrong that children learn at home must be *reinforced*, not only in the curriculum of the public schools but by the example of adults and institutions throughout the society.

People used to say that we transmit values from one generation to the next by resting them on a three-legged stool: the home, the school, and the place of worship. If any leg of the stool breaks, the transmission does not work. The classroom prayer movement, I believe, reflects this model: many of the parents who insist that their children pray in school simply want the schools to reinforce the values taught in the home. And when we are so hard on elected officials for relatively small breaches of ethics, perhaps we are appealing to the same faith: we want our government institutions to reinforce the simple moral truths that we teach our children.

The common objection that Americans cannot agree on values is not only false—it is dangerous nonsense. True, we have trouble on such issues as abortion (although even there, as I noted in chapter 13, our differences tend to be exaggerated). But on the basics, our agreement is broad. Samuel Rabinove of the American Jewish Committee has argued that the values our public institutions (including our schools) reinforce should be *consensus* values—those that are shared across religious traditions.[15] This is not as hard to accomplish as one might think. Some very basic values—the

Golden Rule, for example, and an ethic of loving one's neighbor—are common to every major American religious group. If we cannot agree on such basic truths as these, we will in years to come be unable to resolve the moral crisis threatening our nation.

As it turns out, more than 90 percent of American adults do agree on an American Core—not only on the rules I mentioned but on such notions as respect for others, persistence, compassion, and fairness.[16] It is not that hard to work out such a Core. And if we can't do it, we are not a nation— or, at least, we cannot expect to be a successful one.

Moreover, there is no way to avoid teaching values. Adults do it by example, whether we speak them or not. Television transmits its set of values. So does politics. So do our relationships with family, friends, and neighbors. The question before us is only whether we choose to do it deliberately or by happenstance. And only the first choice can play a significant role in helping our children to learn the skill of moral discernment—and, in so doing, reducing the tendency of the vices to herd.

TOWARD ABSOLUTE EVIL

In chapter 4, I suggested that there are some evils great enough that the person who espouses them cannot possibly be a person of integrity. The time has come to consider what some of those great evils are—and also to ask about the responsibility of people of integrity who find themselves confronted with one. I emphasize that I am talking about evil—not just the fact of being wrong, but the fact of being evil—and, in so doing, I am proposing ideas that are sufficiently beyond the pale that one who holds them cannot do so with integrity, and so is suffering from moral blindness, willed or accidental. In short, as I have said before, I do not believe that one who disagrees with me on a particular proposition of morality or politics is evil—not unless that person espouses one of the evils I mention here.

I cannot prepare an exhaustive list of evils, and so I will list only three— but on these three, much else that is evil in our society depends: racial hatred; violence based on difference; and violence resulting from a closed mind.

Why racial hatred? Surely history has taught us the answer. We have too much experience, in our own nation and in every part of the globe, about what happens when we mistreat people—or just despise people—because of the color of their skin. It is far too late in the human day for any person of integrity to say with honesty, "I have thought the matter through and I have decided to hate those whose race is different from mine."

Why violence based on difference? Because violence is one of the most horrible acts of which the human organism is capable: the deliberate or reckless physical harming of another human. There are times when it is probably unavoidable: for example, in self-defense. But to do it because of a distaste—to lynch black people or Roman Catholics, to batter women, to assault homosexuals—can have no explanation but that one has yielded to evil.

Why violence resulting from a closed mind? Because democracy demands dialogue. The refusal of one citizen to engage in reasoned discussion with another is already an offense against a different civic virtue, civility (the subject of my next book). When this closed-mindedness is accompanied by the same deliberate or reckless harming of another, we have a complete act of evil, for we have committed a terrible act through nothing more than our selfish unwillingness to listen.

I emphasize that this list of great evils is no more than a preliminary effort. I would very much like to hear from readers who have differing opinions—and, in particular, readers who have concrete, thoughtful arguments for which other evils should be placed on the list of those beliefs which no person of integrity can hold.

GENOCIDE: THE GREATEST EVIL

The trial of Adolf Eichmann was an effort to force the world to agree that genocide—the willed and systematic destruction of a people—is so utterly wrong that no limits exist on what we will do to bring to justice those who perpetrate it. And I think the point correct. Genocide is the single most truly horrible evil that it is possible for a human being, or a group of human beings, to commit.

Genocide brings together all three of the evils that I argued no person of integrity can espouse: racism; violence based on difference; and violence resulting from a closed mind. In his autobiography, written after his conversion to the genuine and brotherly Islam of which he found the Nation of Islam a cruel caricature, Malcolm X referred to racism as "the earth's most explosive and pernicious evil." Consider for a moment the two adjectives: *explosive* and *pernicious*. I suppose we all know what he meant by *pernicious*. What could he have meant by *explosive*?

We should think, I suggest, not of explosiveness in the sense that the oppressed may take up arms, although that certainly can and does occur.

We should think instead of the way the racist impulse can explode in the racist and in the fellow traveler of racism, so that suddenly, with little warning, individual mobs may carry out acts of violence against the despised, or, worse, the state may adopt policies of oppression or even destruction. And all at once, having added up racism and the two most evil forms of violence, we have genocide.

Genocide is not a twentieth-century invention. In the Hebrew Bible, entire peoples are wiped out time and again, to the very last man. The Romans (probably) practiced it in Egypt. Europeans practiced it in the Americas. Peoples, as self-defined, were destroyed in Asia, in Africa, in Europe—in short, wherever there were people. But what has forever embarrassed Western philosophy is that genocide could *still happen* after the Enlightenment freed us from the shackles, it is said, of primitive superstition. This must have been what Senator Daniel Patrick Moynihan had in mind in the spring of 1995, when he asked, if the West was truly unwilling to undertake serious military operations to protect the Bosnian Muslims from the Bosnian Serbs, what the twentieth century was for.

Moynihan's question should trouble us. The signal foreign policy accomplishments of the century were the successful hot war against fascism and the successful cold war against communism. The signal domestic accomplishment of the century has been our not yet concluded war against racial oppression. At this writing, Bosnia is a problem that the West has not solved. I do not mean that the West has not solved hatred and violence, which may indeed be the human condition; I mean that the West has not solved the problem of what to do when confronted with an evil so absolute.

How absolute? We saw in the aggression of the Bosnian Serbs the ruthless destruction of another people. Concentration camps. Mass murders. Rape, *evidently as policy*, to ensure an intermixing of bloodlines. For more than two years, the West did little more than wring its hands as it tried to figure out how to protect the soldiers who are for some reason referred to as peacekeepers.

Some critics of American policy have argued that our strange willingness to do little proves that America has no principles other than those that happen to affect our citizens directly—at least none worth fighting for. This may be too harsh, although it may be that there is more to it than we like to think. Still, as some defenders of American policy have argued, there are ethnic slaughters all over the globe, and we can hardly decide to send troops only when the victims happen to win time on CNN.

On the other hand, our inability for so long even to agree to allow the suffering Muslims to buy weapons to protect themselves was a national failure of will for which history, I suspect, will not treat us kindly. We talk much nowadays of character education, which has always been, and remains, a very fine idea. But the principal education for character that we do, we do by example. Virtually every proposed curriculum on values teaches children that genocide is wrong. Virtually every international security agreement states that aggression is wrong. In Bosnia, there is aggression and there is genocide, and America, like the rest of the world, took years to decide that there was something at stake worth fighting for. That dawdling will teach our children far more loudly than any values curriculum that we do not after all mean what we say.

I ask again: What crime could be more horrible than genocide? If we do not see the planned elimination of a people as the horror of horrors, then what, as Moynihan asked, was the twentieth century for? And if we do see it as a horror, then what could more powerfully test our national will? Is that really how America of the late twentieth century is to be remembered in the history books: we will fight to protect our people and our oil, but if the rest of the world wants to engage in slaughter, that is the rest of the world's business?

Bosnia is not unique. We live in a world in which are committed unspeakable atrocities every day. These, too, are tests of our integrity—of our belief in the existence of principles that transcend our self-interest and of our willingness to act consistently with those principles. And day by day, still appalled by our experience of Vietnam, we fail those tests.

I tremble for my country.

But there I go, sounding preachy again. I do not mean to. For I also love my country, its spirit, its generosity, and its warm and wonderful and often clumsy desire to do good. This book has been a small effort to help us figure out how to satisfy that particular desire. In Aristotle's *Ethics*, people would do good because doing good was a habit of the virtuous. In Thomas More's *Utopia*, people would do good without even thinking about it. But we live in a psychologically more complicated time. Doing the right thing rather than the wrong is neither habit nor instinct. It is will.

How can it be otherwise? Aristotle understood the point. So did Plato, so did Aquinas, so did Locke, so did Rousseau, who probably put it best when he wrote that by moving from the state of nature to the civil state, we find that "the voice of duty takes the place of *physical* impulses and right of appetite," so that man "is forced to act on different principles, and to consult his reason before listening to his inclinations."[17] This approach provides the foundation of integrity as I have discussed it in this book: we must make the effort to learn what is right (rather than what we desire) and then to do it. Aristotle placed the intellect over the appetites, Rousseau placed reason above inclination, and the theologians placed God's will above our own. What one sees in every case is the refusal to accept as the measure of morality our choice to do the things that most attract us. To make satisfaction of our desires the only morality is to choose the path away from civil society—away from *civilization*—and back to the state of nature. Valuing the appetites above reason is the path, in fact, toward evil. And that path integrity forbids us to take.

Notes

CHAPTER 1. THE RULES ABOUT THE RULES

1. On cheating by college students, see Karen Thomas, "Rise in Cheating Called Response to Fall in Values," *USA Today*, August 2, 1995, p. 1A. I do not know whether the irony of the headline was intentional.
2. See, for example, *Ryder v. United States,* 115 S. Ct. 2031 (1995).
3. In this I am influenced to some extent by the fine discussion of integrity in Martin Benjamin's book *Splitting the Difference: Compromise and Integrity in Ethics and Politics* (Lawrence: University Press of Kansas, 1990).
4. St. Thomas Aquinas, *The Summa Theologica,* tr. Father L. Shapcote, revised by Daniel L. Sullivan, 2d ed. (Chicago: Encyclopedia Britannica, 1990), 2a2ae, 104, 3.
5. John Wesley, "On the Law Established Through Faith," in *The Works of the Rev. John Wesley,* vol. 8 (London: Thomas Cordeaux, 1811), p. 144.
6. Quoted in Abraham Joshua Heschel, *Maimonides: A Biography,* tr.

Joachim Neugroschel (New York: Image Books, 1991), p. 203. The German edition was published in 1935.

7. W. S. Tyler, *Integrity the Safeguard of Public and Private Life* (Springfield: Samuel Bowles, 1857), p. 6.

8. See Robert Cover, *Justice Accused: Antislavery and the Judicial Process* (New Haven, CT: Yale University Press, 1975).

CHAPTER 2. THE INTEGRITY OF THE UPRIGHT

1. The story is set forth in some detail in Milton R. Konvitz, "Conscience and Civil Disobedience in the Jewish Tradition," in Menachem Marc Kellner, ed., *Contemporary Jewish Ethics* (New York: Sanhedrin Press, 1978), p. 239. Konvitz borrows the story from Josephus's *Antiquities of the Jews*.

2. Quoted in Cathleen Decker, "Gore Says U.S. Needs 'Second Breath of Life,'" *Los Angeles Times*, July 17, 1992, p. A9.

3. Quoted in "McGovern Compares Notes with Dukakis," *New York Times*, November 17, 1988, p. B12.

4. "Quotations of the Day," *New York Times*, September 26, 1988, p. A2.

5. See Andrew Rosenthal, "Dukakis Sharply Attacks Bush on Ethics," *New York Times*, September 29, 1988, p. D28.

6. Quoted in "Jackson Stumps for Mondale," *New York Times*, September 4, 1984, p. B9.

7. "Gov. Deukmejian's Remarks," *New York Times*, August 23, 1984, p. A27.

8. Editorial, "Integrity in Washington," *New York Times*, October 29, 1972, sec. 4, p. 14.

9. Joseph Dana, D.D., *Integrity Explained and Recommended: A Sermon Preached at the North Meetinghouse in Salem, September 8, 1807* (Pool and Polfroy, 1808).

10. For a fascinating discussion of the way the word *integrity* is used (and misused) in debates over how to read the biblical text, see Alan P. F. Sell, *Aspects of Christian Integrity* (Louisville, KY: Westminster/John Knox Press, 1990), esp. chaps. 1 and 2.

11. James M. Gustafson, *Can Ethics Be Christian?* (Chicago: University of Chicago Press, 1975), p. 26.

12. All quotations from *Antigone* are taken from Elizabeth Wyckoff's fine translation, but I will not burden the reader with page numbers. Wyckoff's translation may be found in Sophocles, *The Complete Greek Tragedies*, ed. D. Grene (Chicago: University of Chicago Press, 1954).

13. As Martha Nussbaum points out, where Creon draws a dividing line between those who fight for the city and those who fight against it, Antigone draws a dividing line between those who are members of her family and those who are not. Both of them, then, value persons for the category into which they fall, rather than for anything particular to the person. Martha C. Nussbaum, *The Fragility of Goodness: Luck and Ethics in Greek Tragedy and Philosophy* (Cambridge: Cambridge University Press, 1986), pp. 63–65. This problem, although beyond the scope of the present book, plainly presents a challenge for the moral sense: in particular, there is no easier definition of *prejudice.*

14. Nussbaum, *The Fragility of Goodness,* p. 63.

15. *Catechism of the Catholic Church* (Mahwah, NJ: Paulist Press, 1994), p. 441 (secs. 1790–91) (footnote omitted).

16. For an enlightening discussion of *Antigone* that makes some of the same points as mine, and some very different ones as well, see George Fletcher, *Loyalty: An Essay on the Morality of Relationships* (New York: Oxford, 1993), pp. 27–31.

17. Lynne McFall, "Integrity," *Ethics* 98 (October 1987): 5, 9.

18. Ibid., p. 8.

19. Stuart Hampshire, *Morality and Conflict* (Oxford: Basil Blackwell, 1983), p. 159.

20. Paul Jersild, *Making Moral Decisions: A Christian Approach to Personal and Social Ethics* (Minneapolis: Augsburg Fortress, 1990), p. 21.

21. John Wesley, "On the Law Established Through Faith," in *The Works of the Rev. John Wesley,* vol. 8 (London: Thomas Cordeaux, 1811), p. 151.

22 St. Thomas Aquinas, *The Summa Theologica,* tr. Father L. Shapcote, revised by Daniel L. Sullivan, 2d ed. (Chicago: Encyclopedia Britannica, 1990), 2a2ae, 104, 4.

23. Quoted in Abraham Joshua Heschel, *Maimonides: A Biography,* tr. Joachim Neugroschel (New York: Image Books, 1991), p. 64. The book was first published in 1935 and the English translation first appeared in 1982.

24. W. S. Tyler, *Integrity the Safeguard of Public and Private Life* (Springfield: Samuel Bowles, 1857), p. 6.

25. Bernard Williams, *Ethics and the Limits of Philosophy* (Cambridge, MA: Harvard University Press, 1985), p. 169.

26. For a different response to Williams, emphasizing the role of reflectiveness in helping us to understand and evaluate our own characters, see Jonathan Lear, *Aristotle: The Desire to Understand* (Cambridge: Cambridge University Press, 1988), pp. 186–91.

27. St. Augustine, *The City of God*, tr. Marcus Dods (New York: Modern Library, 1993).

28. Hannah Arendt notes this characteristic of Socrates. See Hannah Arendt, *The Life of the Mind—Part I: Thinking* (New York: Harcourt Brace, 1978), p. 197. I am indebted to Tony Kronman for pointing me in this direction.

CHAPTER 3. WHY IS INTEGRITY ADMIRABLE?

1. Warren Bennis, *On Becoming a Leader* (Reading, MA: Addison-Wesley, 1989), p. 41.

2. Editorial, "Integrity in Washington," *New York Times*, October 29, 1972, sec. 4, p. 14.

3. Some, but not all, of this tale may be found in Steve Gerstel, "Biden Rolls Political Dice on Manion Vote—Comes Up Snake Eyes," June 27, 1986, United Press International [Nexis].

4. Lewis B. Smedes, "The Power of Promises," in Thomas G. Long and Cornelius Plantinga, Jr., *A Chorus of Witnesses: Model Sermons for Today's Preacher* (Grand Rapids, MI: William B. Eerdmans, 1994), pp. 155, 157.

5. Ibid.

6. Anthony T. Kronman, "Specific Performance," *University of Chicago Law Review* 45 (1978): 351.

7. For discussion, see, for example, Howard O. Hunter, "An Essay on Contract and Status," *Virginia Law Review* 65 (1978): 1072.

8. Sandra Salmans, "Schwieker: Odd Man In," *Newsweek*, August 9, 1976, p. 16.

9. Quoted in David Alpern, "Reagan's Last Gamble," *Newsweek*, August 9, 1976, p. 14.

10. See generally the discussion in Burt Solomon, "The Press, the President, the Pits and the Pendulum," *National Journal* 26, no. 4 (November 5, 1994): 2600. See also Thomas E. Patterson, "Clinton's Bad Rep Is a Bad Rap," *USA Today*, August 17, 1994, p. 11A. Patterson is the author of *Out of Order* (New York: Knopf, 1993), which argues persuasively that the press now covers Presidents in an excessively cynical and negative way, giving rise to similarly cynical and negative public sentiment. I discuss this and another study in chap. 6.

11. Bennis, *On Becoming a Leader*, p. 43.

12. John Henry Cardinal Newman, *Apologia Pro Vita Sua* (New York: Longmans, Green, 1947), p. 321.

13. Sissela Bok, *Lying: Moral Choice in Public and Private Life* (New York: Vintage Books, 1989; orig. pub. 1978), p. 178.

14. The classic works on the informing function of brand name advertising are George Stigler, "The Economics of Information," *Journal of Political Economy* 69 (1961): 213, and Phillip Nelson, "Information and Consumer Behavior," *Journal of Political Economy* 78 (1970): 311. For a useful discussion of this work by legal scholars, see William Landes and Richard Posner, "Trademark Law: An Economic Perspective," *Journal of Law and Economics* 30 (1987): 265.

15. I discuss this work in Stephen L. Carter, *The Confirmation Mess: Cleaning Up the Federal Appointments Process* (New York: Basic Books, 1994), pp. 13–14.

16. See ibid., p. 14.

17. I recount the battle over the Guinier nomination in ibid., chap. 2.

18. Editorial, "The Tainted Foster Nomination," *New York Times*, February 10, 1995.

19. Editorial, "A Vote for Foster," *The New Republic*, March 6, 1995, p. 9.

20. For a discussion, not all of which I endorse, of this phenomenon, see Ronald Dworkin, *Life's Dominion: An Argument About Abortion, Euthanasia, and Individual Freedom* (New York: Knopf, 1993) pp. 34–47.

21. Garry Wills has suggested that Dukakis's ultimate defeat—he squandered a double-digit lead in the polls—was based precisely on a perception by a majority of voters that he lacked the passion and spirituality they want in their leaders. Garry Wills, *Under God: Religion and American Politics* (New York: Simon & Schuster, 1990).

22. Lynne McFall, "Integrity," *Ethics* 98 (October 1987): 19.

23. Ibid.

24. Martin Benjamin, *Splitting the Difference: Compromise and Integrity in Ethics and Politics* (Lawrence: University Press of Kansas, 1990), p. 173.

25. Quoted in James O'Toole, *Leading Change: Overcoming the Ideology of Comfort and the Tyranny of Custom* (San Francisco: Jossey-Bass, 1995), p. 24.

26. Quoted in Garry Wills, *Lincoln at Gettysburg: The Words That Remade America* (New York: Simon & Schuster, 1992), p. 138.

27. Pope John Paul II, *The Gospel of Life* (New York: Times Books, 1995), p. 135.

28. "Guilty Plea in Threat to Abortion Opponents," *New York Times*, June 7, 1995, p. A20.

CHAPTER 4. CODA: THE INSUFFICIENCY OF HONESTY

1. Sissela Bok, *Lying: Moral Choice in Public and Private Life* (New York: Vintage Books, 1989; orig. pub. 1978), p. 13.
2. For a general discussion of situations in which the law either requires or forbids disclosure, see Kim Lane Scheppele, *Legal Secrets: Equality and Efficiency in the Common Law* (Chicago: University of Chicago Press, 1988).
3. *Near v. Minnesota*, 283 U.S. 697, 704 (1931).
4. *Snepp v. United States*, 444 U.S. 507 (1980) (per curiam).
5. See *Haig v. Agee*, 453 U.S. 280 (1981).
6. For scholarly criticism of this argument on the ground that the government might otherwise have too much control over information, see, for example, Vince Blasi, "The Checking Value in First Amendment Theory," *American Bar Foundation Research Journal* (1977): 521; Cass Sunstein, "Government Control of Information," *California Law Review* 74 (1986): 902. See, generally, "Symposium: National Security and the First Amendment," *William and Mary Law Review* 26 (1985): 715.
7. *Laidlaw v. Organ*, 15 U.S. (2 Wheat.) 178 (1817).
8. See, for example, Scheppele, *Legal Secrets*; Anthony Kronman, "Mistake, Disclosure, Information and the Law of Contracts," *Journal of Legal Studies* 7 (1978): 1.
9. For a more detailed exposition of these points, see Scheppele, *Legal Secrets*.
10. Robert Pear, "Mondale Eases Pledge to Dismiss Reagan Rights Panel Appointees," *New York Times*, August 8, 1984, p. A1.
11. See Jean Bethke Elshtain, *Democracy on Trial* (New York: Basic Books, 1995). Elshtain is borrowing, with due acknowledgment, from John Courtney Murray.
12. See the very fine extended discussion of this point in Michael Perry, *Love and Power* (New York: Oxford University Press, 1991), as well as the shorter but still convincing treatment in R. George Wright, *Reason and Obligation* (Lanham, MD: University Press of America, 1994), pp. 99–106.
13. Christopher Lasch, *The Revolt of the Elites and the Betrayal of Democracy* (New York: Norton, 1995), p. 87.

14. Fred Korn and Shulamit R. Decktor Korn, "Where People Don't Promise," *Ethics* 93 (April 1983): 445.

15. Jonathan Lear, *Aristotle: The Desire to Understand* (Cambridge: Cambridge University Press, 1988), p. 190.

16. Ibid., p. 191.

17. St. Thomas Aquinas, *Summa Theologica*, II, 2, xcv, art. 1.

CHAPTER 5. THE BEST STUDENT EVER

1. Hannah Arendt, "Lying in Politics: Reflections on the Pentagon Papers," in *Crises of the Republic* (New York: Harcourt Brace Jovanovich, 1972), pp. 3, 7.

2. The most recent classroom prayer figure, as of this writing, is a Gallup Poll finding 71 percent in favor of a constitutional amendment to support it. See Mary Beth Marklein, "Discipline Is No. 1 School Concern," *USA Today*, August 23, 1995.

3. See Ronald Dworkin, *Life's Dominion: An Argument About Abortion, Euthanasia, and Individual Freedom* (New York: Knopf, 1993), p. 13.

4. For a fairly simple explanation of puffery and the reasons the courts allow it, see Ivan L. Preston, "The Definition of Deceptiveness in Advertising and Other Commercial Speech," *Catholic Law Review* 39 (1990): 1035. See also Albert Breton and Ronald Wintrobe, "Freedom of Speech v. Efficient Regulation in Market for Ideas," *Journal of Economic Behavior and Organization* 2 (March 1992): 217.

5. This practice may be defended by use of the substantial economic literature on advertising as information. The basic idea is that advertising does not necessarily *persuade* the consumer to make a purchase, but does *inform* the consumer about the products or services that a firm provides. The advertising will keep the brand name before the consumers, so that when they go to make purchases, they will do so with more information. See Phillip Nelson, "The Economic Consequences of Advertising," *Journal of Business* 48 (1975): 213. See also William Landes and Richard Posner, "Trademark Law: An Economic Perspective," *Journal of Law and Economics* 30 (1987): 265.

6. Erik Eckholm, "The Dark Science of Fund-Raising by Mail," *New York Times*, May 28, 1995, sec. 4, p. 6.

7. Ramona L. Paetzold and Steven L. Willborn, "Employer Irrationality and the Demise of Employment References," *American Business Law Journal* (May 1992): 23.

8. Junda Woo, "Quirky Slander Actions Threaten Employers," *Wall Street Journal*, November 26, 1993, p. B1.

9. See, for example, *Clements v. County of Nassau*, 835 F.2d 1000 (2d Cir. 1987) (dismissing bad-faith grading suit); and *Wallen v. Domm*, 532 F. Supp. 73 (E.D. Va. 1982) (dismissing infliction-of-distress suit).

10. *University of Pennsylvania v. Equal Employment Opportunity Commission*, 493 U.S. 182 (1990).

11. See Stephen Wermiel, "Colleges Lose Case on Secrecy of Tenure Files," *Wall Street Journal*, January 10, 1990.

12. See Michael Sicouolfi, "Many Companies Press Analysts to Steer Clear of Negative Ratings," *Wall Street Journal*, July 19, 1995, p. A1.

13. I discuss the old-boy network and its modern derivation, the "star system," in Stephen L. Carter, *Reflections of an Affirmative Action Baby* (New York: Basic Books, 1991), chap. 2.

CHAPTER 6. ALL THE NEWS THAT'S FIT

1. The most recent classroom prayer figure, as of this writing, is a Gallup Poll finding 71 percent in favor of a constitutional amendment to support it. See Mary Beth Marklein, "Discipline Is No. 1 School Concern," *USA Today*, August 23, 1995.

2. All of this analysis is from Stephen Hart, *What Does the Lord Require? How American Christians Think About Economic Justice* (New York: Oxford University Press, 1992), pp. 156–59. Father Andrew Greeley has written a truly sparkling exposé of the ways in which the lives and beliefs of Roman Catholics defy stereotypes. See Andrew M. Greeley, *The Catholic Myth: The Behavior and Beliefs of American Catholics* (New York: Macmillan, 1990).

3. Quoted in Catherine S. Manegold, "Down and Divided in Buffalo, Abortion Foes Suspend Siege," *New York Times*, April 30, 1992, p. A1.

4. See Burt Solomon, "The Press, the President, the Pits and the Pendulum," *National Journal* 26 (November 5, 1994): 2600.

5. Thomas E. Patterson, "Clinton's Bad Rep Is a Bad Rap," *USA Today*, August 17, 1994, p. 11A.

6. Howard Kurtz, "The Teflon Congress," *Washington Post*, September 4, 1994, p. C1.

7. This study and other relevant data are discussed in Morton M. Kondracke, "Is Newt Paranoid About Media Bias? New Study Says No," *Roll Call*, April 20, 1995. See also the postscript to the paperback edi-

tion of Thomas Patterson, *Out of Order* (New York: Knopf, 1993). The paperback was published by Random House in 1994.

8. Quoted in Kondracke, "Is Newt Paranoid About Media Bias?"

9. Jonathan Alter, "They're on Candid Camera," *Newsweek,* October 31, 1994.

10. Although polls taken at the time of the hearings showed that most responents believed Thomas, not Hill, a Gallup poll taken just over one year later (adequate time, perhaps, for discernment) showed that 51 percent believed Hill and 34 percent believed Thomas. These and other data are discussed in Stephen L. Carter, *The Confirmation Mess: Cleaning Up the Federal Appointments Process* (New York: Basic Books, 1994), especially p. 236 n. 44.

11. See Kondracke, "Is Newt Paranoid About Media Bias?"

12. 501 U.S. 663 (1991).

13. *Branzburg v. Hayes,* 408 U.S. 665 (1972).

14. See, for example, the data discussed in Martin S. Greenberg and R. Barry Ruback, *After the Crime: Victim Decision Making* (New York: Plenum Press, 1992).

15. Quoted in Jamie Stiehm, "Where the Sun Doesn't Shine," *Columbia Journalism Review,* May/June 1995, p. 19.

16. Ken Auletta, "Fee Speech," *The New Yorker,* September 12, 1994, p. 40.

CHAPTER 7. AND NOTHING BUT THE TRUTH

1. For discussion of the wager of law, see F. Pollock and F. W. Maitland, *The History of English Law,* vol. 2 (Cambridge: Cambridge University Press, 1898), especially p. 632. See also T. F. T. Plucknett, *A Concise History of the Common Law* (Boston: Little, Brown, 1956), pp. 113–14.

2. A few years ago, when I wrote a book called *The Culture of Disbelief: How American Law and Politics Trivialize Religious Devotion,* I was disappointed to receive some criticism for referring to God as "He." I was following the religious tradition that has sustained me in difficult times, and I am not inclined to change now. Readers who are suspicious of faith and would prefer a more scholarly justification might profitably examine Francis Watson, *Text, Church and World: Biblical Interpretation in Theological Perspective* (Grand Rapids, MI: William B. Ecrdmans, 1994), chaps. 9–12 of which represent a very respectful argument, taking full account of feminist scholarship, for referring to God as "He."

3. See Helen Silving, "The Oath: I," *Yale Law Journal* 68 (1959): 1329.

4. As of this writing, some 95 percent of adults surveyed say that they believe in God. See Morin, "Unconventional Wisdom," *The Washington Post*, August 27, 1995, p. C7.

5. Roger D. Groot, "The Early-Thirteenth-Century Criminal Jury," in *Twelve Good Men and True: The Criminal Trial Jury in England, 1200–1800*, ed. J. S. Cockburn and Thomas A. Green (Princeton, NJ: Princeton University Press, 1988), p. 3.

6. The first case of this kind was apparently *United States v. Stark*, 131 F. Supp. 190 (D. Md. 1955). Others include: *United States v. Cogdell*, 844 F.2d 179 (4th Cir. 1988); *United States v. Hajecate*, 683 F.2d 894 (5th Cir. 1982), *cert. denied*, 461 U.S. 927 (1983); *United States v. Medina de Perez*, 799 F.2d 540 (9th Cir. 1986); *United States v. Schnaiderman*, 568 F.2d 1208 (5th Cir. 1978). For general background, see Giles A. Birch, Comment, "False Statements to Federal Agents: Induced Lies and the Exculpatory No," *University of Chicago Law Review* 57 (1990): 1273; and Lawrence A. Brown, "False Statements," *American Criminal Law Review* 24 (1987): 567. I am grateful to two students in my 1993 seminar on Law, Secrets, and Lying, Diane Gujarti and Cinda York, for bringing to my attention these and other relevant sources.

7. 18 U.S.C. 1001.

8. Sissela Bok, *Lying: Moral Choice in Public and Private Life* (New York: Pantheon, 1978), p. 83.

9. Ibid.

10. The theory of rational ignorance is most fully developed in Robert E. Goodin, *Manipulatory Politics* (New Haven, CT: Yale University Press, 1980).

11. See Orlando Patterson, "Race, Gender, and Liberal Fallacies," *New York Times*, October 20, 1991.

12. See Akhil Amar, "The Bill of Rights as a Constitution," *Yale Law Journal* 100 (1991): 1159.

13. See James W. Ely, Jr., "The Chicago Conspiracy Case," in M. R. Belknap, ed., *American Political Trials* (Westport, CT: Greenwood Press, 1981), p. 263.

14. Amar, "Bill of Rights," pp. 1183–91.

15. Gerd Tellenbach, *Church, State and Christian Society at the Time of the Investiture Contest* (New York: Harper & Row, 1970), p. 136.

16. Anthony T. Kronman, *The Lost Lawyer: Failing Ideals of the Legal Profession* (Cambridge, MA: Harvard University Press, 1993), p. 12.

17. Gillers's remarks in "Hero or Knave?" (roundtable discussion), *American Lawyer* (July/August 1995): 37.

18. Bok, *Lying*, p. 85.

19. Gillers's remarks in "Hero or Knave?" p. 37.

20. See Kronman, *The Lost Lawyer.*

21. See, generally, American Bar Association Standing Committee on Ethics and Professional Responsibility, *Withdrawal When a Lawyer's Services Will Otherwise Be Used to Perpetrate a Fraud,* Formal Opinion 92–366 (August 8, 1992).

22. Walther I. Brandt, ed., *Luther's Works*, vol. 45 (Philadelphia: Fortress Press, 1962), p. 101.

CHAPTER 8. UNTIL WE ARE PARTED

1. See "The Latest Word on Families," *The Numbers News,* January 1995, p. 1. (*The Numbers News* is a newsletter published by the same company that publishes the much better known *American Demographics.*)

2. See "Relations Between the Sexes," *The Public Perspective,* September–October 1993, p. 88.

3. Michael Walzer, *Spheres of Justice: A Defense of Pluralism and Equality* (New York: Basic Books, 1983), p. 235.

4. Robert V. Levine, "Is Love a Luxury?" *American Demographics,* February 1993, p. 27.

5. Gretchen Craft Rubin and Jamie G. Heller, "Restatement of Love: Tentative Draft," *Yale Law Journal* 104 (December 1994): 707, 710.

6. See, for example, the discussion of the literature in Tom W. Smith, "Can Money Buy You Love?" *The Public Perspective,* January 1994, p. 33.

7. See Lynn A. Baker and Robert E. Emery, "When Every Relationship Is Above Average: Expectations of Divorce at the Time of Marriage," *Law and Human Behavior* 17 (1993): 439.

8. Because common-law marriage requires nothing but the consent of the parties and is often treated by the courts as resting entirely on contract, there has been occasional litigation arguing that it is sex discrimination to refuse to grant common-law marriage status to same-sex unions. So far, this litigation has failed.

9. For a discussion and explanation of some of this literature, see Robert Wright, *The Moral Animal: Evolutionary Psychology and Everyday Life* (New York: Pantheon, 1994).

10. See the discussion in Adin Steinsaltz, *The Essential Talmud,* tr. Chaya Galai (New York: Basic Books, 1976), pp. 129–36.

11. See John L. Esposito, *Islam: The Straight Path* (New York: Oxford, 1991), pp. 94–96.

12. Indeed, a continuing psychological puzzle is why—other than the issue of breach of promise—we put so high a premium on sexual fidelity. My own answer as a Christian is that the mandate of sexual fidelity (at least in marriage) is part of the God-given knowledge of the good that we are called to discern. The legal scholar George Fletcher proposes a different and certainly plausible explanation: "[S]exual acts serve as ritualistic confirmation of the underlying relationship of emotional devotion. . . . Because disloyalty is so easy and so tempting, constant reassurance becomes mandatory." See George Fletcher, *Loyalty: An Essay on the Morality of Relationships* (New York: Oxford, 1993), p. 76. For a discussion of the possible biological components of sexual fidelity and infidelity, see Wright, *The Moral Animal.*

13. Lewis B. Smedes, "The Power of Promises," in Thomas G. Long and Cornelius Plantinga, Jr., *A Chorus of Witnesses: Model Sermons for Today's Preacher* (Grand Rapids, MI: William B. Eerdmans, 1994), p. 156.

14. Ibid., p. 160.

15. Ibid., pp. 160–61.

16. Ibid., p. 157.

17. Karl Rahner, *Foundations of Christian Faith*, trs. William V. Dych (New York: Crossroad, 1986), p. 419.

18. Smedes, "Power of Promises," p. 157.

19. Philip Edgcumbe Hughes, *Christian Ethics in Secular Society* (Grand Rapids, MI: Baker Book House), pp. 161–62.

20. See "Q. When Is a Marriage Not Really a Marriage?" *Newsweek*, March 13, 1995, p. 58.

21. Smedes, "Power of Promises," p. 161.

22. Aristotle, *Ethics*, trs. J. A. K. Thompson (London: Penguin, 1953), book 3, p. 130.

23. Margaret Farley, *Personal Commitments: Beginning, Keeping, Changing* (San Francisco: Harper & Row, 1986).

24. Ibid., pp. 84–109.

CHAPTER 9. TO HAVE AND TO HOLD

1. Adin Steinsaltz, *The Essential Talmud*, tr. Chaya Galai (New York: Basic Books, 1976), p. 133.

2. See, for example, Madeline Kochen, "Constitutional Implications of New York's 'Get' Statute," *New York Law Journal*, October 27, 1983, p. 32.

3. See, for example, the discussion in Ellis Cose, *A Man's World: How Real Is Male Privilege—and How High Is Its Price?* (New York: HarperCollins, 1995), pp. 173–86. The indispensable work on this problem is of course Joseph Goldstein, Anna Freud, and Albert Solnit, *Beyond the Best Interests of the Child* (New York: Macmillan, 1973).

4. See Richard L. Berke, "From the Right, Some Words of Restraint," *New York Times*, September 17, 1994, sec. 1, p. 9.

5. See Judith Stacey, *Brave New Families: Stories of Domestic Upheaval in Late Twentieth Century America* (New York: Basic Books, 1990), pp. 144–45.

6. See Karol Wojtyla, *Love and Responsibility*, tr. H. T. Willets (New York: Farrar, Straus & Giroux, 1994). The English translation was originally published in 1981. The book was originally published in Poland in 1960, two decades before its author became Pope John Paul II.

7. Alimony, money that is paid in order to end a marriage, is a poor analogy. Alimony, properly understood, simply compensates one spouse (usually the wife) "for the opportunity costs she incurs by entering and investing in the marriage." Elisabeth M. Landes, "Economics of Alimony," *Journal of Legal Studies* 7 (1978):35.

8. Aristotle, *Nichomachean Ethics*, tr. J. A. K. Thompson (London: Penguin, 1953), book 9, 1164a13.

9. "Relations Between the Sexes," *The Public Perspective*, September 1993, p. 88.

10. See Bickley Townsend and Kathleen O'Neill, "American Women Get Mad," *American Demographics*, August 1990, p. 26.

11. See Joan Brightman, "Why Hillary Chooses Rodham Clinton," *American Demographics*, March 1994, p. 9.

12. Quoted in Philip Edgcumbe Hughes, *Christian Ethics in Secular Society*, (Grand Rapids, MI: Baker Book House), p. 165. Chrysostom suggested understanding the word *head* as in the relationship of head to body: one cannot survive without the other. But this analogy, meant to solve the problem of the husband who despises the wife, makes a clear statement about which spouse Chrysostom believes the Scripture leaves in actual control.

13. Lewis B. Smedes, "The Power of Promises," in Thomas G. Long and Cornelius Plantinga, Jr., *A Chorus of Witnesses: Model Sermons for Today's Preacher* (Grand Rapids, MI: William B. Eerdmans, 1994), p. 158.

CHAPTER 10. THE INTEGRITY OF FUN AND GAMES

1. Roger Angell, "The Flowering and Subsequent Deflowering of New England," reprinted in *The Third Fireside Book of Baseball,* ed. Charles Einstein (New York: Simon & Schuster, 1968), pp. 27, 34.

2. See, for example, Catharine MacKinnon, *Feminism Unmodified: Discourses on Life and Law* (Cambridge, MA: Harvard University Press, 1987), pp. 117–24.

3. Joey Jay (as told to Lawrence Lader), "Don't Trap Your Son in Little League Madness," in *The Third Fireside Book of Baseball,* pp. 226, 229.

4. Chandler quoted in Tom Callahan, "Scratch Czar's Crown and Find Pure Tin," *Washington Post,* August 30, 1992, p. D3.

5. Quoted in Richard Justice, "Giamatti Reestablishes His Power," *Washington Post,* August 25, 1989, p. G4.

6. See Mark Maske, "Owners Limit Powers of the Commissioner; Scope of 'Best Interests' Clause Narrowed," *Washington Post,* February 12, 1994, p. D4.

7. *Federal Baseball Club of Baltimore v. National League of Professional Baseball Clubs,* 259 U.S. 200 (1922).

8. See Walter Byers (with Charles Hammer), *Unsportsmanlike Conduct: Exploiting College Athletes* (Ann Arbor: University of Michigan Press, 1995).

9. In 1992, students in Washington, D.C., public schools averaged 705 on the SAT, representing a score of 33 percent correct items on the verbal portion and 25 percent on the mathematics portion. Random chance would yield a 20 percent score. For a fascinating discussion of the test scores and other issues, see Gerald W. Bracey, "The Third Bracey Report on the Condition of Public Education," *Phi Delta Kappan,* October 1993, p. 104.

10. Quoted in Rick Reilly, "A Good Joe," *Sports Illustrated,* January 18, 1995.

11. Quoted in Harry Blauvelt, "Brief UCLA Stay Causes Furor About MVP Harding," *USA Today,* June 2, 1995, p. 2C.

12. Tom Weir, Commentary, *USA Today,* June 2, 1995, p. 6C.

13. Quoted in Blauvelt, "Brief UCLA Stay Causes Furor."

14. Alfred Kreymbourg, "Chess Reclaims a Devotee," in Irving Chernev and Fred Reinfeld, eds., *The Fireside Book of Chess* (New York: Simon & Schuster, 1949), p. 6.

15. Quoted in B. G. Brooks, "Colorado Stands By Its Record," *Washington Post,* December 23, 1990, p. D3.

16. William F. Reed, "A Loser in Victory," *Sports Illustrated*, October 15, 1990, p. 96.
17. See Raymond Keene, "Keene on Chess," *The Times* (London), March 14, 1994.
18. See Raymond Keene, "Kasparov in Counter-attack over Rival's Cheating Claim," *The Times* (London), March 18, 1994.

CHAPTER 11. CODA: THE INTEGRITY OF CIVIL DISOBEDIENCE

1. See, for example, Michael Perry, *Morality, Politics, and Law* (New York: Oxford, 1988).
2. Perry, *Morality, Politics, and Law*, p. 118, quoting Kent Greenawalt, "A Contextual Approach to Disobedience," *Columbia Law Review* 70 (1970): 48, 69.
3. Perry, *Morality, Politics, and Law*, p. 118, quoting Greenawalt, "A Contextual Approach," p. 70.
4. As I have been discussing Michael Perry, I should note that he concedes this point: "Nazi Germany is one context. By any plausible standard, contemporary American society is quite another." Perry, *Morality, Politics, and Law*, p. 118.
5. See, for example, Kent Greenawalt, *Conflicts of Law and Morality* (New York: Oxford University Press, 1987); Joseph Raz, *The Authority of Law* (Oxford: Claredon Press, 1979); Michael Perry, *Love and Power* (New York: Oxford University Press, 1990); Philip Soper, *A Theory of Law* (Cambridge, MA: Harvard University Press, 1984); A. D. Woozley, *Law and Obedience: The Arguments of Plato's Crito* (Chapel Hill: University of North Carolina Press, 1979).
6. I make no comment here about the source of the individual's presumptive obligation to *obey* the law. The alert reader will note that I have rested that obligation on the individual's own vision of obeying the law as morally worthwhile, whatever the source of that vision. In this I follow Joseph Raz, *The Morality of Freedom* (Oxford: Clarendon Press, 1986). I discuss the sources of legal obligation in more detail in Stephen L. Carter, *The Dissent of the Governed* (Cambridge, MA: Harvard University Press, 1996). For a forerunner of the arguments made there and in this chapter as well, with explicit and detailed attention to both Raz and Perry, see Stephen L. Carter, "The Dissent of the Governors," *Tulane Law Review* 63 (1989): 1325.
7. Raz, *The Morality of Freedom*, p. 98.

8. Ronald Dworkin, *A Matter of Principle* (Cambridge, MA: Harvard University Press, 1985), p. 110.

9. Martin Luther King, Jr., "Love, Law, and Civil Disobedience," in *A Testament of Hope: The Essential Writings of Martin Luther King, Jr.*, ed. James Washington (San Francisco: Harper & Row, 1986), pp. 43, 49.

10. David Tracy, *Plurality and Ambiguity: Hermeneutics, Religion, Hope* (Chicago: University of Chicago Press, 1987), p. 84. I discuss this aspect of religion in greater detail in Stephen L. Carter, *The Culture of Disbelief* (New York: Basic Books, 1993), esp. chaps. 2 and 3. For a fascinating account of the role of civil disobedience in Judaism, see Milton R. Konvitz, "Conscience and Civil Disobedience in the Jewish Tradition," in Menachem Marc Kellner, ed., *Contemporary Jewish Ethics* (New York: Sanhedrin Press, 1978), p. 239.

11. Martin Luther King, Jr., "Nobel Prize Acceptance Speech," in *A Testament of Hope*, pp. 224, 225–26.

12. Martin Luther King, Jr., "Letter from Birmingham City Jail," in *A Testament of Hope*, pp. 289, 291.

13. Ibid., p. 294.

14. See, for example, Perry, *Morality, Politics, and Law*, p. 108 (U-turn example), and Kent Greenawalt, "Promise, Benefit, and Need: Ties That Bind Us to the Law," *Georgia Law Review* 18 (1984): 727, 763 (speeding and trespassing examples).

15. Ronald M. Dworkin, *A Matter of Principle* (Cambridge, MA: Harvard University Press, 1985), p. 105.

16. Perry, *Morality, Politics, and Law*, p. 109.

17. Carl Cohen, *Civil Disobedience: Conscience, Tactics, and the Law* (New York: Columbia University Press, 1971), p. 103.

18. John Rawls, *A Theory of Justice* (Cambridge, MA: Harvard University Press, 1971). See also John Rawls, *Political Liberalism* (New York: Columbia University Press, 1993).

19. See Stephen L. Carter, *The Culture of Disbelief: How American Law and Politics Trivialize Religious Devotion* (New York: Basic Books, 1993).

20. Martin Luther King, Jr., "A Testament of Hope," in *A Testament of Hope*, pp. 313, 328.

CHAPTER 12. CAN INTEGRITY BE LEGISLATED?

1. Editorial, "A Bevy of Independent Counsels," *New York Times*, May 22, 1995, p. A14.

2. *Congressional Record* 123 (1977): 20,966 (statement of Senator Humphrey).

3. Ibid. (1976): 22,671 (statement of Senator Percy).

4. Ibid. (1976): 22,788 (remarks of Senator Javits).

5. Ibid. (1976): 22,668 (remarks of Senator Ribicoff).

6. Ibid. (1976): 23,074 (statement of Senator Clark).

7. See Gerard E. Lynch and Phillip K. Howard, "Special Prosecutors: What's the Point," *Washington Post*, May 28, 1995, p. C7.

8. See Stephen L. Carter, "The Independent Counsel Mess," *Harvard Law Review* 102 (1988):105.

9. See *Morrison v. Olson*, 487 U.S. 654 (1988).

10. Amitai Etzioni, "We Shouldn't Squander Our Moral Outrage," *Wall Street Journal*, December 27, 1994, p. A16.

11. Alexis de Tocqueville, *Democracy in America*, tr. George Lawrence (Garden City, NY: Doubleday, 1969), p. 105.

12. For a discussion of state efforts to regulate what candidates for office may say and how, see Stephen D. Sencer, "Read My Lips: Examining the Legal Implications of Knowingly False Campaign Promises," *Michigan Law Review* 90 (1991): 428.

13. *Brown v. Hartlage*, 456 U.S. 45 (1982).

14. See Sencer, "Read My Lips."

15. The theory of rational ignorance is developed in Robert E. Goodin, *Manipulatory Politics* (New Haven, CT: Yale University Press, 1980), chap. 2. Goodin argues that rational ignorance combines with other factors to provide politicians with strong incentives to lie, or at least to be secretive.

16. Nat Hentoff, *Free Speech for Me But Not for Thee* (New York: Harper-Collins, 1992), p. 17.

17. *New York Times Co. v. Sullivan*, 376 U.S. 254 (1964).

18. See, for example, Meri Matsuda, "Public Response to Racist Speech: Considering the Victim's Story," *Michigan Law Review* 87 (1989): 2320.

CHAPTER 13. TOWARD AN INTEGRAL POLITICS

1. See Gordon S. Wood, *The Creation of the American Republic 1776–1787* (New York: Norton, 1972).

2. See, for example, "Mistrust of Government at New High, Poll Finds," *San Diego Union-Tribune*, August 1, 1995, p. A7.

3. *The Federalist No. 10* (James Madison).

4. For my earlier discussions of how and perhaps even why our political movements tolerate such views, see Stephen L. Carter, *Reflections of an Affirmative Action Baby* (New York: Basic Books, 1991), chap. 7 (conservative tolerance of racism), and *The Culture of Disbelief: How American Law and Politics Trivialize Religious Devotion* (New York: Basic Books, 1993), chaps. 2, 3 (liberal tolerance of religious bigotry).

5. For a discussion of the incentives that we give candidates to behave in this manner, see Robert E. Goodin, *Manipulatory Politics* (New Haven, CT: Yale University Press, 1980).

6. Christopher Lasch, *The Revolt of the Elites and the Betrayal of Democracy* (New York: Norton, 1995).

7. I use the term *welfare state* understanding full well that it is politically loaded and that most of the benefits of the welfare state go to Americans of the middle and upper classes. See Theodore R. Marmor, Jerry L. Mashaw, and Phillip L. Harvey, *America's Misunderstood Welfare State* (New York: Basic Books, 1990).

8. All the examples come from the following two documents: Stephen Moore and Dean Stansel, *Ending Corporate Welfare as We Know It* (draft report) (Washington, D.C.: Cato Institute, March 6, 1995), and Robert J. Shapiro, *Cut-and-Invest: A Budget Strategy for the New Economy* (policy report no. 23) (Washington, D.C.: Progressive Policy Institute, March 1995).

9. Moore and Stansel, *Ending Corporate Welfare*, p. 4.

10. Ibid., p. 3.

11. Ibid.

12. Ibid., p. 11.

13. This effort is the subject of my earlier book *The Culture of Disbelief*.

14. See Carter, *The Culture of Disbelief*, esp. chaps. 2, 3, and 11.

15. Pliny (the Younger), "Christians in Bithynia," reprinted in *Documents of the Christian Church*, ed. Henry Bettenson (Oxford: Oxford University Press, 1963), pp. 3–4.

16. Fortunately, the district judge's ruling was reversed on appeal. See *Kreimer v. Bureau of Police*, 958 F.2d 1242 (3d Cir., 1992).

17. Minow's comments are quoted in Rushworth M. Kidder, *Shared Values for a Troubled World: Conversations with Men and Women of Conscience* (San Francisco: Jossey-Bass, 1994), pp. 178–89.

18. This proposition has been a staple of recent social criticism. See, for example, Christopher Lasch, *The Revolt of the Elites and the Betrayal of Democracy* (New York: Norton, 1995); Amitai Etzioni, *The Spirit of Community: Rights, Responsibilities, and the Communitarian Agenda*

(1993); and, of course, the work of Mary Ann Glendon and of Robert Bellah and his collaborators.

19. See generally the discussion of this history in Hannah Arendt, *The Life of the Mind—Part II: Willing* (New York: Harcourt Brace, 1978).

20. See Martin Buber, *Between Man and Man*, tr. Ronald Gregor Smith (New York: Macmillan, 1965). The essays in the volume were written between 1929 and 1939.

21. One recent survey found that only 5 percent of voters consider abortion a decisive issue in casting their ballots (according to a 1995 *New York Times* poll, available on Nexis). A 1992 poll found that only one voter in nine even wanted presidential candidates to talk about their views on abortion. See John Brennan, "'92 Republican News Analysis," *Los Angeles Times*, August 16, 1992, p. 6.

22. In the early 1980s, the Congress considered the Human Life Bill, which purported to define life as beginning at the moment of conception. I do not think this would have been a very wise law, but I was astonished at the legion of constitutional theorists who rushed to insist that it was unconstitutional. By far the weakest thread of *Roe v. Wade* (410 U.S. 113 [1973]), one that the Supreme Court almost never mentions any longer, was the insistence that the government is without power to determine when life begins. The only reason offered was that society had reached no consensus on the issue. But because the Human Life Bill would have been an effort by the Congress to demonstrate the existence of consensus, it could hardly be unconstitutional for the reason offered by the Court—not unless what the justices meant was that because the society had never reached any consensus before (which might not even have been true), it would never be allowed to reach consensus in the future. For a discussion of this issue, see Stephen L. Carter, "The *Morgan* 'Power' and the Forced Reconsideration of Constitutional Decisions," *University of Chicago Law Review* 53 (1986): 819.

23. 410 U.S. 113 (1973).

24. These data, which have been fairly consistent for twenty years, are the subject of a thoughtful analysis by Ronald Dworkin. See Ronald Dworkin, *Life's Dominion: An Argument About Abortion, Euthanasia, and Individual Freedom* (New York: Knopf, 1993).

25. See especially *Planned Parenthood of Southeastern Pennsylvania v. Casey*, 112 S. Ct. 2791 (1992).

26. See Stephen L. Carter, "Abortion, Absolutism, and Compromise," *Yale Law Journal* 100 (1991): 2747.

27. Jean Bethke Elshtain, *Democracy on Trial* (New York: Basic Books, 1995), p. 26.

28. For a provocative (if ultimately unpersuasive) suggestion that legislation adopted in a narrow interest rather than the broad national interest might sometimes be unconstitutional, see Cass Sunstein, "Naked Preferences and the Constitution," *Columbia Law Review* 84 (1984): 1689.

29. Bob Herbert, "Renewing Black America," *New York Times*, July 14, 1995, p. A25.

CHAPTER 14. CODA: INTEGRITY, EVIL, AND THE AMERICAN CORE

1. Antony Flew, *God and Philosophy* (New York: Harcourt, Brace & World, 1966), p. 48.

2. See the masterful discussion in Hannah Arendt, *The Life of the Mind—Part II: Willing* (New York: Harcourt Brace, 1978), pp. 13–28.

3. St. Thomas Aquinas, *Summa Theologiae*, 2a2ae, 104, 1, p. 49.

4. W. S. Tyler, *Integrity the Safeguard of Public and Private Life* (Springfield, MA: Samuel Bowles, 1857), p. 9.

5. Moses Maimonides, *The Guide of the Perplexed*, book II, ch. 39, reprinted in Arthur Hyman and James J. Walsh, eds., *Philosophy in the Middle Ages* (Indianapolis: Hackett, 1973), p. 401.

6. F. C. Copleston, *Aquinas* (New York: Penguin 1991; orig. pub. 1955), p. 154.

7. See Stephen L. Carter, *Reflections of an Affirmative Action Baby* (New York: Basic Books, 1991), p. 245.

8. Tyler, *Integrity*, p. 9.

9. Ibid., p. 10.

10. Ibid., p. 25.

11. Isaiah Berlin, *Two Concepts of Liberty* (Oxford: Clarendon, 1958), pp. 52–57.

12. John Locke, "A Letter Concerning Toleration," in *The Second Treatise of Civil Government and a Letter Concerning Toleration* (Oxford: Basil Blackwell, 1946), p. 156.

13. Charles Taylor, *The Ethics of Authenticity* (Cambridge, MA: Harvard University Press, 1991), p. 15.

14. Václav Havel, "In Our Postmodern World, a Search for Self-Transcendence" (address at Independence Hall, July 4, 1994).

15. Samuel Rabinove, "Religion and American Public Life," in David D.

Dallin, ed., *American Jews and the Separationist Faith* (Washington, D.C.: Ethics and Policy Center, 1993).

16. See "Poll Shows Most Prefer Values Taught at School," *Fort Worth Star-Telegram*, October 9, 1994, p. 8. The existence of these broad commonalities is made most obvious by the well-deserved commercial success of William J. Bennett's *The Book of Virtues* (New York: Simon & Schuster, 1993).

17. Jean-Jacques Rousseau, *The Social Contract*, book 1, sec. 8.

Index